Priceless Weddings

FOR UNDER $5,000

(Revised Edition)

PRICELESS WEDDINGS

FOR UNDER $5,000

(Revised Edition)

KATHLEEN KENNEDY

POTTER STYLE

NEW YORK

This book is dedicated to my children,
Nicholas and Michaela Kovalsky.
Hoping they find true love, abundant happiness,
and make many priceless memories.
Looking forward to helping plan their
priceless weddings someday!

POTTER STYLE and colophon are registered trademarks of
Penguin Random House LLC.

Originally published in different form in the United States by
Three Rivers Press, an imprint of the Crown Publishing Group,
a division of Penguin Random House LLC in 2000.

Grateful acknowledgment is made to Penguin Random House LLC for permission
to reprint an excerpt from *It Was on Fire When I Lay Down on It* by Robert Fulghum,
copyright © 1988, 1989 by Robert Fulghum. Used by permission of Villard Books,
an imprint of Random House, a division of Penguin Random House LLC. All rights
reserved.

Library of Congress Cataloging-in-Publication Data

Kennedy, Kathleen, 1965–
Priceless weddings for under $5,000 / Kathleen Kennedy.—Revised edition.
  p.   cm.
1. Weddings—Planning.   I. Title.   II. Title: Priceless weddings
for under five thousand dollars.
HQ745.K445 2015
395.2'2—dc23   2015009055

ISBN 978-0-8041-8576-9
eBook ISBN 978-0-8041-8577-6

Printed in the United States of America

Book design by Claire Vaccaro
Cover design by Jane Archer with hand lettering by Alane Gianetti

10 9 8 7 6 5 4 3 2 1

First Revised Edition

CONTENTS

INTRODUCTION

———•———•———

When I am introduced as the author of *Priceless Weddings for Under $5,000*, I often get one of three responses: "Can you really have a wedding for under $5,000?" or "No way! That's not possible!" or "I was at a great low-budget wedding recently, . . ." and then the individual begins to tell me all of the fabulous details of the day's celebration.

Many people tell me they wish they had a copy of the book when their daughter, son, or they themselves got married. Others ask where they can buy a copy to give as a gift for a friend, a sister, a godchild, or someone else they know who is getting married soon.

However this book ended up in your hands, I hope it inspires you and your fiancé as you embark upon your wedding planning journey. To date, thousands of couples have used this book. They all discovered the very thing I want to share with you: there is no need to mortgage your future for a one-day event. You can have a priceless wedding without spending a fortune!

The idea to write about priceless weddings occurred to me while I was working as a caterer and event planner. My clientele were brides and grooms who were throwing lavish weddings with hundreds of guests and costing tens of thousands of dollars. I had witnessed firsthand the stresses of the big day, the unrealistic expectations, and the inevitable letdown. I saw fights between family members, brides in tears over minor details, and how some couples were so overwhelmed that they really did not enjoy themselves. As one bride I know said, "My wedding day was a blur of chaos and details.

With the whole day so tightly planned out, I didn't even get a chance to say hello to some of my closest friends."

When I got engaged, I vowed that our wedding would not suffer that same fate. We set out and planned an intimate, personal ceremony and reception for a fraction of what my clients were spending. Our day of celebration, relaxation, great food, and good friends was affordable, enjoyable, and memorable. Several of our guests said that they felt they knew us better when they left our wedding than they did beforehand. That, to me, was priceless. Yet all in, it cost under $5,000.

After we got married, other engaged couples began to call and ask me for advice on how to plan a customized wedding with a shoestring budget. I soon realized that there was a need for a budget-planning guide to help couples craft their wedding their way. *Priceless Weddings* was written to empower you to plan and personalize your day so it reflects who you are as individuals and as a couple—without costing a fortune. The book is full of cost-cutting ideas, suggestions on where to splurge and where to save, plus savvy strategies gleaned from years of catering, event planning, and bargain hunting.

In the following chapters, I walk you through the steps I would recommend to you if I were your very own wedding consultant. When I refer to "your inner wedding planner," I am encouraging you to ask yourselves questions, fill out forms, and take the first planning steps as if I were right there next to you. I will work with you to accomplish the following:

- Create a vision and a memorable event that will resonate for you and your fiancé, plus all family and friends who attend.
- Carve out strategies for your wedding, whether you are the do-it-yourself (DIY) type or someone who wants to have it all done for you.
- Save significantly—without it being noticeable or offensive.
- Inspire you, especially by sharing scenarios and tips from recently married couples and wedding professionals.

- Research and do as much as possible online, including planning, preparation, making checklists, building a wedding website, registering, picking music, and sharing photos.
- Execute your ceremony and reception flawlessly.

Throughout the book I focus on special touches and meaningful personal inspirations that you can utilize to add dimension to your wedding, such as family memorabilia (your mother's wedding dress), the story of how you met (a nightclub in Boston), favorite flowers (heirloom roses), or a special venue (a local farm). I will help you build a wedding and reception around a meaningful theme, such as a specific historical period (e.g., "retro vintage chic"), or a philosophy, such as "natural and organic."

In the process of writing *Priceless Weddings*, I had the opportunity to interview dozens of other couples like us, who, for whatever reason, didn't have $5,000 to spend on their nuptials, or who didn't want to spend more than $5,000. I realized that while each wedding was unique, something occurred in all of them that was missing in more elaborate weddings. I heard tales of people pitching in to help in any way they could, and how good it felt to these participants to play an active role in the union of their loved ones. The common thread I felt when brides, grooms, family, and friends described the day's events was the overwhelming feelings of love, joy, and community.

At the end of each chapter and interspersed throughout the book, you will find wedding scenarios that highlight how a specific couple designed their wedding. None of these couples was focused on money or showing off or keeping up with the Joneses. Instead, they devoted themselves to working together to plan, prepare, and partake in the events of a wedding celebration. Whether the couple is tying the knot barefoot on the beach, atop a ski mountain in Indiana, or wearing designer clothes in a chic setting, the weddings profiled within these pages are full of self-expression, originality, and stylishness.

This book is designed to help make your dreams come true. Whether you envision a lavish luncheon or a simple country ceremony, the ideas you find here will help you create memories that last a lifetime, even as they stay within the constraints of your budget. Enjoy these narratives. You will soon be joining the ranks of these couples with your own wedding story to tell.

Chapter One

TEN STEPS TO A PRICELESS WEDDING

———○———

Congratulations! Raise a glass and make a toast to your adventure into the world of wedding planning. By now you have probably called or texted friends and family to report the great news. Maybe you have an engagement ring or a date in mind. But what's next? Where do you go from here?

To make your journey as seamless as possible, I recommend that you focus on ten key steps:

1. Craft a **vision** for your priceless wedding.
2. Determine your **priorities.**
3. Draft a realistic **budget.**
4. Create a **timeline.**
5. **Research** your options.
6. Keep a **wedding notebook** or journal.
7. **Track** all costs, deposits, and payments.
8. **Finalize** all of the details.
9. **Execute** with ease.
10. **Relax and enjoy your wedding!**

If you are raring to go, jump right in and start with step 1. Or consider reading through the entire book, then coming back to start the steps. There is no right or wrong way to proceed. What is important is to decide broadly what you want. Clarify what is most important. Get real about the budget. Then hone in on how to bring it to life. The following is a brief overview of all the steps.

STEP 1. CRAFT A VISION FOR YOUR PRICELESS WEDDING

This is the step that helps you decide what success looks like for you and your beloved. With a broad brushstroke, set down on paper the blue-sky ideas of what success looks like. When you think about the festivities, what do you want to remember most when it comes to the ceremony and reception? Use your imaginations to conjure up the idealized image of your big day.

STEP 2. DETERMINE YOUR PRIORITIES

This is the time to decide what aspects of your ceremony, reception, and the vision you drafted are the most important. Once you have determined what is crucial to both of you—for instance, having live music—your priorities will help you decide where to splurge and where you might want to cut back. Add in the details that you already know now, too. For example, draft a guest list to plug in how many people you think will attend. And if you plan to wear your mother's wedding dress and only need to pay for alterations versus buying a whole new wedding gown, make a note of that.

STEP 3. DRAFT A REALISTIC BUDGET

Now that the word is out that you are tying the knot, have any family members pledged to help financially with costs? Have one or both of you set aside any savings? Can you count on part of your paycheck to cover expenditures? Do you need to consider additional creative financing options? Based on your budget, priorities, and any costs you may already have nailed down, you can estimate how much to allocate per category, such as food, location, clothes, and so on.

RINGS AND THINGS

I f you are still searching for the perfect engagement ring, here are a few of the ways the couples I spoke with cut costs:

- Inherited a hand-me-down or a family heirloom from Mom
- Selected a stone other than a diamond, such as a ruby or a sapphire
- Used a birthstone for the center stone with tiny diamond chips on each side
- Picked out a ring at a pawn shop
- Bought a diamond from a wholesale jewelry mart
- Decided on an Irish claddagh heart-in-hand ring
- Purchased a ring at an estate sale
- Had a graduate art student make it for the cost of the gold
- Reset a ring or a stone they already had
- Designed their own matching ring set—without a stone
- Fell in love with an antique ring at a consignment shop
- Chose a silver ring instead of a gold or platinum one
- Bought a ring with both of their birthstones
- Bid on a ring on eBay
- Bought a ring off Craigslist
- Purchased on TV/online shopping networks, such as HSN or QVC
- Borrowed a ring for the ceremony and then purchased a ring while on their honeymoon
- Bought a smaller stone, planning to "trade up" every five years

One bride and groom, both previously married, had old gold jewelry from their past lives melted and molded into new hammered gold rings in a symbolic gesture of sharing their pasts and forming their new lives together.

STEP 4. CREATE A TIMELINE

You will want to know how quickly you must make decisions. Timelines are going to vary a lot, depending on your priorities and the length of your engagement. If you are having a one-year engagement, you can be a lot more laid-back than if you decide to elope next week. Do note that if you have your heart set on a specific wedding site or other important details such as a designer dress, a favorite minister, or a specific band, nail those down first.

We had eight months lead time between our engagement and our wedding date. Our timeline looked like this:

8 MONTHS IN ADVANCE	Vision statement crafted, top 5 elements prioritized, budget complete
6 MONTHS IN ADVANCE	Location contracted, officiants enlisted, website started
5 MONTHS IN ADVANCE	Photographer booked, dress ordered
4 MONTHS IN ADVANCE	Groom fitted for tux, paper for invitations ordered
3 MONTHS IN ADVANCE	Shoes and veil purchased, florist chosen, gift registry done, wedding newsletter sent out, menu written, help hired, cake ordered
2 MONTHS IN ADVANCE	Music recorded for the ceremony and reception, ceremony and vows written, invitations printed and sent, dress fittings
1 MONTH IN ADVANCE	Reminder cards sent, newsletter and website about weekend festivities created
THE WEEK OF	Wedding license secured, vows finalized, a dinner hosted for out-of-town guests

Post-nuptials	Wedding announcements sent, thank-you cards written and mailed, website updated with photos and video

STEP 5. RESEARCH YOUR OPTIONS

To create a wedding that truly reflects who you and your betrothed are as individuals—and as a couple—use the resources and exercises throughout the book to research options for every part of your special day from invitations and attire to flowers and favors. Chapter 4, Internet Inspirations, will be particularly helpful in brainstorming ideas and comparing prices. Research online, read the chapters and wedding scenarios, attend bridal shows, and call around to get pricing.

STEP 6. KEEP A WEDDING NOTEBOOK OR JOURNAL

While you are researching and when you decide upon any aspect of your wedding, whether it concerns the ceremony or the reception, write it down either in a notebook or a wedding planner (see page 10), or print the details and add the page to the appropriate category, for example, invitations. Keep separate folders for estimates and final decisions. Jot down ideas that you brainstormed and notes from conversations with family, friends, and—especially—vendors. I must have made forty calls before an innkeeper who was fully booked on our date referred me to another inn that eventually became our wedding site. Even after seeing it, we didn't book it on the spot. We took notes, compared it against other sites we saw, and eventually called and negotiated a terrific rate.

MAKE YOUR OWN WEDDING PLANNER

Create a binder to use for all of your wedding notes. The goal is to capture your priorities, your budget, ideas discussed while brainstorming, a record of the phone calls you've made, and any quotes received from potential vendors. To organize your receipts, price quotes, and brochures, it is helpful to add clear plastic pocket dividers to a three-ring binder. Or set up an accordion file with a section for each of the following topics:

1. Ceremony: words, music, vows
2. Reception: food, themes, flowers
3. Apparel
4. Guest list, gift receipt list, etc.
5. Receipts, invoices, contracts, deposits
6. Other: websites, inspirations, etc.
7. Honeymoon

STEP 7. TRACK ALL COSTS, DEPOSITS, AND PAYMENTS

It is important always to have a sense of where you are in relation to your budget so that you don't overspend in one area without cutting back in another. Be sure to keep receipts and contracts in a safe place—and don't forget to read the fine print. Set up payment schedules that will work based on your current and projected cash flow. As one friend put it, "It was really helpful that we didn't have to pay for everything at once. We paid a deposit on our space and negotiated a payment schedule for the catering that we could live with. One month we bought the dress; the next month we booked our honeymoon."

STEP 8. FINALIZE ALL OF THE DETAILS

As the wedding draws closer, you will have to finalize all of the details. This is usually when you decide on the invitations and when to send them, the flowers, the officiant, the vows, and the final guest list. Refer to the checklist on pages 351–52 to be sure you haven't overlooked anything. Keep in mind that planning your wedding should be fun, not stressful. Practice the stress-busting tips in chapter 15.

STEP 9. EXECUTE WITH EASE

The goal is for you to bask in the love of your future spouse, friends, and family, both on and leading up to your big day. For the ceremony and reception, a key recommendation is to delegate as many tasks and responsibilities as possible to someone you trust. The last thing the bride or groom needs is to be worried about cueing the music for the walk down the aisle.

STEP 10. RELAX AND ENJOY YOUR WEDDING!

As I tell my friends and clients, "Don't forget to breathe." Planning your wedding is an exercise in delayed gratification, so it is extremely important that you relax enough to fully experience the day that you labored so hard over. It will be here and gone before you know it.

Keep in mind that not everything will go as planned. No wedding will ever be 100 percent perfect. Like it or not, some details may have to be rearranged at the last minute. Remember: Embrace the journey! At my friend Laura's wedding, the flowers that were delivered were completely different from what she had ordered. At first she was irritated, but then she decided that in the scheme of life and in relation to the importance of the day's events, flowers were not worth getting that upset about.

If at all possible, have a designated wedding coordinator to help direct the big day and attend to details that, as bride and groom, you should not have to think about in the midst of your celebration. This person will also serve as your "bad cop," keeping all participants on course with your timeline. My maid of honor relished this role. She made sure that all deliveries went to the right place, that the wedding certificate was signed, and that everyone stayed out of my dressing room. Her help was invaluable. If something big went wrong, I had given her the go-ahead to make executive decisions. I wanted my focus to be on the groom, our marriage, celebrating the start of a new phase of our lives together, and on being present with all in attendance.

AN ALL-AMERICAN BARBECUE

Kathleen and Gary's Wedding on July 4
55 guests in Bolinas, California

PRIORITIES

1. Great food (many of the guests were chefs and caterers)
2. Location—we wanted it to be local (Northern California) and by the ocean
3. Casual, friendly atmosphere
4. Date—Fourth of July—the anniversary of the day we met
5. Memorable, stylish, and unique

I was twenty-nine and Gary was thirty-one when we tied the knot. Gary and I met on the Fourth of July, two years earlier, while boogie-boarding in the ocean. We decided to get married on the anniversary of the day we met, and we liked the idea that we would always celebrate our wedding date in tandem with a national holiday and fireworks. We had been living together for over a year, but this was the first time our families would come together, so we wanted it to be incredibly special. We also wanted the wedding to be in a place where all our guests could be really comfortable and where kids (we have six nieces and nephews) could have a blast.

LOCATION

We got married at a horse-ranch bed-and-breakfast that was on a cliff overlooking the Pacific Ocean. The interior of the building was nicely decorated with antiques and had enough room to accommodate us inside in case of rain. The inn's two guest rooms were perfect changing rooms for the bridal party and later served as the site of our first night together as husband and wife. The inn's grounds were spectacular—acres of green grass surrounded by eucalyptus trees, a pool, the ocean view, and an amazing herb and wildflower garden. I walked through the garden arm and arm with my brother (who was giving me away) and met my groom in a gazebo under a redwood tree. During the reception, croquet and softball equipment were set up on the lawn for the younger guests, and after lunch we had dancing on the brick patio for all who wanted to partake.

BUDGET

Site and wedding night (a B and B)	$ 750
Dress, alterations, and veil	$ 395
Tuxedo rental	$ 130
Food and beverage	$ 1,650
Cake	$ 275
Photos	$ 325
Video	$ 0
Music	$ 0
Flowers	$ 275
Invitations	$ 110
License	$ 60
Miscellaneous (disposables, favors, etc.)	$ 250
Hairstylist (my splurge for me and my mom)	$ 140
Total	$4,360

DETAILS

We had a very short ceremony, ten minutes in length. I warned friends and family not to be late, so that they would not miss the whole thing. Gary's best friend was deputized as a California justice of the peace for the day, so he was legally able to marry us. I delegated wedding-coordinator duties to the maid of honor, Laura. She assisted with the ceremony, took care that details leading up to the ceremony went off without a hitch, kept the reception running smoothly, and read the prayer of Saint Francis of Assisi (page 312) during the ceremony. My niece was a flower girl, dropping rose petals along the garden path, and my nephew followed as an adorable ring bearer. Our vows were adapted from Marianne Williamson's *Illuminata*.

APPAREL

I wore a white lace bodice with a shantung silk skirt (a real steal at $275) and a short silk-trimmed sheer chiffon veil that hung from a barrette in my hair. Both Gary and his best man wore traditional black tuxedos. My maid of honor wore a three-quarter-length light-green silk dress that matched my rose-and-green color scheme.

MUSIC

We taped our favorite light-rock love songs for before the ceremony, some dancing music for after the ceremony, and Pachelbel's Canon in D Minor for my walk through the garden. The selections included "Love Will Come to You" (Indigo Girls), "A Wink and a Smile" (Harry Connick Jr.), "Make Someone Happy" (Jimmy Durante), and "The End of the World as We Know It (and I Feel Fine)" (R.E.M.).

FLOWERS AND DECORATIONS

My bouquet was made of light pink roses and ivy, tied with pale-pink silk ribbon. Boutonnieres for the groom and best man were matching roses with baby's breath. My maid of honor, my mom, and Gary's mom all wore rose and ivy corsages.

The only other flowers we purchased were two centerpieces, one each for the buffet and cake tables, that consisted of pale pink roses, ivy, and wildflowers in hand-painted window boxes. These planters were chosen not only to decorate the tables but to double as lasting keepsake gifts for my maid of honor and the friend who helped record the music for our wedding celebration. A bolt of extra-wide sheer ivory chiffon (a gift from a friend) was loosely draped around the gazebo. The resulting look was so beautiful that I donated the fabric to the innkeeper to use for future weddings there.

FOOD AND BEVERAGE

Immediately following the ceremony, we had a round of traditional toasts from the wedding party. Then, we gave out picnic baskets and tablecloths to every two people. Our guests spread out on the lawn and feasted on individual cheese trays garnished with wildflowers from the garden. We included some bubbles in the basket, so young and old alike were blowing bubbles into the light breeze.

Most of our guests moved to tables on the patio to eat the main course (see the menu on page 16). The self-serve luncheon utilized upscale disposable paper plates, cups, and napkins, along with china serving platters that were either borrowed or received as wedding gifts. I designed the menu myself, and a friend who used to work for me at a catering company cooked everything on-site. Several items were purchased already prepared: the spare ribs came from a smokehouse, the buns for the sandwiches and the French bread came from a local bakery, the wedding cake came from a culinary school. The cake was decorated with piped grape clusters and marzipan flowers. The cookies were a gift from a friend who owns a deli. They say that brides never eat at their wedding, but there I was, munching happily on ribs, salads, and cake in my white wedding gown.

OUR WEDDING MENU

APPETIZERS

Picnic Baskets filled with
Pesto Brie, French Bread, and Grapes

LUNCHEON BUFFET

Chipotle Barbecued Baby Back Ribs
Country Fried Chicken
Shrimp Salad Sandwiches
Confetti Pepper Potato Salad
Creamy Orange Basil Coleslaw
Farmer's Market Tomato Salad
An Assortment of Fresh Fruit

DESSERT

Peruvian Wedding Cookies
White Sponge Wedding Cake with Lemon Curd Filling
and White Chocolate Buttercream Icing

BEVERAGES

Raspberry Lemonade, Iced Tea, and Sodas
Coffee, Tea, and Sparkling Cider

Chapter Two

ENVISION AND PRIORITIZE

○———————○

This chapter is the kickoff to customizing your wedding. When you are ready to start planning, I recommend making a date with your fiancé to sit down, maybe over dinner or a glass of wine, and talk through what a successful wedding looks and feels like to both of you.

To begin with, I'd like you to imagine your inner wedding planner asking lots of open-ended questions to help further uncover what having a priceless wedding means to you. The conversation may go something like this:

- Do you have a clear image of what you expect for the ceremony and reception?
- Did you grow up dreaming of a church ceremony followed by an elegant soiree, and a classic floor-length, fitted silk wedding gown? Or . . .
- Would you prefer to ditch tradition and elope to Vegas, wearing whatever your heart desires?
- Maybe you are not sure yet and want to do some research and consider all your options?

If you have been leading an "always a bridesmaid, never a bride" life and have attended dozens of weddings, you may know down to the last detail what you want. Now you just need to figure out how to execute your event on a tight budget. Perhaps you have been glued to the television since you got engaged, watching a myriad of weddings, as well as searching the web for ideas.

If, on the other hand, you really do not have a sense yet of what the possibilities are (they are endless!), go ahead and peruse websites, TV shows, and local wedding showcases that will start the ideas percolating.

When you feel compelled to jot ideas down on paper, jump right into step one below and craft a vision statement. Then proceed with step two by filling out the Couple's Questionnaire on pages 26–28 and setting your priorities. On the other hand, if you would feel more comfortable starting with the questionnaire, jump ahead to step two and circle back after completing it.

STEP 1: CRAFT A VISION

Vision statements are inspiring words chosen by the betrothed couple to clearly and concisely convey the tone, theme, and details of their special day. You are ready to write your **vision statement** when you have an overall idea of what you want the wedding to look and feel like, as well as what you hope the guests would say about it afterward. Once complete, your vision statement will help you communicate your needs with wedding vendors and with family members.

If you are early in the planning process and do not yet know exactly what you want the wedding to look or feel like, do not worry. A vision statement can be a living, breathing, ever-evolving document. It is meant to be helpful, not intimidating! You can redraft it as many times as needed.

Here's how to draft your vision statement: Visualize the setting, the time of year, and anything else about the who, what, where, when, and how. Paint an image of details, themes, and the overall feeling of what you want your wedding to be like. What elements are critical to its success? What is essential to include or do, and what is essential not to include or do? Fill out the Vision Notes worksheet (page 20) with the broad view of what you hope to accomplish on your wedding day.

Visions and Vendors

The ability to share a clear vision statement will be especially helpful for anyone you may be working with who has not met you previously. Potential wedding vendors may try to impart *their* vision for your wedding, such as having you agree to a menu they are already preparing for another wedding the same day. Or, they may be trying to up-sell you a BMW when you are perfectly comfortable with and prefer a Toyota. Being crystal clear on what you envision and why enables you to paint the picture of the elements of a successful wedding.

Brainstorming Your Vision

Years ago I stopped making New Year's resolutions and instead picked theme words, or *intentions*, to focus on each year. For example, last year I focused on gratitude, and this next year I am focusing on launching, for example, this book and my son off to college. Setting an intention for your wedding is optional, but it's a great way to start drafting your vision.

With your partner, brainstorm an "intention" of one to five words that evoke the feeling, theme, and/or formality of your nuptials. For instance, for our wedding, we quickly agreed that we wanted it to be stress-free, a celebration, and delicious.

Another fun exercise to help you paint a mental picture of your big day is to imagine many years into the future. You and your partner are celebrating your ten-year wedding anniversary. You are looking back and discussing your ceremony and reception. Here are a few conversation starters to help you conceptualize the details:

- When you look back on the wedding festivities, what do you hope you and your guests feel and remember?
- Was it a large wedding or small and intimate; a traditional celebration or eclectic?
- What were the main elements of the ceremony? Of the reception?

- How did the main elements reflect who you and your partner are?
- What was the setting and time of day? Was it formal or casual?
- What other details of significance color your memories of the big day?

VISION NOTES

Wedding Vision: ....

....

....

....

....

....

Key Elements: ....

....

....

....

....

....

Must-*Not*-Haves: ....

....

....

....

....

....

VISION EXAMPLES

A NEW YEAR'S VISION

Here is a vision statement from Amanda and Peter, who married just after midnight on New Year's in Cincinnati; see pages 29–32 for more.

We want our wedding to be more of a party than a traditional wedding. No cake, no photographer, simple decor, nothing cookie-cutter. We want God and prayer to be integral and our friends to vow they will help keep us on the path of love and growth. Our friends can form a circle of support around us with their hands touching us. Our children should be in the middle of the circle with us. This represents how we hope to continue to build a tight community within our marriage. New Year's Eve will be the prelude to our vows, and New Year's Day marks our new beginning. Every year thereafter we can look back on what worked well in the last year and what we hope to accomplish during the next in regards to our relationship.

THE START OF OUR GROWN-UP LIVES

Here is the vision statement for recent college graduates Kim and Brandon.

Our wedding is the next stage in our lives. We are seeking a traditional church ceremony, a white silk dress, tuxedos, and flowers everywhere, followed by a banquet in the church hall. We plan to serve American fare that will appeal to all. Our wedding cake will be topped with a china bride and groom that we can hold on to for eternity. We will toast with champagne and kiddie cocktails for the younger set. Our crafty family and friends will help us keep the price per person in line so we can invite a few hundred of our closest friends. Though it will be very affordable, it will not feel cheap or chintzy. We are ushering in a new era combining both families and lots of traditions, as well as making a few of our own.

SET AN INTENTION
AND ENJOY THE JOURNEY!

ONE OF MY FAVORITE SLOGANS IS
"Intention, Attention, and No Tension."

As a bride or groom it's ideal to achieve all three.

INTENTION: If you had to come up with from one to five words to describe your wedding day, could you? Write a brief statement formally describing the feelings, emotions, and bonds you desire to create at your wedding—the essence of your vision.

ATTENTION: In the midst of the stress that leads up to and includes your wedding day, keep your attention on one detail or decision at a time. Also remember what your intention is and focus on it. Remember to breathe, smile, and enjoy every moment surrounded by your partner, family, and friends.

No TENSION: Remember what your priorities are, do not sweat the small stuff—*really*, do not sweat the big stuff either. (I know it's so hard, but commit to it right now!) Set the intention to enjoy your engagement, have fun along the way, and relish your wedding planning journey!

MARRIAGE MISSION STATEMENT

Another option that I highly recommend is a Marriage Mission Statement. In today's culture we spend lots of time and energy planning the perfect wedding day. When helping couples plan their wedding, I usually suggest the importance of **spending even more time discussing marriage** and what marriage means to them than spending time planning their wedding.

If you're interested in doing so, you could easily utilize the vision notes form (page 20) and methods, but instead focus on your marriage. Or search for "Marriage Mission Statement" on the Internet. There are lots of websites with examples that could prove beneficial.

STEP 2: CLARIFY YOUR PRIORITIES

One of the keys to an affordable wedding is to decide early on what your top priorities are, taking care not to spend lavishly on areas that are not. Fill out the Couple's Questionnaire on pages 26–28. Your priorities will help determine your vision for your wedding and how best to utilize the funds available. Examples of top priorities: a specific location, a small or large guest list, a religious or spiritual ceremony, great food, live music, or an Alençon lace dress.

Our priority list helped us—and everyone who was trying to help us—to focus on what was important to us and to concentrate our limited financial resources where we most wanted to spend them. For instance, if location is ranked high on your list, start looking and talking about it with everyone you meet. If incorporating religion or spirituality is a priority, this is the time to seek out your minister, priest, or rabbi. Let friends, coworkers, and relatives know that you need help and what your top priorities are. If you already know of specific areas you plan to do yourself or assign to a friend or family member, fill those in on the form also.

If you focus on your top priorities, the rest will fall into place. In other words, don't worry too much about all the details right now. For example, maybe you are not sure what time of day you prefer. Wait, gather more information, and think about it later. When you find the perfect site and determine its availability, you can make that call.

How Priorities Help

For my fiancé and me, location, food, and self-written vows were the top priorities. We asked for and received help from friends and family on other areas, such as music. We kept the guest list under control, inviting eighty guests (of whom fifty-five attended), and we sent out announcements to another fifty friends and relatives.

Once my fiancé and I determined the location and date of our wedding—at a horse-ranch bed-and-breakfast on the Fourth of July—it was easy for us to determine that an all-American picnic would be the theme, that the wedding would take place in the afternoon, and that we would serve lunch.

The priority list also helped us decide what aspects were not as important to us. Photographs were one example. Yes, we wanted them. We even wanted them done professionally. They were not, however, something we were willing to spend top dollar on. Later we would go to bridal shows, read local wedding guides, and get a wide variety of quotes. Eventually we decided on a photographer who was a friend of a friend. Our photos turned out great, the price was reasonable, we got to keep the negatives, and our photographer made us a custom wedding album that I will cherish forever.

CHOOSE
YOUR PRIORITIES

The following list of possibilities is meant to inspire you.

- Style: traditional church wedding, spiritual but not religious, civil, or simple and natural
- Size: large; small, with immediate family only; just the two of us; or just the two of us with kids from our first marriages
- Season: spring, summer, fall, or winter
- Formality of the reception atmosphere: simple elegance, rustic, black tie
- Is there a theme, such as vintage, '20s, '40s, '60s, beach party, other
- Location: beach, park, backyard, summer home, a lodge, farm, destination wedding, at home, our church, banquet hall, other
- Ceremony elements that may be critical for you: a chuppah, blessing of the rings, breaking of glass at the end of the ceremony, Bible readings . . .
- Green: completely sustainable, green where possible, organic food . . .
- Fun, really, really fun: photo booth, dunk tank, carnival games, New Year's Eve, Halloween . . .
- Food: is it a main focus or a nice-to-do? What are your favorite foods or favorite restaurant?
- Adult beverages: is a full bar a priority, or wine with dinner, or a champagne toast?

FILL OUT THE QUESTIONNAIRE AND DETERMINE YOUR PRIORITIES

You and your fiancé can answer the following questionnaire individually or collaboratively.

Skip any questions that you are not sure about and come back to them later. To estimate the number of guests, you should both draft your initial guest lists.

COUPLE'S QUESTIONNAIRE

Bride _____

Groom _____

Wedding Date _____ Time of Year _____

Number of Guests _____ Length of Engagement _____

Location Ideas _____

_____

_____

_____

_____

_____

_____

_____

_____

_____

Prioritize the following in order, starting with 1 as the highest priority. Specify where applicable by filling in the blank or circling the option that best suits you as a couple.

RANKING

_____ Location

_____ Theme

_____ Formal, semiformal, or informal atmosphere

_____ Small, medium, or large wedding

_____ Time of day _____

_____ Catered food: all, none, or partial

_____ Brunch, lunch, tea, cocktails, dinner, desserts, or cake

_____ Catered beverage service, espresso bar

_____ Full bar, beer and wine, partial bar, nonalcoholic only

_____ Vows: traditional, write your own, other _____

_____ Religious aspect: specify _____

_____ Photography: professional or friends, extensive or simple

_____ Video: professional, friends, or none

_____ Hair and/or makeup: professional or not

_____ Bride's dress type: formal, semiformal, or other _____

_____ Number of bridesmaids, if any _____

_____ Bridesmaids' dress type: formal, semiformal, or choose
their own

_____ Groom's tuxedo, suit, or other _____

_____ Number of groomsmen, if any _____

_____ Groomsmen apparel

_____ Theme _____

_____ Color scheme, if any _____

_____ Other priorities _____

_____ _____

_____ _____

_____ _____

DIY projects and person assigned, if applicable:

Rewrite and rank your top priorities here:

1. _____

_____

2. _____

_____

3. _____

_____

4. _____

_____

5. _____

_____

NEW YEAR'S BLISS

Amanda and Peter's New Year's Wedding
50 guests in Cincinnati, Ohio

PRIORITIES

1. For God and prayer to be a central part of their wedding and marriage
2. To literally be encircled with friends and family
3. Prominent inclusion of their three kids
4. More of a party than a wedding
5. Convenience

Amanda, thirty-seven, and Peter, thirty-six, met two-and-a-half years earlier while partnering in a Cross Fit gym. Over time their connection grew, and love blossomed, surprising both of them.

Once they decided to make it official, they spent several months talking about what they wanted to do for their nuptials. It was late November, in the midst of Thanksgiving and the start of holiday season, when they agreed on a date. Their goal was to host a relaxed, nonstressful event that would serve double-duty, ushering in the New Year while celebrating the start of their marriage.

LOCATION

Amanda and Peter were married at their friend Deke's home, a restored 110-year-old, three-story, historic American Foursquare–style mansion. They had been leaning toward getting married in another country. With less than two months to plan, they decided, for reasons of cost and convenience and to make sure close family and friends could attend, to hold it locally instead. Their Punchbowl.com digital invites asked folks to join them to help close out the old year and ring in the new. The celebration started at 8:00 p.m. on New Year's Eve, and the ceremony commenced at 12:30 a.m. New Year's morning.

BUDGET

Wedding/reception site	$ 0	
Dress, alterations, veil, and shoes	$ 220	(dress, alterations, and veil, $120; shoes, $100)
Groom's clothing	$ 0	
Food, liquor	$ 500	(food, $200; liquor, $300; see opposite)
Photography	$ 0	
Makeup, hair	$ 50	
Flowers	$ 380	
Decorations	$ 0	(a present from her maid of honor)
Invitations, music	$ 0	(both digital)
License/minister	$ 35	
Total	$ 1,185	

DETAILS

Amanda's super-creative friends helped to decorate, and the house, decked out in Christmas decor, looked elegant. For the ceremony, Amanda walked down the wooden staircase with her three boys and into the front room, where she stopped right under an ornate crystal chandelier. The only music they set up in advance was the tune "Home," by Phillip Phillips, which played as they came down the staircase. The lights were dimmed, and tall sparkly hurricanes with long-stemmed calla lilies, some set on mirrors with tea lights, were interspersed with arrangements of orange gerbera daisies. Garlands, arrangements of black and white feathers, and Christmas ornaments added cheer to the rooms.

During the ceremony, Amanda and Peter asked everyone in attendance to make a circle around them and, literally, "put their hands on" the couple as accountability partners, who would help keep them on the path of love and commitment. They wanted a relaxed party atmosphere and chose not to have a professional photographer or videographer. They also omitted many reception traditions, including the wedding cake, the garter toss, and the first dance. Friends captured the moments with photos, most of which were candids. In lieu of presents they had a wishing well tree (they used a Christmas evergreen), where guests could put envelopes with contributions toward their reception, honeymoon, and home.

APPAREL

Prior to the midnight hour, Amanda wore a sequined shirt and black pants. Amanda changed into her wedding dress right after the midnight toast. She bought her empire-waist, floor-length sheath dress off the rack at Nordstrom's and had it altered to fit. She absolutely adored the Vera Wang crystal-beaded, open-toe, strappy 5-inch high heels she wore that "nearly cost as much as the dress." Amanda splurged and had her hair done up. A friend spray-painted a headband with white paint and glued on tiny rhinestones, white silk ribbon, and flowers. The finished band was the focal point of Amanda's up-do. As she walked the walnut staircase to take her place with the groom, she carried a simple bouquet of calla lilies.

Peter paired a dark gray suit he had bought previously with an orange tie. Their boys all wore jeans with polo shirts. The couple had not requested anyone else to wear specific wedding attire, as they wanted all their friends and family to be comfortably casual.

FOOD AND BEVERAGE

Amanda and Peter had scheduled a catering company to serve hors d'oeuvres until midnight and set up an omelet bar after the wedding for an early breakfast. They were wondering why the caterer had not arrived at the house by the agreed-upon time. They got a call close to 10:00 p.m. and learned that the catering truck was in a serious accident and would not make it after all. Amanda said, "We have an amazing community of friends. They pitched in, went to the store, and basically catered the wedding themselves. We ended up getting all our money back from the caterer." They feasted on jalapeño popper appetizers, cheese-and-cracker trays, veggie platters, chips with dip, and assorted appetizers, and they drank beer, Bloody Marys, and mimosas.

"Our wedding was everything we wanted it to be," Peter and Amanda agreed.

Chapter Three

BECOMING BUDGET SAVVY

○——————————○

Throughout this book you will find examples of resourceful couples who designed wonderful weddings within their budgets by detailing their priorities and making strategic decisions on where to spend and where to save.

With your own priority list top of mind, the time has come to sit down and write a realistic budget. First, look at all of the possible ways to finance a wedding, such as drawing from your savings, your incomes, and contributions from parents. Then, if needed, consider alternative resources. For instance, some couples move back home to save; others may get a second job, try to sell items on eBay, or take out a loan.

To help you determine your individual budget, tailor the following worksheet to meet your individual needs. Before you do, browse through the book and take a peek at how different couples customized their budgets to their specifications. In some cases, there was no tuxedo rental, so that is not included on their budget breakdown. In other cases, they added a category or item. For instance, my husband and I used disposable plates and added "disposables" as a budget line item. The main focus of this book is the wedding day itself; therefore, the engagement and wedding rings, a rehearsal dinner party, and the honeymoon are not included on the budget sheet, but feel free to add them if you so choose.

Keep in mind that the figures you decide on for individual categories (attire, photographer, location, catering, and so on) will continuously change until you have made your final decisions. Initially, write in pencil and keep updating the budget breakdown as needed.

For example, you may realize that a designer wedding gown is a priority for you and, therefore, budget $1,000 toward your purchase. Then, you happen upon the perfect dress, and it is on sale for the unbelievable price of $425. You would then have $575 to use in another category. Or perhaps the reverse is true. You budget $500 for your dress. Then you try on a $1,200 gown you can't live without. To save money in other categories, you may decide to take on more DIY projects, for instance, arrange your own flowers, or make cheese trays and simple appetizers to save on catering.

WHY $5,000 OR LESS?

- Spending less on your wedding is in vogue.
- You're cash poor.
- You or your fiancé is between jobs.
- One or both partners are still in college or recently graduated.
- A child is on the way.
- This will be a second marriage.
- You're an older couple currently sending kids through college or saving for retirement.
- This is a reaffirmation of vows.
- You want to save money for your future.
- You want the wedding to be about your commitment, not about finances.
- You didn't want your parents to go into debt for a wedding.

- You had only three months to plan it, so you kept it simple.
- Your friend took a loan out to cover wedding costs, and two years later, she and her husband are still paying it off.
- Your parents offered you $20,000 either for a wedding or to help you purchase your first house, so you decided to spend $4,000 on the wedding and use the rest for a down payment on a new home.
- You went all out on your first marriage, but it didn't last. You don't need to repeat the fairy-tale part; you just want the happily ever after.
- It's still a lot of money—especially in times of economic insecurity.

CREATIVE FINANCING: LOANS, SPONSORSHIPS, AND CROWDSOURCING

In recent years, as more couples pay for their own wedding, creative financing has become popular. This is especially true of second and third weddings, nuptials that feature a bride and groom who have been on their own for a while, and couples who do not have many family members or do not plan to invite family. Consider the following options if your budget is only enough for a quick trip to city hall, but you have your heart set on hosting a priceless wedding closer to $5,000.

WEDDING LOANS. Traditional loans might be available, if needed. The amount would be borrowed using some form of collateral as a guarantee, such as a house, car, 401(k), or stocks. However, I caution couples against starting their marriage in debt if at all possible.

SPONSORSHIPS. Some businesses are willing to offer in-kind gifts, such as a wedding cake, catering, flowers, or a donation toward the wedding, in exchange for advertising on the couples' website, in their wedding brochure, or at the wedding. This method requires a significant amount of work as you line up sponsors who see value in billing as part of your wedding, such as a new caterer or florist. The trick will be to pull it off tastefully versus having too many sponsors and pronounced advertising, which might offend some guests.

RAISE MONEY. Get a second job, walk dogs in the neighborhood, move back home for a while, sell stuff on eBay or Craigslist, have a garage sale, open an online store to sell crafts, and so on.

CROWDSOURCING. Consider signing up with a specialty website that will help you raise money by soliciting funds from strangers, family, and friends. This is a great way to fund your reception and your honeymoon.

While getting sponsorships or utilizing crowdsourcing may seem crazy, many couples have successfully used these tactics to pay for all or a portion of their wedding. See pages 49–50 for Internet resources if you are interested in either or both of these options.

COUPLE'S BUDGET NOTES

W̶hen you first fill this out, it is best to write in pencil. Most likely, you will need to make changes to your budget as you move forward.

Amount from bride's salary   _____

Amount from groom's salary   _____

Amount from savings/investments   _____

Contributions from parents   _____

Contributions from sponsors   _____

Contributions from crowdsourcing   _____

Contributions from gifts   _____

Total Amount Available   _____

	Amount Budgeted	**Amount Paid**
Wedding site	_____	_____
Reception site	_____	_____
Dress, alterations, and veil	_____	_____
Tux	_____	_____
Food, catering	_____	_____
Beverages	_____	_____
Cake	_____	_____
Rentals	_____	_____
Photography	_____	_____
Video	_____	_____
Music	_____	_____
Flowers	_____	_____

(continued)

Invitations	_____	_____
Minister, officiant	_____	_____
License	_____	_____
Other _____	_____	_____
_____	_____	_____
_____	_____	_____
_____	_____	_____
Total Budget	_____	_____

TOP TEN WAYS TO SAVE MONEY ON YOUR WEDDING

1. Keep the guest list under control.
2. Use a location that is free or only charges a small fee.
3. Cater it all—or part of the reception—yourself.
4. Wear clothes you already own, such as your mom's dress or a favorite suit for the groom.
5. Rent a dress and tuxedo instead of buying, or use one that was only worn once.
6. Get married privately and have a party afterward.
7. Go alcohol-free or have a champagne toast, then a cash bar.
8. Don't serve a full meal; instead go with a tea, appetizer, or dessert reception.
9. Use a location where you do not need to rent items such as a tent, tables, chairs, and so on.
10. Elope.

Savvy Strategies for Saving Big

Where to save and where to splurge is highly personal and dependent on each couples' priorities. In general, I would recommend splurging on your top priorities and saving anywhere you can, especially if you can DIY. Then save by cutting costs wherever possible to stretch your budget. The following are general strategies; many more suggestions are detailed in the wedding scenarios and the chapters that follow.

- Keep cutting that guest list. Ask yourself if ten years from now you will still be good friends with all the people invited. Instead, limit the guest list to immediate family only, or invite some guests to just the ceremony.
- You'd better shop around. Do your research, let your fingers do the walking. Get at least three quotes for all big ticket items (e.g., catering, reception hall), and negotiate to get the very best deal possible.
- Go for an all-inclusive option, such as a reception hall that will already be decorated, or a pool hall where they throw in the location if you host an open bar.
- Stay flexible on the day of the week and time. Often Saturday and Sunday evening are more expensive. Consider a wedding earlier in the day or on a weekday night.
- Host an off-season event (e.g., a January event could be 25 percent less than one at Christmas).
- Shop the sales (Black Friday, Cyber Monday, after Christmas, summer clearance, etc.) as well as warehouse stores, discounters, close-outs, consignment shops, and garage and rummage sales.
- DIY as much as possible: flowers, decor, invites, favors, and more.
- Rely on talented friends to do your hair and makeup, photos, music, or officiate.
- Beg, borrow (but don't steal) a dress, jewelry, shoes, music.
- Wait until a later date (e.g., put the reception or honeymoon on hold for six months).
- Hold a courthouse wedding, then throw a reception at home to celebrate.

- Use reward points for part of the reception or for the honeymoon.
- Have the ceremony and reception in one location using the same decor.
- Choose a not-for-profit location, such as a church or temple, for a low-cost locale.
- Skip nonessentials such as favors, dress rehearsal dinner, and live music.

MURDER MYSTERY IN A FRENCH BISTRO

Veronica and Chris's Wedding on February 15
13 guests in Highwood, Illinois

PRIORITIES

1. Fun
2. Cheap
3. Intimate
4. Fast and legally binding
5. Yummy food

Veronica, thirty, and Chris, thirty-six, met in Mexico. Veronica was native to Mexico City, and Chris was a business real estate developer from the United States. The couple moved to Illinois to be closer to Chris's four children from a previous relationship.

Chris and Veronica returned to Mexico on vacation and got engaged while kayaking on New Year's Eve. After spending a total of six years together, they often had spoken hypothetically about getting married, but this time he had a ring. A month and a half later, they held their wedding back in the United States.

LOCATION

Veronica and Chris decided to get married at their favorite restaurant, a suburban French bistro named Froggy's. It has a small private wine cellar that boasts elaborate artwork, wainscoting with stone baseboards, white tablecloths, and café chairs. The couple decided it was the perfect location for their ceremony, too. Additionally, they chose to forgo a traditional wedding reception and instead host a "Murder Mystery Dinner." "I had always wanted to attend one," Veronica shared. "When looking for unique wedding ideas online, I found an affordable self-hosting party-planning kit for a murder mystery theme. We decided to go for it."

BUDGET

Wedding, reception site	$ 0	
Dress, alterations, veil, and shoes	$ 150	
Groom's clothing	$ 0	
Food and beverage	$1,600	
Photography	$ 0	
Hair	$ 35	
Flowers	$ 0	(a gift)
Party theme kit	$ 30	
Invitations, music, decor	$ 0	
License, minister	$ 0	
Total	$ 1,815	

DETAILS

The forest green art deco e-vite invitation read that Chris and Veronica "joyfully request your presence at their marriage celebration." It detailed that it was being performed by a judge at 4:30 p.m. sharp and stated, "Dinner and a Murder immediately following the ceremony."

The small foyer to the restaurant's wine cellar served as the ceremony locale. They set a table upfront with a bouquet of flowers. Folding chairs facing the table were there for the guests to use during the ceremony. The judge led a simple, nonreligious service, which included a Bible verse and a poem.

Immediately following the ceremony, they passed out envelopes to all in attendance. Inside was information on each character for the murder mystery: the character's secret objective, background information, and a name tag. From that point on, everything else for the evening was done in character, including the dinner, the toasts, dancing, and so on.

APPAREL

Veronica wore a loose, white sleeveless tunic by designer BCBG. The dress featured an asymmetrical hemline that started right above the knees in the front and went almost to the ground in the back. Gold floral embroidery embellished the neckline. A large midback cutout showed off Veronica's flawless complexion. She paired the dress with her favorite neutral high heels. Chris's mother lent her a diamond solitaire necklace to wear, plus she had on faux diamond earrings and a bracelet. Chris wore a black tux that he already owned.

MUSIC

One of Chris's friends played the solitary song for the wedding. It was an acoustic guitar version of "Baby I Want You," by Amos Lee. The restaurant piped in continuous music to play in the background during the remainder of the ceremony and dinner.

FLOWERS AND DECORATIONS

Veronica chose not to hold flowers during the ceremony. Small white hydrangeas in square vases dotted the tables, four arrangements in total. In addition to the flowers and a few votives, they placed framed pictures from the couple's six years together around the room. The couple chose to keep the decor very simple and elegant, forgoing elaborate props at the wedding and during the mystery dinner.

PHOTOS

Photos were informally taken by Veronica's mom, Chris's brother, and a few friends. They also attempted to videotape the ceremony on a stationary digital camera, but it did not turn out well. Veronica called it "an epic fail!"

FOOD AND BEVERAGE

The menu featured a choice of three courses, including a soup or salad, entrée, and dessert. The couple offered a simplified version of the restaurant menu, with the most expensive entrées removed to help them stay on budget. Dessert was bread pudding—their favorite—or a bowl of sorbet. Sodas, soft drinks, coffee, and tea were also covered. They had planned to ask anyone drinking alcohol to pay for their own, but only one person ordered, and it was only a few beers, so they covered the bill.

NOTES

Joy, merriment, and laughter were abundant throughout the evening. Veronica felt that their wedding was "really perfect! It was adult only, with the ideal amount of people, and everyone had a good time." The game ended when each character had a chance to guess who the murderer was and why he or she did it. Then the real murderer was uncovered. Afterward guests sat, talked, and eventually trickled out.

Chapter Four

INTERNET INSPIRATIONS

o doubt about it, technology has changed the landscape of wedding planning. This chapter will cover the basics of how to use the web to help you plan, prepare, budget, communicate with vendors and guests, write vows, and research the multitudes of details you can customize for your wedding. From DIY websites, wedding blogs, and cost-effective tips, to wedding images on Pinterest and money-saving online stores that are open 24/7, the Internet is an ideal way to research. It's all at your fingertips.

Did you meet your betrothed online? If so, it is not surprising. The Internet is the #1 way couples meet today; 35 percent of couples that married between 2005 and 2012 met through online dating, according to a study commissioned by eHarmony.com, but carried out by an impartial third party. When I wrote the first edition of *Priceless Weddings* in 2000, the Internet was not the integral life-planning and wedding-planning tool it is today. It's easier than ever to compare prices, purchase gently-used merchandise, bid on auction sites, and look for affordable honeymoon deals or wedding rings, all of which can help you save hundreds, even thousands, of dollars.

The Internet has made weddings more creative. Price competition among vendors and suppliers has become fiercer and more transparent. The Internet also has made new couples and their plans more open and visible. Before the Internet, we had little to no information about a couple's upcoming nuptials except what we gleaned from their engagement announcement in the local paper, plus word of mouth and their wedding invitation.

Nowadays, it is commonplace for newly engaged couples to craft their own wedding website, often using free templates that make the work easy. Your site acts as a landing place to share details with loved ones about your upcoming special event. It is also a unique way to introduce your soon-to-be spouse to any family and friends he or she has yet to meet. From your first date to your engagement, most of these templates let you chronicle in story or video form how the relationship unfolded.

Additionally, most sites offer a host of optional tools that will help you and your guests as the big day gets closer. The specifics of the wedding schedule (rehearsal dinner, ceremony, reception, etc.) are included on the site, along with maps to the various locations, links for reserving a room at nearby hotels and inns, gift registry information, and anything else you want to share to help out-of-town visitors plan their trip and enjoy the event.

That's just the beginning of how the web and social media have become an invaluable resource to budget-savvy brides and grooms. Here are some of the many things you can do on the Internet as your wedding approaches:

- Tweet about your engagement.
- Text a friendly reminder to guests if they do not respond to your invitation.
- Change your Facebook status to "Engaged" and post a "Life Event" when the marriage is official.
- E-mail and text vendors instead of calling them, which creates a paper trail (of sorts) if something goes wrong.
- Live-tweet your wedding, posting Instagram and Snapchat photos to a unique hashtag.
- Build your wedding site, purchase a domain name, register for gifts, find wedding apps, create maps and newsletters.
- Collect a database of guest addresses and correspondence, e-mail save-the-date notices, send and track wedding invita-

tions, allow guests to RSVP online, track guest count and, in some cases, menu selection.

- Create a wedding budget, compare actual spending to your estimates, use payment and due-date tracker applications, follow step-by-step event-planning checklists.
- Read advice from bloggers and online magazines covering all aspects of wedding planning, from invitations to dresses to honeymoons. A few to try include Thebrokeassbride.com, Offbeatbride.com, TheKnot.com, Weddingbee.com, or Weddingmusings.com.
- Log onto Yelp.com to see ratings for potential caterers and locations.
- Get inspired with wedding ideas galore on Pinterest. Start your own board; decide on a color palette for your bridesmaids, decor, linens, and florals; identify the specific flowers you want for your bouquet.
- Find the perfect music and lyrics for the ceremony and reception, listen to samples on Pandora, identify songs on the radio that would work using Spotify or Shazam. Make a playlist for the ceremony and reception.
- Bid on the perfect pair of high heels on eBay for less than half their retail price; look for wedding-band bargains on Craigslist.com and honeymoon specials on Expedia.com; shop Etsy.com for vintage or handcrafted reception decor for less than it costs at brick-and-mortar stores.
- Share photos before, during, and after your big day using Instagram, Snapshot, or one of the new wedding apps (such as Weddingparty.com) that you can get at the Apple Store (also available on Google Play).
- Use live streaming to give "front-row access" to loved ones who cannot attend but want to tune in.

The Internet keeps growing by quantum leaps, with sites launching and folding all the time. My hope is that you use the information in this chapter simply as a starting point. Spend some time surfing and decide which tools work best for you. Almost every aspect of your wedding could be planned and procured online. This is a blessing and a curse: the Internet expands your range of choices, but you can get overwhelmed with too many options. Use the Internet for inspiration but don't get bogged down.

As you always do in cyberspace, take steps to maintain your privacy and do not share information with or make purchases from disreputable or unknown sites. If you plan a meeting with a vendor you found via Craigslist or eBay, bring along a friend and meet in public. Use PayPal or another encrypted service that will guarantee your transactions are safe, and print and save all of your receipts from online transactions.

GENERAL SITES FOR WEDDING PLANNING

Many wedding-related websites aim to be one-stop shops covering all aspects of your big day. Each has its own suite of options. Often they will let you create and post a gift registry, find local vendors, make purchases, and create your own wedding website using templates they provide. Some sites are completely free, while others have free content and wedding apps but may charge a monthly or a onetime fee for an upgraded membership that gives you access to premium content or features. Look and compare the options you get. Is there advertising, or will your wedding site be ad-free?

The Top General Wedding Sites

As you peruse the sites for ideas, make sure to pin your favorites to Pinterest or otherwise mark them so you can always go back to these items.

The following are free sites with lots of great information:

THEKNOT.COM. A great site for building a free landing page for your own wedding, with a countdown feature, a place for posting engagement videos, and links to your registries.

BRIDE.COM. A good place to find wedding vendors, services, and bridal shows.

BRIDES.COM. The online site for *Brides* magazine. Good source for wedding dresses and ideas and advice about your ceremony and reception. Includes a budget calculator, registry links, honeymoon planning, etiquette guidance, and descriptions and photos of real weddings.

MYWEDDING.COM. A free site where you can tell how you met, post photos, link to registries, and provide information for your wedding party.

WEDDINGBEE.COM. A site for brides that highlights real weddings and includes a wedding forum to ask questions. Also has a classifieds section for wedding vendors.

INTIMATEWEDDINGS.COM. DIY projects galore on this site that boasts "little weddings, big heart." Lots of gift ideas for bridesmaids and groomsmen, wedding favors, programs, centerpieces, and floral arrangements.

THEFIRSTDANCE.COM. Where wedding planning meets marriage prep, with loads of advice on both. Lots of questions and answers (Q&A), helpful forms, and marriage tests, plus "therapy in a box" tools that will help couples through this stressful time.

WEDDINGBELLS.CA. Unforgettable weddings published about and for Canadians, including fashion and beauty, planning, travel, shopping, real weddings, and contests.

WEDDINGWIRE.COM. Includes planning tools, vendors, dresses, photos, registry, options for creating your own site, travel, wedding forums, budget, and wedding songs.

These are paid sites that will help you build your wedding website:

WEDDINGWINDOW.COM. Some features are free, and others require that you

> ### TIP
>
> Don't just take my word for it. Visit Topweddingsites.com and Top10weddingsites.com for even more sites to visit. You'll find ideas that will inspire everything you need for a priceless wedding.

pay. This sleek, upscale planner site lets you blog; interact with guests, groomsmen, and bridesmaids; and even has a dashboard that will share statistics on how many people have responded, how many are attending, and so on. The biggest drawback is the $14.95 monthly fee (or $79 annually). It's an additional $19 to get a custom.com domain. Works with Facebook, Twitter, LinkedIn, and Pinterest, and is mobile-friendly. It uses HTML5 Editor.

EWEDDING.COM. The various packages offered here range from free to $14.95 per month. Functionalities includes photo storage and display, e-mail, support (if needed), video capabilities for your home page, and background music.

GODADDY.COM. You can purchase a domain name and a unique Internet address, which could include your names or where the wedding will be (such as MaryandJimschicagowedding.com) on this hosting site. You can build your wedding site at Godaddy.com or move to Evite.com or another service. Hosting fees vary, depending on pages and features, from basic five-page sites to a thirty-page site that includes photos, maps, and a video of the engagement story. You decide what you want on the site, and it can be customized at a price.

Wedding Bloggers You Should Know

These are some of my favorite wedding blogs. A few are rather upscale but can be used as a source of inspiration. Log onto Weddingblogs100.com to see an even broader list of bridal bloggers.

- **100Layercake.com:** helps the modern bride to layer her wedding with inspiration and DIY
- **African-Americanbrides.com:** advice for a diversity of brides, budgets, and styles
- **Apracticalwedding.com:** thoughts on staying sane while planning a wedding
- **ABrideonabudget.com:** showcases practical spending advice for fabulous (yet not costly) weddings
- **Thebrokeassbride.com:** bold and original approaches that make the most of your budget

- **Thebudgetsavvybride.com:** helps couples plan a radiant wedding without breaking the bank
- **Eco-beautifulweddings.com:** global, organic, and sustainable wedding style
- **Glamourandgraceblog.com:** includes modern and vintage weddings and theme ideas
- **Groomsadvice.com:** top site for groom-to-groom chat and ideas, plus a registry for men
- **Ilovefarmweddings.com:** romantic, rustic, nature-inspired nuptials
- **Offbeatbride.com:** for those proud to be called weird; their tagline is "Altar Your Thinking"
- **Prettypearbride.com:** for plus-size brides
- **Rusticweddingchic.com:** shabby chic and naturally inspired nuptial ideas
- **Thealternativebride.com:** unique ideas and original themes for a wedding that is YOU

INVITATIONS

Look for invitations that resonate with your theme. The Internet offers templates and forms you can use for printing your own paper mailings, plus many options for going paperless. There are a lot of stationery needs when you're planning a wedding: from your engagement announcement to save-the-dates, the invitations themselves to reception cards and RSVP cards, menu cards to a newsletter you post or send prewedding to familiarize nonresidents with the area, where to stay, and what sites they might want to see while visiting.

Consider paperless invitations for a less formal wedding, or use traditional paper with lined envelopes if you choose to be more formal. The web is also a good place to find brick-and-mortar stationery and card shops, as well as chains like Staples, FedEx Office, Walgreens, Walmart, and Michaels, which offer DIY options for printing. You can either buy invitations and customize them yourself or have the paper vendor print the invitations for you.

These are good websites for paperless invites, eliminating hundreds of dollars traditionally spent on invitations:

- Evite.com
- Grenvelope.com
- Paperlesspost.com
- Punchbowl.com

Many websites offer cute invitations and/or invite paper to purchase and print from your home computer. Either way you can save a bundle over traditional stationery stores through these websites:

- 123print.com
- Invitationsbydawn.com (handcrafted options including wood invites)
- Iprint.com
- Vistaprint.com
- Weddingpaperdivas.com (offers a free matching wedding website if you order invitations through them)
- Zazzle.com

TIP

Search for unique custom bridal and bridesmaids dresses on Etsy .com. Use the search tool to look for individual bridal shops and handmade bride and bridesmaids gowns. For instance, The Peppy Studio (previously Craftingsg), sews custom gowns made in Singapore featuring the color and style of your choice from $59.

BRIDAL AND BRIDESMAID ATTIRE

When I first got engaged, I spent over a hundred dollars on wedding magazines to look at wedding attire. With the Internet as a resource, brides no longer have to make that initial investment. It is free to surf department stores, bridal salons, designer sites, online magazines, Pinterest, and photos that recent brides and grooms have posted for the world to see. By the time you get to a store to try on dresses, you should be self-educated on the styles you like that fit your budget. Further, by checking online first, you can track down where to get the best deal on the dress of your dreams. Plus, online clearance racks will have more merchandise than a store. For more on saving money while shopping for wedding attire, see chapter 6. For additional online inspiration, look at general and blog websites, Pinterest, and apps. Here are recommended online stores to get you started searching for bridal attire:

- Anntaylor.com
- Belk.com
- Bridalandveiloutlet.com
- Bridalmart.com
- Davidsbridal.com
- Etsy.com
- Jcrew.com
- JJshouse.com
- Lightinthebox.com
- Macys.com
- Nordstrom.com
- Simplybridal.com
- Talbots.com
- Target.com

Bridal Attire Rentals

Buying a once-worn or consignment gown or renting a wedding gown will slash the price of buying a new designer dress for a one-day occasion. For more on renting instead of buying, see page 97. Here are some online options to consider:

- Borrowingmagnolia.com
- Littleborroweddress.com
- Rentaweddingdress.com
- Renttherunway.com

TIP

Save priceless money for your bridesmaids. Dress rentals can cost hundreds less. For instance, at Little borroweddress.com, starting at just $50, you can choose from eighteen colors and a variety of different patterns.

Previously Worn Bridal Attire

For individual used dresses try Craigslist and eBay or shop local vintage, thrift, and consignment stores such as Goodwill. Preowned wedding and bridesmaids dresses, shoes, and accessories such as veils are plentiful online:

- Oncewed.com
- Preownedweddingdresses.com
- Resaleshopping.com
- Thethriftshopper.com
- Vowtobechic.com
- Woreitonce.com
- Wornoncebridal.com

Attire Accessories

Veils, gloves, shoes, and other accessories may be substantially less expensive if you compare prices online before purchasing them. The bridal warehouses listed previously (page 53) are a good place to start your search. Here are a few additional websites that focus on accessories:

- Bridalgloves.com
- Shoebuy.com
- Simpleveil.com
- Zappos.com

GROOM AND GROOMSMEN ATTIRE

I advise grooms to try on tuxedos and suits several months in advance of the big day. Entry-level tuxedos can be purchased at JCPenney.com for $99, which is lower than many rental rates. The groom needs to decide if it makes sense to have his groomsmen rent, or if he would prefer everyone purchase his own tux. If he goes the rental route, once the company and style are decided on, your attendants can sign up with their measurements and a credit card. The company sends the appropriate rental via mail, along with a return box, in time for your event. The day after the wedding, all they need

EBAY

A virtual mall of consumer-to-consumer stores, eBay primarily sells its wares through auctions. In many categories, weddings included, you can save 50 to 90 percent off retail prices. There is also a Buy It Now feature where you can purchase an item immediately if you are willing to pay the stated price. Wedding-related items are plentiful, some new, such as never-worn dresses, invitations, signage, and theme props, and some previously used or worn, including shoes, veils, jewelry, and tuxedos. You can even bid on honeymoon packages.

to do is drop it back in the return box. Here are a few of the national rental options:

- Menswearhouse.com
- Tuxedosonline.com
- Tuxship.com

FURNITURE, TENT, AND THEME RENTALS

You can rent just about anything for your wedding, usually through a local rental company. A chuppah or arch and folding chairs may be needed for the ceremony if your location does not provide them. Reception options include tables, linens, carafes, chafing dishes, china, candelabras, glassware, silverware, platters, and a dance floor. For outdoor weddings, renting a tent is advisable so that weather issues do not put a damper on the festivities. The following are national rental companies to consider. In addition, I also recommend searching online for a combination of words, such as *discount*, *wedding*, or *event rental*. Also be sure to input the city closest to your location.

- Classicpartyrentals.com
- Galacloths.com
- Hobbylobby.com
- Rentalhq.com: this site will help you locate local vendors for your wedding rental needs.
- Rentmywedding.com

FOOD

Pinterest is a wonderful resource for menu and food display inspiration. General wedding sites, weddings featured online, and wedding blogs will also have mouthwatering photos and compelling menu ideas. To find caterers and restaurants to provide delicious food, try Yelp.com, Urbanspoon.com, or your local chamber of commerce.

If you are catering your own wedding, purchasing food, platters, and silverware or utensils at wholesale prices will help save a bundle. Or try the furniture, tent, and theme rental sites listed above and see if you can find a local place to borrow the plates, silverware, and platters at an even lower cost. Search online to find local restaurant food suppliers, such as Cash & Carry (smartfoodservice.com) and Gordon Food Service (gfs.com), or visit a membership club such as Samsclub.com or Costco.com. Try the recipes and suggestions in chapter 10, and review the foodie recipe sites below for even more options.

- Marthastewartweddings.com
- Realsimple.com
- Southernliving.com
- Wilton.com

DIY, THEME, AND DECOR

Theme supplies can be purchased at big box, party, and specialty craft stores. After you decide on your location and take stock of what your caterer and location vendors have to work with, use general wedding blogs and online magazines to search out DIY projects that will add ambience without costing a fortune. These are some places to purchase items:

- Factorydirectcraft.com
- Hobbylobby.com
- Michaels.com
- Orientaltrading.com
- Partycity.com
- Weddingdecor.com

ETSY

Etsy.com is an e-commerce website that is a virtual marketplace of boutique seller pages. Consumers can purchase handmade and vintage items, plus some factory-made goods. It's a great place for deals on art supplies, crafts, wedding party gifts, invites, bridesmaids' dresses, and theme decor. As many of these businesses are run out of the owners' homes and there is little to no overhead compared to a brick-and-mortar store, the savings are passed on to you, the customer.

I searched for *wedding* on Etsy.com, and over two million items came up, with over one million of them customizable. The items being sold included wedding candles, flower girl dresses, cake toppers, brooches, artificial flowers, wedding arches, jewelry, favors, gifts, gift bags, foodstuffs, invites, sparklers, wedding lights, and customized favors.

FLOWERS

Admiring the stunning wedding bouquets, corsages, and centerpieces online makes me want to get married all over again. The sites below deliver affordable floral options and DIY project supplies right to your doorstep.

- **Bloomsbythebox.com:** tutorials, videos, projects, and the supplies to bring the bouquets, centerpieces, boutonnieres, and more, to life
- **Fiftyflowers.com:** wholesale and bulk flowers or DIY arrangements, rose petals, corsages, and customizable packages
- **Flowermuse.com:** stunning customizable DIY packages
- **Thebridesbouquet.com:** individual bouquets, corsages, centerpieces; packages starting as low as $99 (bridal bouquet, four boutonnieres, four corsages, and a centerpiece)

MUSIC

The sites listed below are resources to help you find, sample, and save the music you choose for your ceremony, reception, and dancing. In many cases you'll want to purchase the song and/or utilize the premium edition (a feature you need to pay for) to get or make playlists without advertising.

- **Foreverwed.com:** browse wedding song lists.
- **iTunes.com:** preview, buy, and download all the songs you need for the ceremony, reception, first dance, cocktail hour, and dancing.
- **Pandora.com:** listen to your favorite style of songs and music. The site is free, but with a paid subscription you will be able to customize playlists and listen without advertisements.
- **Shazam.com:** gets songs for you that you don't know; make your own playlists.
- **Spotify.com:** use lists from this website to be your own wedding DJ.

- **Weddingmusic.com, Weddingmusicproject.com, Wedding music101.com:** recommendations and excerpts of wedding tunes help you decide what to purchase.

PHOTOGRAPHY

To save big money on wedding photos, ask an amateur shutterbug friend to help chronicle your big day. Afterward, compile the shots he or she took, along with pictures from wedding guests, by uploading to one of the sites below. Once the photos are compiled, you can pick which ones you want to put in a custom wedding album, plus order loose pictures in a variety of sizes. You also can e-vite your family and friends to order (and pay for) their own prints.

- Weddingparty is an app for collecting and sharing photos from the engagement through your honeymoon.
- Wedpics.com and PhotoCircle are designed to store and share wedding photos.
- Also consider Walgreens.com, Walmart.com, Shutterfly.com, and Target.com.

GIFTS AND REGISTRIES

For wedding gifts, plus gift ideas for parents, the wedding party, and wedding favors, check out the following options. Traditionally, it is not considered in good taste to share registry information on your invitation. However, it is appropriate to post details on your personal wedding site and potentially on your e-vites.

- **Cardavenue.com:** a registry for gift cards
- **Crowdsource.com:** enables guests to pitch in together for a large gift purchase, such as money toward a new car, or several medium-sized purchases, for example, a biweekly share or membership in a community supported agriculture (CSA) program.

- **Hatchmyhouse.com:** features a visual representation of the house the couple hopes to build or buy, with guests contributing toward an item at a specific price (for example, $200 for a window).
- **Honeyfund.com:** a nontraditional honeymoon registry that allows guests to purchase unique adventures during the honeymoon instead of linens and glassware. For instance, the wish list could include "romantic dinner for two," "airfare to Hawaii, 2 needed," or "swimming with the dolphins, 2 needed." The prices would also be included.
- **Myregistry.com:** a one-site registry that compiles all store registries into one locale
- **Themanregistry.com:** provides men's wedding planning resources, including groom and groomsman gifts
- **Uponourstar.com:** a registry for donating toward a home, a car, college funds for kids, money toward paying off wedding debt, and more
- **Zola.com:** a "reinvented wedding registry for the modern couple." You can register for anything from trips to cookware, and scan UPC codes to add additional gifts to your wish list at any time. There is a gift grouping option that lets multiple people go in toward something large, such as "a weekend in wine country." Guests can choose to donate whatever they want toward the present.

In addition to the above options, many specialty stores, such as Crate & Barrel, Pottery Barn, Target, and Williams-Sonoma, offer traditional registries online. If there is a store where you are interested in registering, check with them to see if they offer both online and in-person registry services.

TRAVEL

The following are resources to aid an away-from-home wedding and your honeymoon travel needs. In addition, check for special deals on well-known sites like Expedia.com, Orbitz.com, Priceline.com, and Travelocity.com. Plus, search hotel and airline sites directly.

- **Bestdestination.com**: resort and vendor reviews for destination weddings
- **Destinationweddings.com**: packages for the honeymoon and weddings away from home
- **Kayak.com**: review flights, hotels, and car rentals on multiple search engines at one time
- **Tripadvisor.com**: for consumer ratings on hotels, travel sites, and tourist destinations

LIVE STREAMING

Loved ones from across the country and around the globe can support your nuptials without ever leaving home. Skype .com, HangWith app, Upstream app, Apple's FaceTime app, and YouTube Live Stream allow you to share your wedding live at no cost.

A paid media service that could be worth the investment is I Do Stream (idostream.com). From a few hundred dollars and using your own camcorder, you can broadcast high-quality footage of your wedding live to up to fifty simultaneous viewers on five continents. A higher-priced, all-inclusive equipment-rental package includes a laptop, an HD camcorder, a tripod, software, shipping charges to you, and return shipping for the equipment. The service even sends an e-vite with the wedding date, time, and log-in codes to your potential web viewers.

PINTEREST INSPIRATION

Pinterest is a free social-networking platform that acts as a virtual bulletin board—customizable with your ideas or someone else's. When you find something online—an image, a blog post, an inspirational quote or a photo—you can pin it to your board for everyone to see. It helps you organize and share ideas. There are *lots* of wedding ideas on Pinterest to choose from, pinned there by brides, grooms, caterers, wedding consultants, and other vendors.

Start by registering. Then create boards for ideas you find inspirational and worth saving, for example, recipes, wedding attire, wedding themes, and wedding words (for invites, poems, readings, etc.).

YOUTUBE

YouTube can be a *huge* online resource if you are a visual and/or auditory learner. You'll find tutorials on DIY projects, videos of others' weddings, wedding songs, dances, wedding speeches, and wedding bloopers. After your wedding, you can privately post wedding videos. Use the search engine on YouTube to find public videos that are relevant by typing in phrases such as "wedding flash mobs," "dancing lessons," "how to write your own wedding vows," or "how to do an updo hairstyle."

MESSAGE BOARDS

Message boards are often part of the larger wedding websites, as well as smaller sites produced by individual bloggers. A message board is an online support system. If you send a query, chances are someone out there has gone through something similar and will reply. TheKnot.com, Weddingwire

.com, and many blogs have their own message boards for anyone navigating through the wedding-planning process.

CRAIGSLIST

Check this classified-advertisement website for bargain-basement prices on items such as lights, chair covers, candles, linen, centerpieces, favors, rings, shoes, photo booth props, and wedding dresses. Craigslist also lists estate, garage, and rummage sales, any of which could produce some low-cost treasures.

WEDDING APPS

There are thousands of wedding apps. Virtually anything that you can do on a computer has a mini or "lite" mobile app version that will help you capture the basics. There are a lot of photo apps, including Photo Booth, which takes four quick pics in a row and arranges them in a strip similar to one from an old-fashioned photo booth. Later you can print the photos, save them, and add them to an online scrapbook. Other photo apps include frame makers, movie and slide makers, poster makers, and photo stickers.

Here are several wedding-related apps worth taking a peek at:

- Appy Couple (yes, it's "Appy," not "happy"): shares information and photos from your engagement through your honeymoon
- Bridal show: lists local and national vendors
- Bridal Shower Games
- Best Budget: offers a wedding budget calculator

- Hair MakeOver: lets you upload a photo and "try on" different hairstyles before your big day
- Meetup: shares the dates for the sessions and groups you join, from wedding dance lessons to DIY wedding groups, LGBT weddings, and bridal fairs. You decide what to attend.
- Wedding LookBook: The Knot has a beautiful app for this.
- Weddinggawker: allows you to look at other people's weddings for inspiration

THE "BIG LEBOWSKI" OF WEDDINGS

Chelsea and Jesse's Wedding on September 6
175 guests in Omaha, Nebraska

PRIORITIES

1. Sticking with the theme of their first date
2. Not stuffy
3. Relaxed and fun
4. More of a party than a wedding
5. For both to be part of the planning process

Chelsea, twenty-six, and Jesse, thirty-five, met while working for a telecommunications center. When they married, they had been dating for three-and-a-half years.

On their first date, they watched *The Big Lebowski*, starring Jeff Bridges. Every year on the anniversary of their first date, they watched the movie again, drank White Russians, and went bowling. Six months before they were even engaged, Chelsea spotted save-the-date cards with *The Big Lebowski* theme.

The cards stated, "the Dude proposes, the Dudette abides." From that point on they agreed that if and when they got married, they wanted to have a *Big Lebowski*–themed wedding.

LOCATION

True to the movie theme, the invitation they sent out was ransom-note-style, printed on glitter paper using a Cricut machine. The font was a match of the one featured in the movie's title sequence. The invite read:

> The Dude & His Lady
> Invite you to a day of bowling,
> boozing, food, and a wedding.

In addition to the unique handmade invitations, the couple also worked with a friend who was a computer coder to set up their own wedding website. One of Chelsea's pieces of advice is to let people contribute their talents to make your day extra special.

The nuptials were exchanged in a local vintage bowling alley, complete with a marquee-sign announcement. They held the ceremony and exchanged their vows right on the bowling lanes. Guests were told in advance to dress as favorite characters from the movie. The only decor was glow-in-the-dark stars which they hung around the bowling alley.

BUDGET

Dress, alterations, veil, and shoes	$ 750
Groom's clothing	$ 350
Site rental	$ 0 (waived due to bar use)
Liquor	$ 1,300
Unlimited bowling and shoe rental	$ 300
Photography	$ 600
Videography	$ 900

Makeup, hair	$	50
Flowers	$	90
Decorations	$	200
Invitations	$	350
License, minister	$	35
Total		$4,925

DETAILS

Jesse's friend Luke was ordained online by the Church of the Latter-Day Dude, a part of the Religion of the Big Lebowski.

There are no obligations to join the other 225,000 Dudeist Priests. However, you will have to "vow to uphold the principles of Dudeism; to just take it easy, to be *dude* (easygoing) to everyone [you] meet, and to keep [your] mind limber," as well as affirm that "the ordination is for [you], not someone else, or for [your] dog or whatever."

Chelsea shared that neither of their families are super religious, so the ceremony was "short and sweet." And instead of just the bride making an entrance, Jesse wanted to have a special entrance also. The officiant welcomed everyone and shared a brief story about the couple. They chose to skip readings but wanted to share a "unity cocktail" as part of the proceedings. With a spotlight on them and black lighting everywhere else in the bowling alley, the couple strolled toward the bowling pins, where they proceeded to pour the ingredients for a White Russian into a drink shaker, mixing it together, drinking it arm and arm, and declaring it their signature cocktail for the evening. They then walked back to the officiant and continued with the wedding vows and exchange of rings.

APPAREL

Chelsea was trying to match the green velvet robe that "Dude's lady friend" wore in the movie, but eventually she gave up and went with a black-and-green full-length prom dress. It was fitted on top, with cap and trumpet sleeves, a sweetheart neckline, black tulle, and green sequin beading. She wore sparkly green patent leather heels and later changed into bowling shoes. On her head was a vintage pillbox hat with a veil in front and feathers on one side.

Jesse channeled Dude's attire wearing a vintage Pendleton sweater, pajama lounge pants, and a bowling shirt. Groomsmen wore brown-and-yellow bowling shirts, and the bridesmaids wore matching yellow vintage-inspired dresses.

MUSIC

They used the soundtrack to *The Big Lebowski* for the ceremony. They also had a playlist they made on Spotify.

FLOWERS AND DECORATIONS

Chelsea ordered gerbera daisies and pinned three together on each of the bridesmaids. "We did not tell the florist they were for a wedding so they wouldn't overcharge us." They put empty coffee cans randomly on tables as added props.

PHOTOS

"We splurged on photos and video. For our big day we hired two videographers plus a photographer from 8:00 a.m. to 9:00 p.m. We also spent $400 on engagement photos. If we had needed to save, that would be an area we could have cut back on," stated Chelsea.

FOOD AND BEVERAGE

The largest charge of all was the bar bill, which also covered use of the bowling alley. They had the White Russian signature cocktail, plus two kegs of beer and bottles of wine, most of which went untouched.

The dinner was provided by a food truck that set up outside in the parking lot. They served Italian sausage, bacon-wrapped hot dogs, sliders, garlic fries, and, for the kids, chicken fingers. Guests were told to go get food whenever they wanted. There never seemed to be too much of a backup, and the line moved fast. All agreed the offerings were delicious comfort food—much better than standard wedding fare.

For dessert, Chelsea's mom set up a cupcake buffet and used multi-tiered cupcake stands to add height to the display. She made twenty-four dozen of various flavors and toppings, including some based on the movie, such as White Russian Dudecakes, Nilest Black Magic Dark Chocolate Cupcakes, and Red Velvet for Maude, plus she baked some with Fruity Pebbles both in the batter and mixed into the frosting.

Chapter Five

LOCATION, LOCATION, LOCATION

○——————○

These days, anything goes for your wedding location. From tying the knot while skydiving to a traditional backyard or church wedding, your choice of a venue will play a large part in defining the tone of your celebration. Some couples know immediately where they want to tie the knot, some couples may have several ideas and need to narrow down their list, and others may have no clue.

If you need help deciding where to get married, answer the questions on pages 26–28 and start brainstorming with friends and family until you find your perfect location. Here's what you'll find in this chapter:

- A questionnaire to help you with your location priorities
- An A-to-Z location-brainstorming list
- Questions to ask when calling sites
- What to look for on location
- How to negotiate the best contract

My hope is that you have already completed the Vision Worksheet and Couple's Questionnaire in chapter 2. If not, please do so before proceeding. Those worksheets, coupled with time spent researching on the Internet, reading magazines, attending wedding shows, and so on, will definitely help you as you move along in the planning journey and select a site. Here are a couple of additional details you will want to nail down before beginning the fun task of scouting wedding sites:

- Write out your guest list. When you know the size of your celebration, you'll know how large or small a locale you will need (see pages 287–90 for more on guest lists).
- Decide on a season, possible dates, and an approximate time for your celebration. You will need these to inquire about site availability. However, if you have a well-known location in mind, remaining flexible will help ensure that you can book the site.

LOCATION QUESTIONNAIRE

Answering the following questions will jump-start your location search. Don't worry about replying to questions that aren't applicable or that you haven't yet decided on.

Approximate date _____ Time _____ Number of guests _____

What town or area do you want to get married in? _____

What places in that area are special to you as a couple? As individuals?

_____

Do you want to get married in a church or synagogue? _____

Do you already have a few locations in mind? _____

_____

Do you want your wedding and reception to be in the same location or in two separate locations? _____

What is your favorite place as a couple? _____

Where did you spend your first date? _____

Where did you get engaged? _____

Where is your favorite park, restaurant, hotel, etc.? _____

Do you, your family, or close friends have a house or other site that would be suitable for a wedding and reception and that would not cost you money to rent? _____

Is there a theme that you would like associated with your wedding and reception? _____

_____

_____

_____

_____

_____

_____

What activities that you do as a couple might you want to include in your wedding or reception (such as hiking or walking on the beach)? _____

_____

What else is important to you with regard to your wedding and reception?

_____

_____

_____

_____

_____

_____

_____

_____

_____

This section will help you and your fiancé brainstorm together as well as with friends or family. Before you go through the list, reflect on your priorities and try to visualize the type of party or event that would truly symbolize who you are as a couple to the guests whom you are inviting. Have a paper and pen or a notebook available to jot down ideas that sound good to you.

A   An **art gallery** may be ideal for a small group, depending on the size and price of the gallery, or find an **arbor** in a local park and tie the knot under the trees. An **arboretum or botanical garden** will provide such lovely scenery that you'll save lots of money on decor. Many **aquariums** have party rooms to rent, and **amusement parks** often have wedding packages that are all-inclusive. An **antique shop or mall** would add character to your special event.

B   The **beach** is always a romantic setting for formal or informal weddings. Large and small **boats** or **barges** appeal to land and water lovers alike and can work for brunch, lunch, cocktail, or dinner receptions. A **bed-and-breakfast** is a great location for all size weddings, and an added bonus is the availability of accommodations for out-of-town guests. Sunrise, midday, or sunset on a scenic **bay** is always a good bet. A **barn** makes a good backdrop for a rustic celebration. Or tie the knot in your favorite **bar**.

C   Traditional wedding locations include **churches, chapels,** or a **courthouse.** The local **community center** is usually quite reasonable to rent for the day and often includes tables and chairs. A **country club** has the benefit of in-house caterers, which may be a pricey alternative, but not if you are only hosting a handful of people or having a breakfast or afternoon tea. Some **catering companies** have their own on-site locations, which can run the gamut from reasonable to exorbitant, based on your tastes and the size of your wedding. Other ideas include tying the knot at a lakeside **cottage,** a **cabin,** a **campsite,** on a **cruise ship,** in a **coffeehouse,** or at a **café.** You might want to investigate your **alma mater** or the local **college campus,** because there are often great deals to be had at such sites. Also consider a **combination** wedding and honeymoon in one; run away to a European **castle,** vacation at an all-inclusive resort that handles weddings, or tie the knot at a **casino** that has affordable wedding packages.

D A wedding in the scenic **desert** can be ideal, especially when it is winter elsewhere.

E Horse lovers may be sweet on the idea of an **equestrian center** celebration, and Southerners may like the idea of eloping to the **Everglades.**

F Scenic sites abound, such as a **field** in summer, a **flower garden** in full bloom, a redwood or evergreen **forest**, a working **farm** (complete with animals and a red barn), the county **fairgrounds**, or aboard a **ferry** with the view of the water and a nearby city.

G A golf lover may want to exchange nuptials on the **golf course**, and a hopeless romantic may choose to locate a **gazebo** in a nearby park. Or plant a **garden** in your own yard.

H Don't overlook the obvious locations, for instance, your **home** or the home of friends or relatives, or consider renting a home on the beach or in the woods. Also consider a **harbor** with a scenic view, local **historical sites,** veterans or town **halls,** and local **hotels.**

I Both **inns** and hotels can have the advantage of catering, parking, and guest rooms on location.

J A **Japanese garden** makes a great backdrop for a midday tea celebration and great wedding photos, while a **jazz club** could be perfect for either a semiformal or a black-tie affair.

L **Lakes, lawns, lodges, lofts, libraries,** or a **log cabin** are all fabulous locations.

M Inquire for rates at a **museum,** a **military club,** or a **meditation center.** Find out if permits are needed to join in marriage on a local **mountaintop.**

N Instill patriotism and scenic beauty in your wedding at a **national park.** Inquire at a local **nursery** if you can wed there; with so many plants and flowers you should save on the location and the decor.

O An **orchard** in full bloom with apple blossoms, cherry flowers, or fresh fruit would make a blushing bride appear even more beautiful.

P Choose your site from any number of **parks:** county, state or national, or pick a favorite **picnic spot,** a fishing or boat **pier,** rent a **party boat,** or book the **penthouse** at a local hotel and exchange your vows there. A restaurant **patio** would also work well.

R Look into your local **recreation center,** check into **retreat locations,** find out more about a favorite **restaurant** or **resort,** consider a **rose garden,** a horse **ranch,** a **racetrack,** or a **Renaissance fair.**

S A **ski lodge** could be the perfect winter destination, the local **senior center** may be quite a bargain, or the **synagogue** may be your ideal.

T Try for the **town hall,** the **temple,** or a **tearoom.** Tie the knot on the **train** or a **trolley** or under some type of **tent**—circus, backyard, rented.

V A **vineyard** has year-round natural beauty, and the wine is often included with the price. Also inquire about **vacation rentals, village halls,** and historic **Victorian homes and B&Bs.**

W How about a wedding in the **woods,** by a **waterfall,** or on the **wharf?** Or find a wonderful **wedding chapel** that suits your needs.

Y Renting a **yacht** for a few hours is not always as expensive as it sounds. And don't overlook your own or someone else's **yard**—front or back.

Z Not only will you get great photo ops, but a wedding at the **zoo** will bring out the kid in all of your guests, young and old alike.

Bear in mind your priorities and your budget. If you keep the cost of the site down or book a location at no charge (like your own backyard), there will be more money for you to spend on other priorities, such as the wedding dress or the food. But if location was on the top of your priority list, maybe this is the place you want to spend the big bucks. It's all up to you!

MONEY-SAVING TIPS

Brainstorm first about the type of locations that appeal to you and then about how you can have the location of your dreams without paying full price. Although many sites may appear to be way out of your price range, it is always worth calling just to gather information. Renting the botanical gardens may not be feasible, but do they let people get married in the rose garden for free or, at a nominal charge, while the park is open? Can you get married at the zoo and rent one of the picnic areas for the event as opposed to renting the whole pachyderm building? Even renting out a small yacht may be affordable if the $400 cost includes a three-hour cruise for up to fifty people. And three hours isn't long enough for the ceremony *and* a full meal, so you will save money on catering by serving just hors d'oeuvres or cake and champagne.

Keep thinking about ideas and alternatives and brainstorm ways to make your perfect places more affordable:

- Try booking off-season or at odd hours or on days that aren't as popular.
- If you are looking into parks, try renting a small area instead· of the whole park, or find out any parks that may let you have your event there without charge. Some parks won't guarantee you access to a certain area but may leave it first come, first served. You can assign a close friend or family member to arrive very early in the morning of your wedding to claim the location. (Note: It is always wise to ascertain that some sort of rain shelter is nearby.)
- Consider hosting the wedding and reception in one location. This saves money by not having to staff, decorate, and rent two different sites. Also, some of the most affordable locations are halls that are attached to a church or other house of worship. You can use your own caterer or do the food yourself. State parks, village halls, and municipally run buildings and parks are also very affordable options.
- Time of day matters, too. If you book your location for breakfast or high tea, you may save money on the room rental as well as big dollars on the food and caterers. Dinner is the

most expensive meal, and evening is the most popular time of day to rent a banquet site. Keep in mind that day or night, Saturday is the day of the week that most weddings are held. Choosing to wed on a Sunday, or even a weekday, can really cut back on your costs.

- Consider hosting the wedding at a restaurant, especially one that has a nice view or area in which to hold the ceremony. In a restaurant setting, you often save money because you won't need rentals (tables, glassware, etc.), and everything is included in the per person food and beverage charges. Some places may have a balcony or patio adjacent to their seating area. If so, the ceremony could be held outdoors, with the reception to follow inside. They may charge a cost for the room rental, though in many cases as long as your food and beverage meet a minimum, the space is included.

- When you are calling around to inquire about sites, don't mention right away that you are getting married; instead say that you are hosting a party. When a bride and groom walk in the door, the business sees dollar signs. If they don't know that the quote they are giving you is for a wedding, they won't have time to jack up the prices or give you special wedding brochures with more expensive prices and catering options.

CHAPELS OF LOVE

One possible locale for budget-conscious couples to consider is the traditional wedding chapel. Found all over the country, chapels have styles that vary widely from quaint cabins in the woods to ornate Victorian homes equipped with closed-circuit television and full wedding-planning services. Most chapels have a nondenominational minister to perform your ceremony, so you share intimacy and a spiritual element without dogma.

In Las Vegas, "the wedding capital of the world," you can choose from many nontraditional chapel themes. For example, an Elvis wedding comes complete with costumes and music, a drive-through wedding chapel is a twenty-four-hour possibility, or you can forgo the outrageous and opt for elegant luxury in a Bellagio Hotel wedding chapel.

(For more on Las Vegas, see page 335.)

WILD AND CRAZY WEDDING LOCATIONS

For those who yearn for an adventurous union, try tying the knot while involved in one of these activities:

- Bungee jumping
- In-line skating
- Roller skating
- Horseback riding
- Hiking
- Ice skating
- Kayaking
- On safari
- Skydiving
- Scuba diving
- Skiing
- Snowboarding
- Snowmobiling
- Riding in a hot-air balloon
- Riding on a roller coaster

The Pros and Cons of Wild and Crazy Wedding Locations
Pros:

- They are unique.
- You are doing something you love and that you love to share with your fiancé.

A WORD OF CAUTION

Don't procrastinate when looking for a wedding site! If you wait too long to start calling around, some venues may not be available. Popular locations may be reserved up to one year in advance. On the other hand, don't omit a location from your list if you are pulling together a last-minute wedding—you may get lucky and book a cancellation slot.

Remember, the date, time, theme, type of food, and so forth will all be influenced by your location choice, or your location choice might be influenced by the date, time, theme, size, and type of food.

- You get an adrenaline rush while tying the knot.
- Your guest list will be very short.
- You may be too scared about the stunt to have second thoughts about the wedding.

Cons:

- The guest list is limited to those participating in the sport.
- Special arrangements will need to be made for guests with physical limitations.
- There is a potential for danger—which can be both a pro and a con. On the one hand, it spices up the day; on the other hand, if you or your fiancé gets injured, there goes the honeymoon!

FINDING YOUR VENUE

After you know the size of your wedding and the type of location that you and your fiancé desire, it's time to localize your search to the area you would like to get married in. For many couples, this can be very easy because they want to get married close to their current home or at least within driving distance. For others, often first-time brides, it can be much more difficult if they want to get married out of town, such as where they grew up or in their favorite city or town, which may be out of state. If this is the case, making a trip to your wedding city early in the planning process will help you narrow down wedding-site choices. You will want to investigate the suggestions described below, or have someone who lives where you want to get married do as much of the legwork for you as possible. (Also see chapter 14 for more hints on handling the details of out-of-town weddings.)

Where to Look Locally

A great place to start your search for the ideal wedding or ceremony locale is the **Internet.** Search for "wedding sites," "special event locations," or "event planning" and enter your zip code or the name of your area. See pages 48–50 to get more ideas on how to search for sites online.

Visit **bridal shows, bridal malls, and bridal outlet shops** nearby or in the city closest to you. These one-stop shopping locations have all kind of information for you on everything from caterers to tuxedo rentals and disc jockeys. Booths may be set up by individual locations that are trying to rent their wedding sites. You can gather the information in person that you would normally need to get on the phone and on a tour of the property. You can shop for dresses and wedding cake, plus take home a show guide that will have contact information for all vendors and site locations.

If you are having a church wedding or a wedding at one location and are searching for a separate reception site, talk to the **wedding coordinator** or **minister** on-site. They not only have experience with lots of brides and grooms, but chances are they have been invited to receptions at a variety of locations and will have insights to share on everything from locations to musicians. Also, talk to as many **brides and grooms** as you can. If they are newlyweds, they have already been through this search-and-gather process and may be able to give you a few new ideas.

Call the **park districts** in your area. They often handle not only the parks but some of the historical locations, the town hall, and recreation centers or senior centers. Also call the **chamber of commerce** and the **visitors' or tourist bureau** for your area. They usually have handouts and publications from rental locations, and they may know of buildings or vacation rentals that are available but not published anywhere. Local **realtors** may also have a line on nice houses or estates that are available to be rented by the day or weekend.

Scour **local magazines and newspapers**—especially during their annual bridal issues, which often are published in January or February. These newspapers sell advertising to sites that are well known for hosting weddings and special events. Also, look online under "event planning," "wedding," or "party." Some areas even have special phone books devoted exclusively to event planning and wedding vendors. You can usually find a variety of phone books at your local **library.**

The **library** may also have **local wedding guides** or **books** on the shelves that really lay out what is available close to you. Another good idea is to look at **travel books** for your area. They may list some backroad locations that are close but not well known. If you have started dress shopping, your sales-people have likely heard of many cool places to wed. Ask them if they have any location or vendor tips to share.

Don't rule out using a **caterer** as a resource for finding the perfect site. If you already know that you want a specific caterer or wedding planner to work with you, you might as well get your money's worth and let them help you find the locale. Some caterers have exclusive rights to premier sites, and in order to rent the location, you have to use that caterer for your event.

Be vocal about your search; let family, coworkers, acquaintances, and everyone you come into contact with know you are looking for a wedding site. Often a suggestion for a location comes from someone who previously held or attended an event in a location that is not listed in any guidebook or website. Word of mouth is a great location reference.

SOME OF THE BEST THINGS IN LIFE ARE FREE!

With legwork and creativity, it is possible to find a venue that is completely free. Keep in mind, though, that in some cases, a free locale could end up being costly if you need to rent a tent, tables, chairs, and other items, while a restaurant with a patio, which might include all of those items if you pay for a certain amount of food, could end up being cheaper. Make sure you look at the whole package and all incidental costs before deciding.

Besides the usual backyards, parks, and nature settings, consider off-beat location ideas such as getting hitched in the Walmart where you met, or at a business you frequent or perhaps one that a friend owns, such as a book-store, antique mart, flea market, florist, or garden center. To make it worth their while, call local media and invite them to cover the wedding as a special interest story. One friend of mine married at the top of the ski hill where she and her hubby met. Anyone who wanted to witness the blessed event had to pay to get in the park, be fully equipped, and take the lift to the top for the exchange of vows. Afterward, the attendees met in the chalet for appetizers and spiked hot chocolate.

QUESTIONS TO ASK BY PHONE

After you come up with a list of potential sites to investigate, divvy up the names and phone numbers with your partner and set a timetable to complete all the calls. The following is a list of questions to ask when you are calling around for site information and availability. Tailor the questions to your individual needs.

- What is the cost for the rental? Is it a flat rate or an hourly rate?
- How many hours do you get for this price? What if the party runs overtime?
- Are there certain times of the day (or the week, or specific seasons), when the location price is discounted?
- Will there be staff on hand to help with the location? Are their services included in the price?
- Is the location public or private? Do you get exclusive use of this area, or can the public wander in?
- How convenient is this site to get to? Is there adequate parking?
- Is there handicap access (if needed)?
- How many guests can the space accommodate?
- Is there an appropriate site for the wedding ceremony?
- Is my wedding date available? What else is happening on the property that day?
- Is music allowed on-site? Is there a piano, a stereo or speakers

for an MP3, or a public address (PA) system included in the rate? Are there restrictions as to types of music and noise levels (i.e., is amplified music allowed)?

- Is there a kitchen? Is there a caterer list that we have to choose from, or can we bring our own food or caterer? Are kitchen facilities available? Are they included in the price? What kind of equipment is in the kitchen?
- What type of equipment is included in the rental price— tables, chairs, glassware, plates? Will the location's staff set up the banquet area? Is there an extra charge for this?
- Will the staff clean up the space and break down the equipment?
- Is there a dance floor? A coat area? Changing rooms for the wedding parties?
- Is an alcohol license required for the day?
- Will there be decorations on-site that will help save money, such as flowers in bloom, antiques, Christmas decor?
- If hosting a theme wedding, does the site lend itself to what you have in mind? For instance, if you want a "green" themed event, are sustainability practices used at this location and in the building design, such as reclaimed wood walls and bamboo flooring, and are recycling and composting programs in place? (For more on green and theme weddings, see chapter 7.)
- What are the rules and regulations for using the site? (For example, some sites do not allow you to use candles. You need to know this before you buy two hundred tea lights.)
- What are the cancellation fees and refund policies?
- Is there an alternate location in case of bad weather?
- Is a security deposit required? If so, when is it refunded?

After you and your fiancé have called the locations you are interested in and compared notes, narrow down your selections to the top three to five.

Then make appointments to see the locations, preferably when an event or wedding is taking place.

When you get to the location, revisit the preceding questions and see for yourself if the picture painted by the person you spoke to was accurate.

WHAT TO LOOK FOR IN A WALK-THROUGH

In addition to the aforementioned questions, pay special attention to the following areas during your walk-through:

- Take a look at how much parking is available and the distance your guests will have to walk to the wedding or reception site.
- Is the room or area comfortable for the size of your party, without being so big that you would need a lot of decorations to fill the room?
- What kind of decorations or theme would work best in the room?
- What kind of traffic flow does the room have?
- What kind of lighting is there? Is it on a dimmer?
- Are restroom facilities adequate? Is there furniture for your guests to rest in?
- What type of climate control is there? Is the room too hot or cold or perfectly comfortable?
- What type of ventilation is in the main room? The kitchen?
- Take a look at the kitchen area and note the size, the cleanliness, and the equipment. Whatever location you choose, you will probably want to go back for a walk-through of the kitchen with your caterer, if you are using a caterer.
- If the location checks out well, scout out the perfect spot within the site for holding your ceremony. Some sites have several to choose from, and you will want to let the management know well in advance what your choice is.

FIRST IMPRESSIONS

What did your instincts say to you? Did you feel as if this was the right place? Could you envision yourself celebrating your wedding here? Can you afford it? Is the date that you want available? Will the site be able to accommodate the size and special needs of your party? Your caterer or theirs? What kinds of facilities are included? Is there a kitchen, guest rooms, changing rooms, tables, chairs, linens, silver? What kind of additional expenses will you incur as a result of picking this location? For example, will you need to rent a tent in case of rain, or do they have indoor accommodations?

SPECIAL CONSIDERATIONS FOR OUTDOOR WEDDINGS AND RECEPTIONS

- Investigate if inclement weather is common at this time of year. What is the likelihood of rain, fog, winds?
- Find out if there is a covered location or a building to go into in case of rain. If not, can the area be tented? (This could be a big added expense.)
- If possible, look at the site after a big rain to see how the ground handles it. There is nothing you'll want less when you are walking around in a white wedding dress and high heels or a brand new tuxedo than to be wading in mud puddles!
- Double-check the bathroom availability, accessibility, and cleanliness.
- Find out if electricity is available. Are there heaters or lights for the area?
- Are there indoor or outdoor cooking facilities? Some outdoor locations have no facilities at all or bare-bones picnic tables and barbecues. You will need to know this when you are planning your menu. If that is the case, can a food truck park on the premises for catering?

ENVISION THE SEASON OF YOUR WEDDING

When my husband and I went to look at our future wedding site, I almost vetoed it because it was the dead of winter and nothing was in bloom. If we hadn't asked to see photos of the summer season in the garden, we would have never known how lucky we were to have found such a fabulous, affordable locale. Even so, the pictures didn't completely do the site justice.

When we returned six months later for the rehearsal walkthrough, the sheer beauty of the grounds took my breath away. There was no way that I could have imagined what the incredible wildflower and herb garden would have looked like in the midst of summer or how the redwood and eucalyptus trees would sway and fill the air with their enchanting aromas. I was delighted that my groom talked me into booking the location six months before.

Once you have decided on a site, the next steps involved are negotiating a great price, finalizing your contract, and paying a deposit to hold your wedding date and time. The following tips will help you with these:

- Find out what other, if any, incidental charges may be added to the bill. Have these spelled out in your contract. Try to negotiate for them to be included in the main price; the extra charges can add up very quickly.
- What type of payment plan is required? What kind of a deposit must you leave, and when are the other payments due?
- Pay as small a deposit as possible and charge the deposit to a credit card to ensure you have recourse if there are any problems with the location.

- Your contract should state the date of your event, what room(s) or part of the property you have access to, what hours you are allowed on location, including any rehearsal time needed and any other services you are contracting them for. Include all prices and all due dates for payments.
- It is important to get everything in writing. You need to get everything in writing, so you can hold the site management accountable in case the person you spoke with leaves or forgets what was promised.
- Bring your contract with you on the day of the wedding, so if there are any discrepancies about the bill, you can clear them up before final payment is rendered.

I NOW PRONOUNCE YOU SPOUSE AND SPOUSE

Connie and Nancy's Wedding on June 24
7 guests at the Courthouse in Skokie, Illinois

Spiritual Ceremony on July 22
7 guests in Lake Como Park, Saint Paul, Minnesota

PRIORITIES

1. To pledge their love for each other
2. To get married soon after gay marriage was legalized in Illinois
3. To have a separate spiritual ceremony officially recognized by the Christian church
4. To have close friends and family as witnesses
5. To celebrate cost effectively

Connie and Nancy, both retired businesswomen, had been a couple for over sixteen years when they officially tied the knot. Having met decades earlier while working in publishing at the same company, they learned they lived only a block apart. They became fast friends, often hiking, biking, and going to concerts together. They had thought about getting married along the way; however, they did not see a point in running off to California, Hawaii, or elsewhere if their marriage was not going to be recognized in their home state.

When gay marriage was legalized on June 1 in Illinois, they said, "Let's just do it!" They married three days later in a courthouse ceremony. They arrived at 3:00 p.m. With three couples in front of them, they were married by 3:15. Afterward they took their friends and family out for dinner.

BUDGET FOR ILLINOIS WEDDING

Wedding	$ 0	
Dress, jacket, hat ribbon	$ 200	
Flowers	$ 0	(gift from Connie's daughter)
License ($50), ceremony ($20), copy ($15)	$ 85	
Dinner, including tax, tip, toasts	$ 600	
Minister	$ 0	
Total	$ 885	

DETAILS

Fifteen years earlier they had given each other pinky Möbius bands as partner rings. They decided to exchange wedding bands during the ceremony but thought there was no need for engagement rings. Connie opted for a plain yellow gold band, while Nancy chose a matching rose gold ring.

APPAREL AND FLOWERS

Connie wore a multicolored dress with three-quarter sleeves and a jeweled neckline. Nancy had on a cobalt-blue shell, white cropped pants, and a textured cotton-seersucker blazer that matched the palette of Connie's dress. Connie wore her black Mary Janes, while Nancy had on white slip-on shoes. They had matching straw hats dressed up with cobalt-blue ribbon to tie the look together, and matching bouquets of peach, pink, and orange roses wrapped in green tissue paper.

FOOD AND BEVERAGE

After the civil ceremony, they took their guests to McCormick & Schmick's for dinner. A snug private roomette was preset with chilled glasses and prosecco. They ordered off the menu. At the end of the meal, a complementary chocolate lava cake with a sparkler in the middle was presented to Nancy and Connie.

CEREMONY IN MINNESOTA

Connie and Nancy both yearned for a spiritual celebration in addition to their courthouse nuptials. A lightbulb went off for both of them when they learned that a cousin from California who was also a Presbyterian minister was planning to visit the Twin Cities in July. They called her and asked, "If we travel to where you are staying, *would you officiate a Christian ceremony for us while in town?*" Thankfully, she agreed. Before they arrived, another friend scouted sites for them. They decided to get married at a nearby public Japanese garden.

They drove to Minnesota as part of a preplanned long weekend visiting lots of relatives and friends. On the day of their spiritual ceremony, they wore the same outfits as the original wedding. They chose to just walk in and have the minister perform the ceremony, as they were not able to make reservations beforehand. Nancy shared that no one bothered them, and "we were able to have all the privacy we needed." A friend played several songs on the recorder as her gift to them. Guests took photos on their cell phones and on an iPad and sent them to the couple later on. Afterward they went out for cocktails with the group.

When asked what advice they would give others who are embarking on same-sex unions, Connie suggested to "keep your wedding simple. The simpler it is, the less stressful it will be. If it's too elaborate, you will be leaving yourselves open to potential disappointment."

Nancy chimed in with her advice: "Be very clear on why you are getting married." When asked to explain further, she added, "I wanted to formally pledge to Connie that I will be faithful, truthful, and honest, and love her all of the days of our lives." Connie exclaimed, "Ditto for me."

Chapter Six

WONDERFUL WEDDING WEAR

ere comes the bride, all dressed in white . . . or champagne, or vintage rose, or pale ocean blue. You name it, these days a bride can wear any color she wants to her wedding. Most still choose white, but don't let that stop you. Whatever you and your fiancé choose to wear, let it be uniquely your style.

Weddings have a lot to live up to—a lifetime of daydreams and fantasies about how wonderful they will be. My goal is to help you find your dream dress as painlessly as possible. This chapter is designed to assist you in your search to

- find the right gown, tux, veil, and shoes
- save hundreds of dollars when buying a wedding dress
- consider once-worn gowns, rental dresses, and vintage options
- choose a dress, hair style, and bling to accentuate your best features
- dress the groom in a wardrobe fit for a king (and possibly for free!)
- attire the bridesmaids, groomsmen, moms, and flower girls without breaking the bank.

Time to do a check-in with your inner bridal consultant. Are you leaning toward formal, traditional, classic, royal, modern, contemporary, playful, flirty, or beach chic? What fabrics and styles resonate most with you? Let's get to work finding a tasteful, lovely gown that will achieve your ideal at a cost you can afford.

FOR THE BRIDE

Here are some tips to help you in the hunt:

- Start your search right away. It may take you a while to find the perfect gown, and it will take even longer if you have to order it from the manufacturer or you need to have it altered.
- Look online at Pinterest and other websites, as described on pages 52–54. Bridal magazines are a great resource, too. Thumb through them at your local library or purchase them at a bookstore or grocery store.
- Put ads for gowns that you adore, swatches of dress fabrics, pictures or printouts of bling, shoes, and other things that you come across and *love* in your wedding binder. It's too easy to get inspired and then lose the information. Better to save everything you like until you've narrowed down your choices to "the one."
- Determine how much you are willing to spend and stick to your budget. Reexamine your priorities by referring back to your Couple's Questionnaire answers on pages 26–28 and see where your money should go; then allocate a bottom-line dollar amount to the dress, the shoes, the groom's wardrobe, the accessories, and so on.
- Avoid extra-fancy bridal salons, except to do research on what style of gown is most comfortable. Note that these salons have to mark up their merchandise to cover the cost of the chandeliers and cappuccino. You can probably get a better deal elsewhere.
- Keep in mind that most salespeople work on commission— the higher the price of the gown that they sell you, the more

they make. Don't let them convince you that the most expensive dress is the most flattering!

- Bring along a girlfriend or relative who will give you an honest, objective opinion of what you look like in each dress that you try on and can steer you toward the styles, silhouettes, fabrics, and cuts that accentuate your best features.

- When you go to try on dresses, wear the undergarments that you plan to wear the day of your wedding, or you may determine too late that they are incompatible. I have heard about a few nightmares: a bra displaying way too much cleavage, lingerie showing through, and the dress that was so tight with the addition of special undergarments that the buttons wouldn't close.

- Comparison shop until you drop! Look at alteration policies and pricing, ordering time, refund rules, guarantees, and the overall quality of each shop's work and compare them against each other. Whenever possible, get referrals to find out what other brides think of the salons, outlets, or tailors that you are considering.

- Be certain that the gown you choose fits the theme and season of your celebration. Ask yourself if you want your wedding to be formal, semiformal, or informal, traditional or eclectic, and choose a dress style to match. Also, make sure the dress style fits the location. A long velvet dress with a five-foot train wouldn't be right for a summer wedding on a mountaintop, but it would fit a traditional winter church wedding.

- Ask yourself these questions while trying on the gown: Can I sit, stand, and dance comfortably? Can I hold my arms over my head and move them around without worrying that the dress might tear? Can I take a deep breath comfortably? Will I be able to get in and out of the car with ease?

- Be extremely careful about ordering the right gown size based on manufacturers' sizing charts. The sizes on the dresses do not correspond to normal ladies' and women's sizing, and they all vary from designer to designer. The same is true for bridesmaids' dresses.

- Never order a dress a size smaller, gambling that you will lose weight before the wedding. It is much easier and more cost-effective to have the dress altered close to the wedding than it is to have to a dress taken out because of overly optimistic miscalculations.

- Realize that if you absolutely fall in love with a very expensive style that you know you can't afford, you can create your own version of it by sewing it yourself or hiring a tailor to do it for you. You can also explore online bridal warehouses, or look for a similar style in a consignment shop.

- Write down all quotes on the dresses that you are interested in. Compare at home by going online and researching where to get the best deal. If it's a fair price, go back and place your order. There is no need to buy on impulse or to let a salesperson pressure you into a purchase. The only time you may need to move fast is if there is only one available, such as a consignment or once-worn dress, or at a sample or close-out sale. In that case, see if you can put the dress on hold for twenty-four hours. It's a good idea to carry a smartphone or tablet so you always have it handy to do price comparisons. The goal is to make sure you feel the price is right before making the commitment.

- Find out what extra services, such as steaming, pressing, or storage, you will need to pay for, and what is included in the price of the gown.

- Before committing to a dress, find out how long it will take to be delivered. Don't cut the delivery date too close to your wedding date! Imagine if something goes wrong, and a different gown shows up on your doorstep due to human error.

Leave yourself some leeway. Time to spare also helps if there are flaws or sizing problems that need to be addressed.

- When you decide on a dress, get the delivery date written into your contract. Double-check that the store will be held responsible if the dress is delivered late or if there is a problem on the manufacturer's end. Otherwise, if there is a problem and the store blames the manufacturer, you could be forced to buy another gown on rush order—an enormous, unwelcome expense on top of money already spent.

- Always pay by credit card. It will be easier to get a refund if the unexpected happens. Also keep all receipts, sales slips, and the contract in your binder. Bring it with you whenever you go back to the store for a fitting.

GAME PLANS FOR SAVING MONEY ON A NEW DRESS

By all means, treat yourself to a visit or two to your local **bridal salon or full-service wedding mall,** but avoid buying from them until you have examined all of your options. The prices on their dresses are often out of control. Many of their so-called sales are just overblown prices "marked down" to regular prices with a hefty commission built in for the salesperson and the store owners.

Many **department stores** and their online equivalents have wonderful special occasion and bridal selections. Try JCPenney, Macy's, Nordstrom, Target, Ann Taylor, Talbots, Sears, J.Crew, or any regional stores you prefer, such as Belk or Lord & Taylor. Looking at Nordstrom online, I found a decent selection of dresses under $500. But I really hit the jackpot when I clicked their link to "Reception Dresses." Dozens of casual white off-the-rack dresses popped up. You can even take a peek at prom dresses; if the size and style fits, go for it (and line your pockets with the savings)! Success is all about how resourceful you are.

The popular cable television show *I Found the Gown* claims to offer 50 to 80 percent off retail pricing at their store, Vows, in Massachusetts. (Their online store can be found at Bridepower.com.) To see if there is a similar wedding dress outlet near you, search for "designer wedding dress warehouse" and enter your zip code. For online stores, leave off the zip code and play around with the words *bridal* or *wedding*; *gown* or *dress*; *wholesale, discount, outlet,* or *warehouse.* You can do similar searches for bridesmaid dresses.

Liquidation sales or sample sales can often be found online or in the newspaper. Be careful of any gimmicks and pricing that seem too good to be true, and remember that these dresses were marked down for a reason. Chances are they weren't handled with the utmost care prior to sale day, so be sure to inspect carefully before purchasing.

Bridal warehouse stores save you money because they often sell their own dress designs, so you avoid a retail middle person. One example is **David's Bridal**, with thousands of off-the-rack bridal gowns in stock to choose from. Buying a gown here (not to mention accessories) can save you hundreds of dollars. Also, watch for their $99 dress sale, which is held several times each year. (Call 800-399-2743 to find a location in your area, or log onto Davidsbridal.com.)

TIP

When shopping **outlets, sales, wholesalers, and discounters,** it's always advisable to triple-check what you buy because there is usually a no-return or no-exchange policy. Expect some wear and tear as they are **close-outs, discontinued brands or styles, sample sizes,** or have been around a few seasons and have been tried on several times. Look especially at the overall workmanship, the seams, the hem, the beading or trim, and make sure that if there is an issue, it can be fixed easily. Also inspect the dress for any dirt or stains that aren't removable.

More Money-Saving Dress Tips

Borrow an heirloom dress from Mom, Grandma, or a friend of the family. This option not only saves lots of money but it adds sentiment to your wedding day celebration. Even substantial alterations are still cheaper than a new dress.

Consider renting a dress. You can save well over 50 percent of new dress prices by renting your attire at a local bridal salon. Search online or in the phone book, because while these handy cost-cutting stores are hard to come by, it's often worth the search. This option is best suited for brides who don't need (or already have) a dress to pass on to any future generations. See page 53 for online resources.

Local **antique stores, vintage shops, and online versions** thereof may bear fruit if you are seeking a vintage era or retro gown. Or perhaps you want to make a theme out of your favorite historical time period, for example, the Victorian age or any decade from the 1920s until now. Also try searching for gowns or historical attire for rent at a **costume shop.**

Consignment shops, thrift stores, and rummage sales are definitely worth checking into. Goodwill often has dresses at rock-bottom prices. Church sales and garage sales are other options that can save you a bundle.

GREAT FIND!

A bride who wed in Martha's Vineyard wore a white, handmade Italian lace Ungaro cocktail suit that she bought in a Boston-area consignment shop for $160 (the original $1,800 price tag was still attached). "Perhaps because we were older, the idea of a big white gown and a multi-tiered wedding cake never resonated for me," Cate explained. For her two attendants, Cate found gray-and-cream Italian silk tunics marked down from $400 to $40, and her fiancé's mother sewed lightweight gray pants to match.

A bridal suit can be a chic alternative for nontraditional brides or brides who have already worn an elaborate wedding gown and don't have the desire for a repeat performance. A San Francisco bride who chose to forgo a wedding gown opted for an off-white, woven silk pantsuit from Saks instead. This off-the-rack designer outfit cost her $395, but she was so pleased with her choice that she has already worn it on several non-wedding occasions.

Search **eBay.com, Craigslist,** and other online discounters (see page 54) for formal, modern, or vintage dresses that are being auctioned off or sold at a fraction of the original cost. Sometimes they are samples or last year's collection, or they may be gently worn. **Online, print classified ads, and Goodwill** also may have gowns, tuxedos, and wedding rings for pennies on the dollar of the original price.

Consider a bridesmaid dress. You'd never guess it, but many bridesmaid dresses from upscale designers can easily pass for a wedding gown. If you find a designer that you love, ask if you can view the same designer's line of bridesmaid dresses and separates. You probably will have to try on the outfit in a color other than white, but they will have fabric swatches of all the shades available.

There are a few other pluses to buying a bridesmaid gown: turnaround time is much quicker on bridesmaid dresses than on wedding gowns, and some stores even have a variety of colors, styles, and sizes in stock.

Tailor-make a wedding gown. This was definitely an option I considered after looking at the exorbitant prices of gowns and then comparing them with prices on bridal material in fabric stores. Prices vary greatly when comparing seamstresses. You'll need to shop around locally and online, get references, and see samples of their work. As in most areas of the wedding industry, tailors who specialize in weddings charge much more than those who do not. It is important, however, that you choose a seamstress who has experience sewing wedding attire, because mistakes made with silks and lace can be very expensive. For this reason, many seamstresses will insist on sewing a simple muslin gown first and then using that as their pattern.

A BEAUTIFUL BRIDES(MAID) DRESS

After days of frustration searching for a dress that I loved, I tried on a two-piece bridesmaid dress from Watters and Watters. The sample was a gold skirt with a white lace top, and it occurred to me that if I were marrying for the second time, the combination of white lace and colored silk would have been ideal. Instead, I asked if it was available in white. To my surprise (and delight), it was. I got so many compliments on my dress, and whenever I let someone in on my little secret, she was stunned! Also, if you choose a two-piece skirt and top set, as I did, changing is so much easier, as is using the restroom. Plus, it was a snap to hang and store afterward.

If you or one of your relatives loves to sew, **sewing your own gown** can save you oodles of money—up to 80 percent off wedding dress prices. Bear in mind that the fabrics are hard to work with, and making your own dress is a big leap for a part-time sewing enthusiast with minimal experience. The major pattern companies have dress patterns that you can personalize by choosing your own fabrics, beading, lace, and so on.

WEDDING DRESS SILHOUETTES AND OTHER OPTIONS

Silhouettes and Styles

Choose from formal, semiformal, informal vintage, playful, or contemporary in a variety of silhouettes and styles.

A **ball gown** has a form-fitted bodice and a floor-length skirt. Built-in tulle and/or a fabric lining adds fullness and texture to the skirt—picture Cinderella's elegant gown.

A-line or princess showcases long vertical lines and seams that are slimming to most body types, and features a nonfitted bodice; a princess has a more flared skirt. Either style can make a bride appear taller, and, because it is not too formfitting, it readily hides flaws. It can be casual or ballroom formal, depending on what fabric is chosen. Usually fitted on top and then at the bride's waist, the dress flares into an A shape.

- Within this style, there are several variations. An **empire** waistline falls right below the bust. The small bodice and high waistline minimizes a thick waist. Women with larger busts and hips may choose to avoid this style.
- **Drop-waist** styles work best for hourglass figures or for someone who is tall and lean.

Mermaid style hugs the body, showcasing a woman's curves, and flares out at the knees. It's ideal for brides with curvy figures who want to show them off.

The **sheath** is simple, sleek, and chic; it is best for a woman without figure flaws—it accentuates slim figures and soft curves with fabric that drapes well. The formfitting, slim skirt often has a detachable train. Added embellishments, such as a sash or jewelry, work well with a sheath.

Consider these options as well when selecting or designing your dress:

Skirt styles can be full, sheath, princess, or flowy. There are options in **lengths** as well: short, long, or tea length (to the ankle) with a straight or asymmetrical hem.

Here Comes the Train

A **sweep train** just touches the floor, a **chapel train** extends a yard past the floor, and a **cathedral train** (like Princess Di had) extends seven or more feet from the waist and is usually weighted so that it will fall correctly. Trains should either be detachable or fold into a bustle for easy movement during the reception.

Most trains have a wrist hoop, so the bride can lift the train off the floor without resorting to bending down to scoop it up.

A DIY trend gaining popularity is to purchase a very simple gown, for instance, a satin cowl-neck bridal gown at Target for $99, then embellish it to make it uniquely yours. This would work equally well with a very basic vintage or thrift-store gown, something off the rack, or a hand-sewn sheath or dress pattern in white or a color of your choice. Add rhinestones, beading, or crystal bling and a belt or sash; sew on trim, appliqué, or lace; or pin on a brooch or fabric flowers. If you go with a white or a pale dress, this can be an ideal opportunity to add a "pop" of color, be it something matching your bridesmaids, the groom, your theme, or just a favorite color that works, from neutral shades to burgundy, metallic gold, or even black—almost anything goes.

Neckline Options Are Varied as Well

- A **jewel** neck is similar to a T-shirt, with a round neckline that sits right below the base of the throat.
- The **halter or V-neck** draws the eyes up to the face and down to the waist; both options are dramatic, sexy, and slimming, and show off your shoulder and arms. These necklines can be backless or paired with either a full or partial back.
- **Off the shoulder** features sleeves that sit right below the shoulders, showing off the collarbone and arms. Similar to a strapless but with added support, it looks great on well-endowed brides.
- A **bateau, boat, or Sabrina** is a conservative neckline that falls an inch or two below the collarbone, resulting in a wide curved line that extends almost to the shoulders. It is an elegant, tailored, and feminine look reminiscent of Audrey Hepburn's character in the movie *Sabrina*.

- A **portrait** neckline is slightly lower than a boatneck but still follows the collarbone. This style has a shawl-like addition that drapes over the shoulders, accentuating the arms and calling attention to the bride's face and neck.
- The U-shaped **scoop** neck can cut high or low.
- The **square** neck is similar to a scoop but the lines square off.
- A **strapless** has no sleeves or shoulders and is often cut straight across the bust line. It is flattering on most body types. A-lines are often strapless.
- **Spaghetti straps** are also flattering to most figures. The neckline usually is cut straight across the bust, and thin straps on each side support the bodice.
- The heart-shaped **sweetheart** neckline can be covered with a sheer fabric overlay so not too much is exposed.

Sleeves Are Available in Several Different Styles That Can Vary in Length: short, long, or three quarters

- **Fitted** sleeves are long, extending to your wrist, and are great for slim arms.
- **Bell** sleeves are fitted on top and flare at the wrist.
- **Cap** sleeves are short, just covering the shoulders.
- **Puff** sleeves are puffed off the shoulder and can be short or long sleeved; a long-sleeved puff may be called a **Juliet**.
- **Poet or kimono** style is a long sleeve with a taper that flares out at the bottom.

SHINE IN YOUR FAVORITE HUE

When it comes to **color**, brides today have been inspired to try almost every color of the rainbow—whatever suits them best. Although white, off-white, and ivory are traditional, colors often appeal to brides who have been down the aisle previously wearing white. Alternatives include contemporary hues such as silver, gray, black, iridescent, muted gold, pale blue, emerald green, cobalt, purple, and vintage shades such as rose or lavender. You also might consider combining a white bodice and a colored skirt, or vice versa.

Fabric

From polyesters to rayon, silk, and brocade, there is a huge range in fabrics for wedding dresses. The season, personal preference, and budget will factor in greatly. Crepe, sheers, acetate, and cotton are light, while brocade, damask, jacquard, and velvet are heavier. And there is a whole range in between: silks (such as shantung, charmeuse, chiffon, organza, damask, and taffeta), satins, taffeta, linen, cotton, and many more. Unless you are sewing the dress yourself, the best place to get educated on the options is in a bridal salon or outlet where you can see, feel, and experience the differences and benefits of each option.

Embellishments

Your gown can be adorned with trims, ruffles, appliqués, lace, buttons, beads, bows, piping, rosettes, pearls, and/or sequins on necklines, hems, collars, waistlines, backing, and/or cuffs. Some gowns are embellished all over.

THE RIGHT GOWN
FOR THE RIGHT SEASON

SPRING/SUMMER

Choose lightweight fabrics and simple designs; tea-length or garden-style dresses, off the shoulders and backless; eyelet linen, lace, silk chiffon, and other sheers; short sleeves or sleeveless.

FALL/WINTER

Heavier fabrics and more ornate designs work well—brocade, velvet, heavier lace, taffeta; more elaborate trim, higher necklines, full sleeves, and long skirts.

WEDDING GOWN RX: HELP YOUR DRESS FLATTER YOUR FIGURE

Women of average height, weight, and bustline:

They are extremely fortunate, since they have the widest array of dresses available to them and can pick from most styles and designers. But the rest of us can flatter our features by choosing (or avoiding) different styles and fabrics.

For a shorter and/or petite woman:

- Use vertical dress lines and a longer veil to extend the silhouette.
- Consider a V neckline and a natural waist.
- Avoid too many ruffles, large appliqués, and tiers.
- Opt for fitted or cap sleeves.

For a small bustline:

- Utilize lace, ruffles, and trimmings in the sleeve and bodice.
- A fitted waist can accentuate the bustline.

- Wear a pushup or padded bra (be sure to bring it with you for the fittings).
- Full sleeves and ornate veils can add dimension.

For tall and slender ladies:
- Select off-the-shoulder sleeves or long.
- Pick a full skirt and/or train.
- A V-neck or wide neckline can be flattering.

For wide hips:
- Choose a full or flared skirt.
- Princess gowns are a good choice as they draw eyes upward.
- Wear a full veil.

For full-figured women:
- Select plain style lines: princess or A-line.
- Avoid body-hugging styles, low necklines, and ruffles.
- Look for a smooth, tailored fit that is neither too tight nor too roomy.
- Select simple sleeve styles; if your arms are heavy, avoid sleeveless dresses.

ACCESSORIES

Once you have picked out your gown, you will want to start searching for accessories that complement your dress style. From a traditional veil to a garter belt and shoes, decide which accessories you want to purchase and what your budget constraints are. Don't forget to include *something old, something new, something borrowed, and something blue.*

Headpieces

The most cherished accessory for many a bride is, of course, the **veil.** Veils are usually made with tulle, netting, lace, or organza. Many styles attach to a headpiece, barrette, or comb. Often, fresh or dried flowers, beads, and multiple layering are a part of the design. The length of the veil can vary from shoulder length all the way down to the floor or cathedral length. For convenience after the ceremony, some veils have removable parts so the bodyline of the veil can be taken off without having to readjust the headpiece.

If you are considering a veil or a headpiece, here are a few things to keep in mind to help you choose something right for you, while saving money:

- Choose a style that complements the dress you chose.
- The more formal your wedding, the more formal your veil should be.
- Choose a style that will flatter your face and figure.
- Make sure you can move freely in your headpiece, without the possibility of losing it.
- Ask florists what they charge for a veil made with fresh flowers and tulle. It is usually far less than buying a veil from a bridal salon.
- Comparison shop for the veil in all of the same venues as the dress (outlets, sales, etc.).
- Consider forgoing a veil altogether and instead wearing a bridal hat, fresh flowers in your hair, hair combs, jeweled barrettes, or a tiara.

Shoes

Shoes can set you back a bundle if you aren't careful. If you are planning to wear a full-length gown, keep in mind that your shoes will be covered for most of the celebration. Consider wearing shoes that you already own, borrowing shoes from a friend, renting shoes, or purchasing new shoes from a discount or outlet store. If you are set on having fancy wedding-style shoes, buy a pair of plain white satin pumps from a non-wedding vendor and decorate them yourself with a glue gun and crystal beads, lace, or bows.

Be sure to consider the height of your groom, and choose shoes that will balance out your heights. For instance, if the bride is as tall as or taller than the groom, ballet slippers are an excellent option for comfort and price. For a shorter bride, high heels may be the best possible choice. Make sure that whatever you select is comfortable and that you can walk in them with ease and grace. If you buy new shoes, be sure to break them in before the big day. The last thing you want is to find yourself slipping and sliding down the aisle on new leather soles, or limping at your reception.

Other Accessories

Decide which of the following you want to beg, borrow, or buy:

Jewelry (earrings, necklace, bracelet)
Gloves
A clutch or a money purse
Pantyhose (several pairs, just in case)
A slip
A frilly garter
Special lingerie
A shawl or pashmina

HAIR

Decide how you want to wear your hair and be sure it complements the rest of your wedding attire, especially the headpiece or veil. The best way to save money on your hair is to style it yourself, or have a friend or family member style it for you. If you are set on having your hair professionally styled, compare prices and consider going into the salon the morning of your wedding, instead of having the stylist come to you. A few weeks in advance would be the ideal time to take care of hair maintenance, such as touching up the color, adding highlights, or putting in extensions. If you plan on having a professional do your hair on the day of the wedding, it is advisable to do a trial run prior to the main event. If doing it yourself, use a volume enhancer before styling, and shine spray afterwards. Practice a week beforehand to make sure you like the final result.

For DIY hair inspiration and how-to tutorials, check out Pinterest and YouTube.

Classic Wedding Updos

- **Bun:** A rounded twist on the side or high on top of the head.
- **Chignon:** A low bun at the base of the neck is a classic look.
- **French twist:** This elegant look for medium or long hair twists a ponytail upward, tucking in the ends and pinning it.
- **Vintage:** High glamour best describes this retro rolled-back look.
- **Partial updo:** Hair on the crown and sides is pulled back and pinned. The back of the hair is left straight or in soft romantic curls.
- **Braids:** Classic, French, or reverse French can be formed into a bun or left down.

> ## TIP
>
> Ask your bridesmaids to keep an eye on your hair and makeup. Have them signal you if it needs to be touched up. The last thing you want is to get your photos back and see that your hair looked messy or lipstick was missing—or even worse was on your teeth.

MAKEUP

Unless you are splurging on a professional makeup artist I suggest purchasing cosmetics from a department store or cosmetics store and have their staff makeup artist instruct you on applying the makeup yourself; for instance, Sephora, Ulta, Bare Minerals, or Aveda boutiques, or try makeup counters such as Lancôme, Bobbi Brown, or MAC. Consider going into the store or a salon the morning of your wedding for a makeover session with the products you previously purchased. The cost of the cosmetics and/or the charge of having the staff assist you is usually much less than hiring someone to come on-site to help. Avon or Mary Kay Cosmetics salespeople may be willing to come to your location for no charge.

Spray-on tans and/or body lotion with shimmer have become popular ways to make your skin glow. Temporary or professionally applied false eyelashes are another option that many brides splurge on for such a momentous occasion. The important factor is to not go so overboard that you feel uncomfortable. You should feel like a dressed-up version of yourself, but still yourself!

NAILS

Getting or giving yourself a manicure a few days prior to your main event is a low-cost way to ensure that beautiful hands and nails show up in all of your photographs. A no-chip manicure is my favorite. It costs a little more but lasts longer, and since it dries before you leave the salon, if you do it a day or two before your rehearsal, you are almost guaranteed that it will be intact for the wedding. If you are wearing open-toed shoes, or if you plan to kick off your heels and dance barefoot or in flip-flops, a pedicure would be another wise investment. Plus, a mani-pedi is a great way to de-stress.

FOR THE GROOM

Once you have determined how formal you want your wedding to be and what season it will take place, the groom's wardrobe can be selected.

If you are having a casual wedding, the groom may choose to purchase a suit or wear one he already has in his closet. Darker suits, such as black, gray, or navy, create a cohesive look if all the groomsmen pair them with matching shirts and ties. Tan and neutral suits, especially in lighter fabrics, with or without a tie, are also popular for modern grooms. Tailored fitting is the key for all, making sure they look casually polished. If the groom is in service to our country, a military dress uniform is appropriate for any level of formality. Dark trousers and a light sport coat (or vice versa) also work well paired with a button-down oxford. For a very relaxed beach-style wedding, matching linen or Hawaiian shirts paired with dress trousers are a fun alternative look worthy of consideration.

For traditional formal weddings, the groom, his attendants, and the dads rent their attire from a formal-wear shop. The groom registers at one store for the outfit of his choice, and the attendants come in at their leisure to get fitted for similar attire. Large chain formal-wear stores have the advantage that groomsmen in all parts of the country can get fitted in their own locale, and the store will send the information and reserve the attire at the store closest to the wedding site. Usually the groom and each member of the wedding party pay for their own clothing. Tuxedos, morning suits, and tails are available from these stores in a variety of colors, styles, and sizes. The time of day, formality of the celebration, and the season of the year should be taken into account when picking out formal wear.

Check out two or three different stores to compare prices, availability, rental contracts, and service before choosing which formal-wear store to go with. Ask if the store has any bridal show specials. I came across one such sale that gave the groom free attire if six other men were renting from them, and another sale that gave $40 off each full tuxedo rental. For each groomsman, prices start as low as $59 for a vest and go up to more than $200 for a whole ensemble, including everything he needs—any choice of suit, tux, vest, tie or ascot, cummerbund, shirt, and studs.

BUYING VERSUS RENTING A TUX

If you may need a tuxedo again soon after the wedding, buying a tux may be the right decision for your groom. On a recent trip to a formal-wear store, I spotted a new tux (with pants) on sale for $250. The same store also sold used tuxedos for $150, and all of the accessories that were normally rentable could be purchased either new or used. JCPenney's features a $99 tux, which makes more sense to purchase than to rent elsewhere.

Vintage stores, consignment stores, and thrift shops, as well as online resources like eBay and Craigslist, are also viable options for purchasing formal wear and semiformal wear at a discount.

Here's a short list of what to look for at a men's formal-wear rental store:

- Investigate the condition of the garments.
- Look at the selection of designers and styles.
- Check into the availability of sizes in your selected style.
- Find out the time parameters of the rental return.
- Ask if accessories are included in the rental price (gloves, hat, vests, cummerbund, studs, bow ties, etc.).

A tailored suit can be a fabulous option for a less formal wedding—either a new purchase or an old favorite dressed up with a new shirt, tie, and shoes. Groomsmen are usually asked to wear a similar color suit and tie. Make sure the color of the suits complements the bridesmaids' attire.

It is a good idea to appoint one groomsman to be in charge of returning all the rented merchandise to the store the day after the wedding. This saves the hassle of several separate trips and keeps the groom from worrying about his returns while on the honeymoon.

BRIDESMAIDS AND ATTENDANTS HAVE BUDGETS, TOO

You want to cut costs without sacrificing style; your bridesmaids and groomsmen will have the same goal in mind. Although participating in a loved one's wedding can create deeper friendships, it is often a very expensive undertaking. If participants need to travel to and from an out-of-town location, pay for lodging, buy gifts, miss work, *and* purchase their wedding attire, it can set them back hundreds of dollars. When you are deciding on dresses, tuxedos, and accessories for the wedding party, pay attention to whether or not you are making choices within their budget restrictions.

Bridesmaids' outfits come in just about any color of the rainbow that you can imagine, from lilac to pomegranate to green or gold. Fabrics, formality, lengths, and styles vary greatly, too. Priorities include having the colors match your wedding vision and theme, as well as the color scheme of the ceremony and reception locales. Most brides set out with the objective of choosing a bridesmaid's dress that can be worn again post-wedding. But because of differences in taste (regarding style, fabric, design, and fit) between the bride and her wedding party, a bridesmaid's dress is often banished to the back of the closet after the big event.

You can minimize your attendants' expenses and ensure that they'll wear the dress again by going shopping with them and helping them pick off-the-rack dresses from a department store. Another suggestion is to let the members of your wedding party choose what they want to wear, or give them a shade, a color, or a fabric to choose from and let them pick out a style that is right for them. You can also look into the option of renting. Or look at some of the online Etsy options where custom bridesmaid dresses start at just $59; see page 57. See the Internet options on pages 52–54 for more online recommendations.

Don't forget to let your attendants know if they need to purchase special shoes or shoes in a particular color and style, for example, medium-heeled black pumps. Even if all of the dresses are different colors or styles, similar shoes can tie them together for a more uniform look.

A bride in Detroit told me that she wanted her bridesmaids to wear bright jewel-colored formal gowns. She went to JCPenney's "special occasion" department with the whole party, and each woman picked a formal dress in her favorite style and shade, plus they all wore black dress shoes of their choice. When lined up with the bride, the groom, and the groomsmen dressed in black tuxedos, the effect was formal and dramatic. All of the formal dress selections chosen cost under $100, and one of them was even on sale for $25.95.

FLOWER GIRLS

You can either ask the flower girl to wear a miniature version of the dress the attendants are wearing, or you or her parents can buy a dress in a color and style that suits the formality and theme of your wedding. If you are renting the bridesmaid gowns, consider renting the flower girl's dress as well. If you or a member of your family is handy with a needle and a thread, sewing is another possibility. Also look online for once-worn or inexpensive alternatives.

RING BEARERS

Miniature tuxedos, linen suits with shorts, satin or velvet short sets, and suit jackets with pants are all options for this member of the wedding. Check out men's formal-wear stores for rental availability or consider buying, or having the parents buy, an off-the-rack outfit that complements your wedding colors.

MOMS

Let the moms and mothers-in-law feel free to choose their own outfits. If it is important to you that they match the colors of your wedding, let them know in advance what you are planning. It is a good idea for both moms to be in touch with each other about the color and length of their attire, so that one mom is not ultraformal while the other is ultracasual in a clashing color.

DADS

Dads usually match the formality of their attire to the groom and groomsmen. If they are all wearing morning suits or a tux, the dads should sign up for the same at the same men's store. If they are wearing the suit of their choice, the dads can do the same.

A TALE OF TWO WEDDINGS

Kristi and Marlin's Nuptials on July 13
9 guests in Pentwater, Michigan;
60 in Fresno, California

PRIORITIES

1. Convenience
2. Affordable for everyone to participate
3. Time constraints (they wanted the nicest wedding they could pull off ASAP)
4. To get married in Pentwater, Michigan
5. To hold a reception in Fresno, California

Kristi, thirty-six, and Marlin, thirty-four, initially caught each other's interest on Match.com. He was a business-school grad student and a fan of many genres of music, summer art festivals, and performing arts, including poetry readings. A natural beauty, Kristi is a tall, blue-eyed blonde who was impressed with all that Marlin knew about music, plus she thought it rare for a man to like poetry and art. She was a talented writer who was completing her master's degree in English. Kristi was touched when, on their first date, Marlin waited outside in the cold winter weather just so he could hold the door open for her.

The couple dated for several years, initially during grad school, then long distance for a year and a half, eventually moving together to San Francisco. They lived there for three years before getting engaged.

While in Santa Cruz for the weekend, the ring was burning a hole in Marlin's pocket. He was self-consciously trying to determine where to propose: the pier, the boardwalk, or the Ferris wheel. Finally Kristi asked him, "What is wrong with you—you are unusually quiet?" Right then and there he drew a heart in the sand with his finger, got down on one knee in the middle of it, pulled out the ring, and asked her to become his wife.

LOCATION

For over twenty-five years, Kristi's dad had been spending a week or more vacationing in Pentwater, a beach town on the east side of Lake Michigan. Marlin had been there once to meet the family and had felt very welcomed. It was a very private, crowd-free beachfront, with clear blue water reminiscent of the ocean. Marlin, who has born and raised in California, was blown away when he first visited. "You can't see the other side, it is so big," explained Marlin. "It feels just like the ocean."

Kristi and Marlin discussed holding the wedding there to make it convenient for Kristi's dad, Tom, who had been battling leukemia for more than ten years. Kristi's dad had already rented a house for a week, one that he had been in many times before. They were all looking forward to being together. The wedding was to be held at sunset on the patio deck overlooking the lake. Both the home and deck were situated high atop a cliff, with a steep drop down to the beach and a breathtaking view.

At the time, they did not know how severely ill Tom was. Unfortunately, he did not live to see them wed. They called the homeowner to cancel the reservation after Tom passed, and she offered them the home, rent-free, because of all the years Tom had taken such good care of it. Kristi and Marlin decided to move forward, marrying there in honor of her dad.

BUDGET FOR MICHIGAN WEDDING

Wedding, reception site	$	0
Hotel (3 nights for bride and groom)	$	550
Dress, alterations, veil, and shoes	$	150 (dress, $100; lingerie $50)
Groom's clothing	$	60
Food and beverage	$	250

Arbor	$	100
Photography	$	0 (gift)
Makeup, hair	$	0 (her sister did it)
Flowers	$	240
Decorations	$	0 (a present from her maid of honor)
Invitations, music	$	0 (both digital)
License, minister	$	155
Total	$	1,505

DETAILS

The couple had been given $3,000 in contributions from their families, so even though they held two events, most of the costs were covered.

They found a minister in Michigan through PentwaterCelebrations.com. He included a small talk on what marriage means, a moment of silence in honor of Kristi's dad, plus the vows the couple wrote. Kristi's stepdad's brother photographed the wedding as his gift to the couple.

APPAREL

Kristi found a never-worn gown in a Berkeley, California, consignment shop. Affordable at only $100, the floor-length, strapless gown was a slightly sheer blend of silk and satin, with beading on top and a ribbon-tied back. Kristi's mom altered it to fit perfectly. Kristi borrowed her sister Julie's Steve Madden sling-back slipper shoes. She also borrowed rhinestone-and-pearl earrings and a bracelet. Julie pinned flowers and beads into Kristi's hair.

Kristi's niece, four, was the flower girl, and her nephew, one and a half, was the ring bearer. They wore matching navy blue outfits.

MUSIC

The couple made an iPod playlist featuring romantic tunes and artists such as Lionel Richie, John Legend, and Michael Jackson. For the ceremony,

Kristi's brother, Danny, played an acoustic guitar version of Stevie Wonder's "Fools Rush In" as the bride entered. Later he played "If I Fell" by the Beatles. Afterward, her stepdad joined in on slide guitar, and they had a sing-along of love songs.

FLOWERS AND DECORATIONS
Kristi and Marlin married under a white arbor they had rented and adorned with silk flowers. Vases of red roses with white calla lilies dressed up the dining room. Kristi had a bouquet of red roses wrapped in silk ribbons. Everybody had either a rose wrist corsage or lapel boutonniere.

FOOD AND BEVERAGE
A local grocery store and deli was the caterer of choice for the small reception dinner. The $250 price included one waiter, nonalcoholic champagne, passed appetizers, and a cheese-and-fruit platter. The dinner menu consisted of steak au poivre with potatoes, salad, asparagus, dinner rolls, and a two-layer (one vanilla, one chocolate) wedding cake decorated with flowers.

THE CALIFORNIA RECEPTION
Their second reception was a semiformal luncheon. Marlin wore a navy suit he owned, plus a button-down shirt and tie. Kristi wore a wedding dress her mom, an excellent seamstress, made especially for this second event. It was an A-line, blended fabric halter gown in wedding white that went to the knees. She and Marlin briefly reenacted their exchange of vows for the sixty guests present at the California event.

BUDGET FOR CALIFORNIA RECEPTION
Wedding/reception site	$ 0
Hotel	$ 220
Dress, alterations, veil, and shoes	$ 0
Groom's clothing	$ 0
Food and beverage (plus cash bar)	$ 734

Photography	$	140
Disposable cameras	$	35
Flowers	$	125
Decorations	$	50
Favors	$	40
Invitations	$	60
Total	$1,404	

DETAILS

Marlin's family was very close, so it was important to him that they formally celebrated his marriage and got the opportunity to spend some quality time with his new wife.

Marlin and Kristi made their own invitations using paper they bought at Office Max and a template they found online. They picked out a fanciful cursive font, printed the invites, and addressed and mailed them.

The location of the Fresno reception was a hotel Marlin frequented while traveling on business. He had always been impressed with their food, service, and facilities, so it seemed ideal for their very special event.

The wedding luncheon was held from noon to 4:00 p.m. in a private banquet room. They decorated with maroon, silver, and white balloons and linens. The addition of red roses in vases helped cheer the room up further.

The menu consisted of Mediterranean chicken breast with rice pilaf, artichokes, and olives, mixed greens salad, and assorted breads—plus chicken strips for the kids. A cash bar was available. A marble sheet cake provided a delicious dessert. As the guests were leaving, the couple handed out See's Candies, a West Coast favorite.

The room had an excellent sound system, and Marlin utilized the playlists from the earlier ceremony, with extra tracks added for dancing. A staff photographer took photos of guests with the happy couple. Kristi and Marlin gave out prints as Christmas gifts.

Chapter Seven

HOT DECOR + COOL STYLE

○———————○

This chapter is designed to help you demystify the decorating experience. Bringing your wedding fantasies to life can involve a lot of hard work behind the scenes—designing, planning, and purchasing everything prior to the big day. We will explore the details that need to be taken care of and identify several ways to save money while creating your ideal ambience.

With our goal of creating a wedding that truly reflects who you and your betrothed are as individuals—and as a couple—our first order of business is to review your vision and your priorities, along with the who, what, when, and where that you have already decided on for your ceremony and reception.

WEDDING THEMES

The theme itself may be crystal clear based on your vision, priorities, location, or other decisions you have already made. If not, use the following ideas to brainstorm further with your betrothed and other members of your family and wedding party.

Wedding themes may start in one narrow area, then build to become a full-textured, thoughtful, larger theme that sets an undertone for almost all of the features of your wedding, from the decor and centerpieces to invitations and guest book, your bridal dress to the attendant's clothes, and beyond. For instance, what starts simply as a rustic theme could end up becoming a September wedding featuring an outdoor ceremony followed by a reception in the barn, with wooden tables and chairs, fall colors, sunflowers, a country-western band, line dancing, and a bonfire after dark.

There are a lot of aspects to consider. Your theme may evolve from one or a combination of the following:

- Season and holiday: spring, summer, fall, winter; New Year's (see pages 29–32 for an example of a New Year's wedding), Valentine's Day, Fourth of July, Thanksgiving, Christmas
- Location, whether the actual location of the wedding or a location you re-create—a vineyard, art gallery, rose garden, mountainside, Parisian café, Smoky Mountain cabin, your favorite place (the restaurant you went to on your first date?)
- A memory or memento, such as your grandmother's 1940s wedding dress
- Something that you, as a couple, want to share with your guests:
  - First date (see pages 12–16 for an example of a couple who did this)
  - A hobby, such as traveling, camping, or traveling on cruise ships
  - A sport, such as baseball, skiing, surfing, or golf
  - Green or organic themes (if that is important to your lifestyle)
  - Photography, especially if that is your hobby or if you have a good set of photos that traces how you got to this place
  - Favorite flowers, such as roses or spring cherry blossoms
- A color or color scheme: monochromatic or a pairing of two, three, or more colors
- A vintage period in time that you enjoy: the Renaissance, Victorian period, or the roaring '20s
- Style of wedding: traditional, formal, casual, cocktail, modern, contemporary, black tie

- Atmosphere: rustic, garden, whimsical, country and western, or carnival or prom theme
- Time of day and/or meal: breakfast, lunch, dinner, high tea, dessert bar, champagne and hors d'oeuvres

Consider how your theme can have different interpretations based on descriptors, elements of style, creativity, colors, decorations, and your vision. For example, the following are different renditions of a garden-party wedding theme:

A WHIMSICAL GARDEN PARTY might have elements of Alice in Wonderland. It could be indoors or outdoors, perhaps with a giant chessboard and croquet on the lawn, a groom who wears a top hat, a topsy-turvy Mad Hatter cake, clocks, and tea candles in teacups. Light blue and white would be a good color scheme, with spring garden flowers here and there.

A SUMMER GARDEN PARTY would be outdoors, maybe at a botanic garden or nursery or on a patio, with lots of flowers in bloom in the ground and in pots, and umbrella-covered tables covered with floral patterns over solid-colored linens. Food could include grilled vegetables, vegetarian entrees, a salad with nasturtiums, champagne with edible flowers, rose-hibiscus tea.

HIGH TEA could be indoors, evoking a garden or an atrium/greenhouse. The menu would have dill-and-cucumber sandwiches, tuna or chicken salad on mini croissants, fruit, and mini scones with berry jam, petits fours, chocolate-dipped strawberries, and tiny cupcakes instead of a wedding cake. Teapots from garage sales filled with silk or fresh flowers would look nice on each table.

Use your imagination and creativity to design a theme that is right for you, or forgo a theme altogether. If you forgo a theme, move forward focused on the style and formality you already have decided on. Pick colors for the reception and attendants, and then skip the remainder of this section. Or read through and see if any ideas spark your interest.

If you decide to focus on a theme, you may or may not want to let your guests know what it is in the invitation. For example, you could state, "Kindly wear Roaring Twenties attire" or "Ladies are requested to wear hats and gloves." Keep your themes appropriate to the season of your wedding, for example, an autumn harvest party in October. Use props you own, or borrow or rent them to help set the stage. Decide ahead of time if just your reception or the entire wedding will be centered on this theme.

The theme suggestions below are meant to help you brainstorm ideas. The Internet, especially Pinterest (see page 62), various blogs (pages 50–51), and general sites (pages 49–50) such as TheKnot.com, have full-color examples of what couples have done at all budgets, big or small. I recommend you peruse examples of recent weddings on these sites and collaborate with your team (bride, groom, attendants, family) to decide what works best for you. Open a Pinterest account if you do not have one, and start a memory board to help bring your theme to life.

Here are some possible wedding themes to consider:

ANTIQUE ECLECTIC. Purchase a variety of mismatched invitations, glassware, vases, tables, and chairs at amazing prices by visiting rummage and garage sales. Dinner would feature a comfort-food buffet laid out on picnic tables covered with vintage linens. Borrow friends' antique cars to take you to the wedding and reception, and wear your mom's or grandma's wedding dress.

AUTUMN HARVEST OR SUMMER VINEYARD. Grapevines, vegetables, and fresh fruit work together to adorn the tables. Add champagne grapes to your bouquets and centerpieces for an apropos touch. Local wines and lemonade will quench your guests' thirst, while wooden barrels can serve as cocktail tables; top them with empty wine bottles filled with wildflowers.

BASEBALL. Consider marrying at a minor league ball park before or during the game, or perhaps at a sports bar. Or wed at home or a rental hall and feature your favorite team's colors and signage throughout the event, from invites and thank-yous, to casual jerseys to marry in. A baseball signed by you and your betrothed with your wedding date on it could be a fun favor and reminder of the special day.

BEACH PARTY. A wedding at the beach can be formal or casual, whatever you prefer. Consider a beach barbecue or clambake, followed by volleyball or swimming, or have an acoustic guitar serenade the sun as it sets. Serve mai tais and frozen cocktails, hold a limbo dancing contest, and use tiki torches for outdoor lighting. Invite guests to wear casual or semiformal beachwear.

CARNIVAL OR COUNTY FAIR. Booths or food trucks feature a variety of fair foods, from hot dogs and Polish sausage to burgers, chicken on a stick, lemonade, funnel cake, shish kebabs, potato salad, and blue-ribbon pickles. Have a ring toss for the kids, and perhaps a circus tent, cotton candy, a photo booth, and ball toss with tin cans and penny prizes. Decorate with balloons and streamers of colored tickets. Design the dessert as a potluck cake or pie contest. Huge rainbow lollipops and penny candy make good decorations. Perhaps have a popcorn stand, along with ice cream bars in a self-serve freezer.

CHERRY BLOSSOMS. For this theme you could include a spring menu with honey ham and asparagus and deviled-egg appetizers. Fans painted with cherry blossoms could be at every place setting and double as a favor. An archway or chuppah wrapped with cherry blossoms could serve as a feature of the ceremony site, while details like pink tea roses with cherry blossoms could be highlighted in the bridal bouquet, centerpieces, and on the wedding cake.

COUNTRY AND WESTERN. Ask the men to bring their ten-gallon hats and women to wear square-dancing skirts and be ready to do the Texas two-step. Hiring a dance instructor to give a one-hour lesson would be an inexpensive add-on that could get everyone onto the dance floor. A few bales of hay, some sunflowers, and a scarecrow or two would add to the ambience. Serve barbecued ribs, chicken, beef, and beans. Yeehaw!

FAIRY TALE, CINDERELLA, OR HAPPILY EVER AFTER. A ballroom or any large, open room with a dance floor can be the centerpiece of this theme. Decorate with glass slipper centerpieces, pumpkins and ivy spray-painted gold, plus the bride can arrive in a horse-drawn carriage, wearing a princess gown and tiara with veil.

GARDEN PARTY OR AT-HOME WEDDING. A backyard or local park in the spring or summer season can make a perfect backdrop for a wedding. Consider a canopy in case of rain or if there is a need for shade. Chalkboard signs and menus add to the decor, along with potted plants, lanterns with tea candles, and centerpieces of tin watering cans filled with flowers.

HEARTS AND FLOWERS. Use flowers and heart shapes to decorate the reception site. Some possibilities include floral wreaths or posters in heart shapes around the walls of the room, rose-covered arches, candied hearts on the tables, and baskets of fresh or silk flowers.

HOLLYWOOD MOVIES. Rent out an old theater and have your names placed on the marquee. Project a movie showing how you met, perhaps with photos of you and your betrothed as babies and progressing up to the engagement. Your invitations might be designed to look like movie tickets, and you might dress in a 1940s hairdo with a vintage movie-star-like dress. Waiters can dress like ushers. A popcorn stand, hot dogs, ice-cream-fountain concessions, snow cones, and candy apples highlight the menu. Or base the entire theme on your favorite movie; see pages 64–68 for a bowling-alley wedding based on a couple's first date film, *The Big Lebowski*.

HONEYMOON OR AN ON-LOCATION WEDDING. Whether you dream of a casino-based fantasy theme, Disneyland, or a tropical wedding in Jamaica, leaving home can help cut down the stress and inspire a wedding theme. See Chapter 14.

LUAU. Whether you're in Hawaii or not, a luau—complete with roasted pig, ukulele players, hula dancers, and floral leis—can be delicious and will make for noteworthy memories.

MEXICAN FIESTA. Mexican food, great beer and sangrias, staff in colorful costumes, tables covered with bright cloths, and a mariachi band are major elements of this fun-filled theme wedding. Turn your backyard or a hall into the party headquarters. Or feature Brazilian or Ecuadorian food instead.

NATURE OR CAMPING. An eco-friendly theme might feature a campfire cookout menu, compostable disposables, and rose-tree cuttings to plant at home as party favors. The wedding could be held in a park or alongside a 1950s-style trailer. You might even have several families camp together or stay in a lodge or log cabins so the wedding can take place in nature.

NEW ORLEANS JAZZ. NOLA food choices could include gumbo, catfish, rice and beans, cocktails, beignets with chicory coffee, and an espresso cart. Perhaps feature a jazz band, colored beads and Mardi Gras masks, Beale Street signs on tables as decor, and even spontaneous parades led by a trumpet player during dinner. *Fun!*

PERIOD WEDDING. Roaring Twenties or Flashback to the Fifties, here is where the Great Gatsby dress code or poodle skirts belong. Add the specific music, foods, drinks, and decorations of the era, and it's a hit.

PICNIC. This is perfect for an outdoor wedding, usually in the spring or summer. At my wedding we served picnic appetizers followed by a barbecue; for the menu, see page 16. See another example of a picnic theme on page 177.

PROGRESSIVE WEDDING. This wedding theme takes place in several cities or locations, usually because the couple lives in a different area from their families. The ceremony could be in one city, followed by receptions in various locations (hosted by family members) over the following weeks. The original wedding attire could be worn at each event, and wedding videos can be shown at each party.

RENAISSANCE. If you like this style, consider renting period dress for wedding attire, and possibly getting married in a themed specialty banquet hall, such as Excalibur in Las Vegas or at a local Renaissance fair. Or host a small group at one of Medieval Times's many locations.

ROCK AND ROLL. Elements of this retro theme may include leather and lace on the bride, a black-and-white theme with pink or red as an accent, an actual guitar and a black permanent marker as a guest book, transportation in a borrowed 1950s or '60s car, and using albums as a base for floral vases and forty-fives as the tables' number signs. The cake could be in a guitar shape or look like stacked albums. Paper flowers made out of music sheets can be a DIY project for the decor.

SEASIDE SUNSET. Marry at sunset and pray for clear skies! Your centerpieces might be fishbowls sitting on a round mirror, filled with layers of sand topped with seashells and a candle in the middle. Additional votives around the centerpiece add soft lighting as the sun goes down. You could serve cioppino or paella, or a surf-and-turf combination like beef tips with shrimp fettuccine and broccoli rabe. Or my favorite: lobster rolls with chips and slaw. Other options include sushi and tempura, or chowder and fish-and-chips. The reception might even be in a coastal seafood restaurant, or food trucks could cater the themed food at home or in a banquet hall. Details might include a mermaid-style wedding gown, and your bridesmaids and linens could have theme colors like shades of ocean and sand. Toothpick umbrellas in the drinks and sand buckets with potted plants on the buffet tables add to the ambience.

SOUTHERN SUMMER WEDDING. Old-fashioned hospitality is the hallmark of this theme, including mint juleps, a soul food banquet, formal attire, a Dixieland-style band, and a rented or borrowed southern estate.

THE STORY OF US OR OUR LOVE STORY. Chronicle how you met and what sparked your romance using framed pictures or a slide show projected on a wall. Your wedding program and wedding website could describe favorite dates, shared hobbies, vacations taken together, and aspirations for the future. The main decorative element is lots and lots of photos—in frames on the tables, or perhaps clipped onto a clothesline across a room or the backyard. Have old favorite things from your attic as centerpieces and decor, such as trophies, stuffed animals, artwork, or family photo albums. Have the DJ play a trivia game with little-known facts about the couples and the families.

VICTORIAN. Choose period costumes or not, and include lots of flowers: fresh and dried arrangements as well as Victorian tussy-mussy bouquets. Don't forget the ribbon and lace. A certain formality is an important part of this theme, and a high tea celebration works well.

WINTER WONDERLAND. This wedding is all white, with plenty of miniature lights, sleigh bells, white ribbons, and ornaments. Add just a splash of color with antique-style Christmas ornaments or snow knickknacks, such as a sled, skis, scarves, and muffs. You could also hire antique-costumed carolers.

There are many elements of style that will help bring your theme to life:

- A palette of colors perfect for the season
- Formality of the theme, atmosphere, and attire
- Your ceremony and reception sites, the wedding program, guest book, menu cards, and escort cards or table assignments

- Musical choices before and during the ceremony, during dinner, and afterward, whether a prerecorded digital playlist, a live band, or DJ
- The look of your tables including the gift table, buffet tables, guest tables, linens, and table settings
- Flowers, including the bridal and bridesmaids' bouquets, corsages, boutonnieres, buffet table decorations, and centerpieces
- The menu selection and style of service (buffet, passed appetizers, food truck, family style, preplated, traditional)
- The cake, other desserts if relevant, party favors or takeaways, open bar, beverage service, espresso cart or coffee/tea

A GREEN OR ECO-FRIENDLY WEDDING

Consider going green, which will work with nearly any style you choose. Here are some suggestions on how to do it:

- **Engagement ring.** Start with an ethically sourced (conflict-free) diamond or an heirloom hand-me-down.
- **Invites.** Send out seed-infused invitations, reply cards, thank-you notes, and envelopes with wildflower or herb seeds and post-consumables. Guests simply plant the paper, water it, and watch it grow. To see the many varieties or place an order, log onto Botanicalpaperworks.com. Wooden invites are also beautiful as they take less paper for printing and make good keepsakes.
- **Location.** Stay nearby, ideally somewhere very natural. Avoid leaving a big carbon footprint. A green

restaurant, a public venue like a park, a local farmer's market, a historic farm, a museum or zoo, an eco-friendly hotel, or a yoga studio are all possibilities, as are natural surroundings, such as a beach, lakefront, preserved area, or vineyard.

- **Transportation.** For traveling from hotels and homes to the wedding and reception sites, consider renting a trolley or arrive by canoe if going to an island by your lake house. The groom could come by bicycle. In cities there are Zipcars and electric taxis, or you could borrow or rent a hybrid.
- **Colors.** Seek out natural hues—greens, browns, beige, ocean blue, sunset colors.
- **Gown.** Acquire a once-worn or heirloom gown, rent one, or buy or commission a gown made with organic cotton and/or other organic fibers. Make your own veil and a special dried flower-and-antique-brooch bouquet, featuring your grandma's rhinestone jewelry and flowers from dates with your fiancé.
- **Flowers.** Use wildflowers for the bridesmaids' bouquets, black-eyed Susan boutonnieres, and centerpieces featuring secondhand and vintage vases filled with wildflowers.
- **Edibles.** Serve organic and sustainable options as much as possible. Use recycled paper if menus are printed. Make sure the coffee and chocolate are fair trade and/or organic.
- **Skip the rice.** Rice can be a danger to humans, who may slip and fall, and to birds, because it is not easy to digest. Instead, hand out tissue-paper confetti wedding poppers that are biodegradable.
- **Special touches.** Donate money to a fund for water in third world countries, or plant trees to offset the wedding's carbon footprint.

FLOWER POWER

Your personal tastes and desires will come strongly into play when you are deciding what type of flowers and how extensive the floral budget will be. Let's start by taking a closer look at the three main areas where you may wish to use flowers for your wedding.

TO DECORATE THE WEDDING SITE: altar arrangements or a floral chuppah (a wedding canopy used in Jewish ceremonies), pew decorations, possibly a wreath at the entrance

TO DECORATE THE RECEPTION SITE: table centerpieces, buffet table arrangements, reception guest tables, garlands, room decorations, cake table, guest book table

FOR BRIDAL AND WEDDING PARTY ARRANGEMENTS: the bride's bouquet, the groom's boutonniere, and bouquets, boutonnieres, or corsages for the attendants, groomsmen, mothers and fathers of the bride and groom, and flower girl. You may also include a "throw" bouquet so the bride can keep the real thing to dry or press as a remembrance.

How to Find a Florist

While you're flipping through magazines or clicking through Internet blogs to see how couples are dealing with their wedding flowers, decide how much or how little of the actual arranging you want to do yourself. Read through this chapter and get a preliminary feel for what you may want to do, whether or not you can do it, or if you require professional expertise. Then go out and get some quotes from wholesale flower shops and professional florists to see if your fantasy is appropriate to your bottom line.

To find a florist, check with family, friends, and recent newlyweds to get a referral, if possible. You can also get referrals from other vendors you may be talking to about your wedding—for example, photographers or caterers. Scout online, visit wedding shows, look in the Yellow Pages, and peruse local bridal magazines or newspaper ads. Also, check to see if there is a horticulture school in your area or a university that offers continuing-education classes in flower arranging. Check with the instructors at the school to see if any promising students are available to design the flowers for your wedding.

We found our florist on a visit to a local mall. Strolling through, I saw a small glass-enclosed kiosk in the middle of the shopping center. I peeked inside and really loved the floral arrangements and freshness of the flowers that I saw. When I asked the saleswoman if they did wedding flowers, she showed me a wedding portfolio with photographs from events in different price ranges and gave me several references to call. I told her that I was on a limited budget, and she was extremely helpful in assisting me with ideas and suggestions on ways to save money.

Here are a few tips I've discovered along the way that will help you save a bundle:

- Doing the flowers yourself, or having a friend do them, will cut costs dramatically. If you don't feel confident about your arranging skills, try looking for a florist with low overhead, for example: a grocery-store flower shop, a florist working out of his or her home, or a part-time florist who can afford to decorate your wedding without significant markup.
- Do some of the flowers or decorations yourself and hire a pro to do others. You can decorate the reception hall yourself and hire a florist to do the bouquets, corsages, and boutonnieres for you.
- If you do hire a florist, you can save hundreds by having a friend pick the flowers up at the shop and set them up on location for you.
- Buy flowers through your local wholesale flower market, wholesale warehouse club, or at a farmer's market. Consider what flowers are in season and if there are garden flowers or wildflowers in the yards of any of your friends and family.
- Keeping the wedding party small can save money by not having to buy as many bouquets or boutonnieres. By the same token, the fewer guests you invite, the fewer reception tables

you will need to decorate, thus saving money on centerpieces that need to be purchased or made.

- Although marrying near a holiday can make individual flower bouquets cost more, many churches and banquet halls will already be decorated with flowers, so you will save money. For instance, at Christmas your local church altar may be blanketed with gorgeous red, white, and pink poinsettias, and the banquet room may have a decorated Christmas tree with colorful lights and garlands set up. In addition, your caterer may have holiday-themed ornaments to use on the buffet table. Check with your vendors to see what decorations will be available.

- Even if your wedding date isn't near a holiday, there still may be decorations available through your church, banquet hall, and caterer. I spoke with quite a few couples who spent no money, or just a small rental fee, because they used preexisting silk flowers and decorations provided by their church. Silk flowers generally cost 50 percent less than live flowers, so even if you have to buy them you will save money (and you'll get to bring them home to decorate your new surroundings).

- One cost-cutting hint is to get married in a location that has a garden in full bloom. This keeps both floral and decoration costs to a minimum and provides a natural wedding theme. Our location had a fabulous wildflower and herb garden, with plenty of trees and lawn. We only spent money on personal flowers and two arrangements: one for the cake table and one for the buffet table. Our location coordinator gave us edible flowers from her garden to help brighten the food, and she had several small vases inside the house filled with wildflowers.

- Find out if another couple is marrying at your location on the same day, and ask if they want to share decorating costs. If you find an amenable couple and you can come to terms on the flowers you both want in the arrangements, you save money on altar flowers, pew decorations, and the aisle runner, as well as tabletop and room decorations.

FABULOUS DECORATIONS FOR FREE

One lucky Illinois couple got the use of a tent and complete decorations (flowers, lights, dance floor) for no charge, saving thousands of dollars. If they hadn't asked if there were any upcoming events, they wouldn't have known to piggyback their event to occur the morning after a very upscale wedding.

Types of Flowers

Check with your florist or flower market to find out what flowers are in season at the time of your wedding and which varieties are the most affordable. Also ask about durability in heat, if applicable, and if colors are available that match the theme colors of your wedding.

ROSES are the most traditional wedding flower and the most popular, with literally hundreds of varieties, colors, sizes, and hues to choose from. They are available year-round, and their cost varies, based on the variety chosen. The use of the rose has come to be synonymous with the phrase "I love you." Spray roses are especially affordable because they have multiple buds per stem. For affordable reception table centerpieces, place miniature spray rose plants in wicker baskets; you can often purchase these roses for under $5 at grocery-store floral departments.

ROCK BOTTOM ROSES

Vanessa, a bride who married recently in New Orleans, Louisiana, was shocked when she initially got quotes from local florists that would take up half of her entire budget. To save money, she decided to do her own flowers, with the help of her seven bridesmaids. She ordered flowers a week in advance from Sam's Club. She asked what type of roses would be available and ordered thirty dozen to arrive the day before her wedding. The roses came in orange, pink, burgundy, red, white, white with pink, and yellow; they were $10 to $12 per dozen. Including floral supplies, filler greenery, and the roses, she spent a total of $395.

The day they received the roses, she and her bridesmaids cut and conditioned them with a powder Sam's Club gave them. "The conditioner helps the buds open up and extends their longevity," Vanessa explained. For her bouquet, she used two dozen roses that were pure white or white with a tinge of pink, and made an old-fashioned nosegay.

Vanessa's wedding was at home, and they decorated rooms of their house, as well as the buffet table, with five large rose arrangements. For the arrangements, they used crystal vases that Vanessa and her groom, Steve, had received as wedding gifts. They also wired roses and draped tulle around their backyard gazebo and a trellis that Vanessa's dad had built for the occasion. After the ceremony, Vanessa's bridesmaids all placed their bouquets around the wedding cake to decorate the table.

OTHER FLOWERS to consider include the following, which are listed with the season when they are in abundance. They may be available at other times, but they could cost more. The garden flowers listed can be purchased through a nursery or perhaps found in your own or a neighbor's backyard. If you love wildflowers, see if your wedding season coincides with a blossoming in local fields or meadows.

SPRING: calla lilies, cherry blossoms, daffodils, delphinium (through the fall), daylilies, forget-me-nots, heather, hyacinth, lilacs, lily of the valley, freesia (through summer), narcissus, peonies, sweet peas, tulip

SUMMER: aster, calla lilies, Canterbury bell, columbine, daisies, delphinium, hydrangeas, larkspur, lilies, lily of the valley, garden flowers (see below), sunflowers

FALL: anemone (fall to spring), bouvardia, marigold, puffy hydrangea, sunflower

WINTER: daffodils, dogwood, hyacinths, holly, poinsettia, ranunculus

YEAR-ROUND: baby's breath, carnations, chrysanthemum, daisies, gardenia (very fragrant but pricey), orchids, roses, spray orchids, alstroemeria, gerbera daisies, gladiolus, iris, stephanotis

GARDEN FLOWERS: asters, bachelor buttons, fruit blossoms, marigolds, magnolias, Queen Anne's lace, pansies, snapdragons, sunflowers, zinnias

WILDFLOWERS: columbine, lilacs, lavender, lupine, violets, larkspur, zinnias

Types of Bouquets

Whether you are doing your own flowers or hiring a pro, you need to understand bouquet terminology. The following are the most common types of bridal bouquets. Often bridesmaids will have a bouquet in the same style as the bride's, but smaller in size.

BIEDERMEIER: a concentric circle of individual colored flowers (creating a striped effect), wired into a lace collar.

CASCADE: an elaborate floral arrangement with ivy and flowers that appears to be draping down from the main bouquet.

CLASSIC BOUQUET: a dense bunch of flowers, usually set into a bouquet holder or Oasis, that can be hand-tied so you can still see the stems, or wrapped in silk ribbon, ballerina-style.

NOSEGAY: round bouquets with flowers and greenery either tightly wired or tied together, or sitting inside a small Victorian-styled handheld vase called a tussy mussy.

BLOOMING GOOD IDEAS

Flower trends are constantly evolving, as are price, availability, and demand. Remaining flexible and choosing seasonally available varieties can help you save a bundle. Consider the following approaches when choosing your bouquet, attendants' flowers, and floral decor. You may want all the flowers to be similar, or perhaps you want the bride to carry a classic bouquet while the attendants have multiple colors, and the reception hall would be decorated in one or two hues that match your overall color scheme. Choices include:

- Classic colors, such as white, pale pink, ivory, and muted pastels, add a formal, traditional elegance to almost any decor. Imagine a cascading bouquet with blouse-white and whisper-pink garden roses. Accentuate with light-hued seasonal flowers such as hydrangeas, peonies, or ranunculus. Planted white orchids with light pink or purple accents can be purchased at big box stores or home improvement retailers and would offer a striking yet cost-effective strategy to adorn the tables. Large abundant displays of whatever hue and blossoms you purchase for the bouquet can do double-duty by marking the landing spot for the bride and groom on the altar and afterward serving as the centerpieces at the buffet tables.
- Monochromatic bursts of color and/or monofloral arrangements make a splashing statement and add an artistic element to any ambiance. Start by picking a favorite color and/or one that works well with your color scheme. Then decide if you want variations of blossoms in that hue or prefer the look of one type of flower in the same color. You can use a classic natural or muted color, such as white or pink, or select a rich, vibrant shade, for instance, crimson, cobalt blue, hot pink, green, or orange.

- A mélange of colors works well for a rustic, seasonal, or country wedding, but it can also work in formal classical arrangements. Ideas range from mixing two or more colors. For instance, white daisies with yellow centers, or several shades of spring tulips, or seasonal garden/wildflowers in hues as varied as nature's palette.
- Nontraditional elements and nonfloral options have become even more popular interspersed with fresh flowers or on their own. Consider incorporating jewelry, pins, colored wire, candy (think candy flowers and cotton candy), antique silverware, beads, pearls, and feathers. Dried, silk, papier mâché, felt, tissue paper, or blossoms made from rolled music sheets can also be used on their own or blended in. Likewise, infusions of fruits and vegetables, for example artichokes, a stalk of Brussels sprouts, bunches of champagne grapes, grapevines, olive branches, and/or herbs add whimsy and a natural touch to classic arrangements.

Additional Floral Ideas

BRIDES should consider carrying a single flower or a cluster of two to three stems, such as a hydrangea, a single calla lily, or a few roses or tulips tied together. Or carry a bunch of natural blooms—peonies, hydrangeas, lilies, daisies, orchids, roses, or freshly picked wildflowers—so no "arranging" is needed. Use the aforementioned nonfloral ideas (see box above) to add an eclectic element of surprise.

BRIDESMAIDS can make small clustered nosegays, for example, or a small bunch of roses cut short and arranged in a tight cluster with all of the buds touching one another. Or tie a medium-sized bunch of wildflowers with twine. Like some modern brides, bridesmaids can carry a single flower instead of a bouquet. Or choose a nonfloral item in place of a bouquet. For instance, pine cones and wheat for fall options. Christmas tree branches and holly berries tied with a velvet ribbon make a wonderful holiday option.

DIY YOUR FLOWERS?

In addition to visiting wholesale flower markets or nurseries, check to see if there are any reputable growers at a farmers market nearby, or scout out a "pick your own" flower farm and have an outing with your bridesmaids a day or two before you tie the knot.

Huge savings on floral hair arrangements are also possible if you make your own. Start by wiring together flowers that match your bouquet. Then attach them to a hair comb, barrette, or headband. This could be used as-is or you could add veiling from a craft store for a traditional look. For step-by-step how-to instructions, peruse the web or find a video on YouTube.

BOUTONNIERES AND CORSAGES can be made by pinning three to five small tea roses together. Or use buds from the flowers you bought for the bouquets and centerpieces. Succulents with leaves are an off-the-beaten-track option for groomsmen. Squares of material placed in suit pockets also work well if the groom is not a fan of flowers. Instead of corsages for the mothers, consider giving them long-stemmed "peace" roses as part of the ceremony. During the processional, as the bride approaches the groom's mother, she hands her a rose, and concurrently the groom hands his soon-to-be mother-in-law a rose. This simple gesture acknowledges the peace that exists between the families and makes the mothers a very special part of the ceremony.

FOR THE BUFFET, consider using leaves, branches, or fruit, either as is or covered with gold or silver spray paint. Orange, cherry, or apple blossoms, lemon leaves, fall foliage, ivy, pears, or apples all create a bountiful effect. Or decorate the buffet with miniature potted fruit trees, dried herb bunches or fresh potted flowering herbs, planter boxes full of flowering bulbs, or bushel baskets placed on their side with farmer's market vegetables or fruit cascading out.

FOR THE DINNER TABLES, get creative with the vessels for your center-pieces. Purchase clay pots at a home-improvement warehouse store and fill them with herbs, flowers, or plants such as geraniums, rosemary, lavender, or pansies. If you enjoy crafting, paint the clay pots with the names of the bride and groom and the date of the wedding. Eclectic cut-flower arrangements can be made by borrowing small vases from friends and family, and arranging three or more vases at different heights, clustered at the center of each table and filled with a variety of flowers.

Found items have become popular as the centerpiece for wedding reception decor. This trend started with mason jars but has extended into antiques, such as milk bottles, watering cans, vintage tin food cans, wooden recipe boxes, or small fruit crates. Scour flea markets, Goodwill, and garage and rummage sales for the perfect find. Any vessel that can be filled with cut or planted flowers and works with your wedding theme is an option.

To create layers of interest, stack alternate textures, such as colored rocks, pebbles, sand, shells, cranberries, fruit slices, or key limes and kumquats inside a tall, wide cylindrical hurricane candle holder, a clear square vase, or a round glass bowl. Top with water and a few floating flowers and candles.

For an evening wedding, place your centerpieces onto a round or square glass mirror, and surround them with lit votive candles or twinkle lights. This works well if you spray-paint bottles of different heights and shapes in a unifying color.

If you have a casual beach theme, shells and pebbles could be strewn directly on the table surrounding the pots. Table embellishments could include edibles, such as salt water taffy in its wrapper.

Other suggestions for centerpieces include fresh or dried floral wreaths with a large candle placed in the center, ivy or floral topiaries, and sheaths of wheat. Fishbowls filled with marbles and goldfish make a fabulous center-piece and would also serve as gifts that guests can take home.

GIVE FLOWERS AS GIFTS. One bride who I interviewed had bought tea-pots at garage sales and flea markets that she later filled with flowers and used as reception-table centerpieces. After the celebration, she gave each member of her wedding party a teapot as a gift for participating. For our wedding, I bought hand-painted aluminum planters for the two buffet table arrangements; they were filled with the same flowers as my bouquet. Afterward, I gave my maid of honor one of the planters, and I gave the other to a friend who helped with the music.

FOR ROOM OR ALTAR DECORATIONS, consider buying potted plants, such as Boston ferns, or potted flowers instead of fresh-cut flowers. If you need a lot of greenery to decorate a bare room or tent, consider renting plants for a day. If you are marrying at one location and hosting the reception at another, assign someone to bring your wedding decorations to the reception hall to add ambience to both with the same arrangements.

ADD EDIBLE FLOWERS to your buffet table, passed appetizer trays, or individual dishes. Use flower petals as wedding decorations and sprinkle them on the cake table.

FOR A FLOWER GIRL'S BASKET, fill a wicker basket with rose petals and tie the basket with a bow in your wedding colors. As the flower girl walks up the aisle or path toward the altar, she drops petals for the bride to step on. If your ceremony site outlaws the dropping of petals, have her hand wedding guests individual buds from spray roses or small handmade silk flowers. The ring bearer's pillow should match the color of the ribbon on the flower girl's basket.

Research Pinterest, wedding websites, and DIY magazines for even more floral and decor recommendations.

TIP

Aisle runners are often purchased from your florist or arranged through a rental company to decoratively cover the side aisles at a church wedding. Although their use can add a traditional formal touch, consider saving money by forgoing the runner. Instead, have ushers escort all the guests up the center of the church, which usually has a runner already in place.

DECORATION IDEAS

Theme props are items that add interest to your décor without breaking the bank. For instance:

- **Candles and votives** add mood inexpensively, and **candelabras,** either borrowed or rented, can infuse a touch of class or formality to the buffet table. **Tiki torches** can light up the night at an outdoor wedding (and may help to keep the bugs away).
- **Twinkle or icicle lights** will add a festive feel, whether indoors or out.
- **Bows, ribbons, tulle, lace, and fabrics** such as satin, silk, or taffeta can add style on buffet tables, stairways, gift tables, and gazebos. They can even be hung from windows or used to decorate doorways.
- **Balloons** can be used to mark wedding locations from the street, as an element in colorful table centerpieces, or in larger outdoor arrangements such as archways or garlands.
- **Place cards** that are handmade or computer-generated can add a formal touch to the dining tables, as can **escort cards** as guests enter or **menu cards** that highlight what you're eating.
- **Candies** in the shape of hearts, like cinnamon Red Hots or pastel Sweethearts, or **heart-shaped confetti** can be sprinkled on the dining tables or the buffet tables for a touch of color.

FLORAL NOTES

Wedding Date _____

Flowers in bloom during my wedding season: _____

_____

Circle what you need and indicate the quantity, making any specific notes for each of the below:

Bride bouquet type, color, flower types _____

Flowers for hair _____

Bridesmaids, how many and what kind of bouquets _____

Mother(s) of bride _____

Mother(s) of groom _____

Grandmothers, other relatives to get corsages _____

Groom, groomsmen _____

Father(s) of bride _____

Father(s) of groom _____

Ring bearer _____

Flower girl, plus basket of flowers or petals needed _____

Centerpieces for tables _____

Flowers for buffet _____

Additional notes: _____

_____

_____

CELEBRATING THE JOY OF LIFE

Antonia and Donn's Wedding on April 14
120 guests in Napa Valley, California

PRIORITIES

1. A peaceful location that would be highly memorable (not a church or enclosed place)
2. Being with family and friends (including six adult children and two grandchildren)
3. Expressing their love in a public way
4. Creating a ceremony in which they share their vows and support each other
5. An element of surprise combining the celebration of the half-century mark for Antonia's fiftieth birthday

As Antonia's birthday approached, she began to plan a really special party that would include her children and the children of her then-boyfriend, Donn, sixty-three. Donn and Antonia (Toni) had met twelve years earlier on a cruise ship: she was a travel writer and he was onboard with a photographer, working as a model for the cruise line. They stayed in touch for over nine years before Donn moved from Los Angeles to the Bay Area, and they began to date formally.

After several years of dating, Donn asked Toni to marry him. They decided to dovetail her prearranged birthday party with a surprise family-only wedding the next morning. They only told their children and a few close friends about their plans, and they asked everyone to "keep it under their hats." They considered the event their wedding reception, and invited 120 guests to the celebration, which was aptly themed *Joie de Vivre*, meaning the "Joy of Life."

LOCATION

Their pre-wedding reception (Antonia's birthday party) was held at a rented barn in Napa Valley, California, that Toni found through a friend. "The barn had a bar, tables, chairs, a large kitchen, and plenty of parking." During the party, Toni and Donn announced to the crowd their love for each other, and their intention to get married in a private ceremony the following morning. In the spirit of the theme of the party, they asked everyone to celebrate their joy.

At 8:45 the following morning, eighteen members of their immediate family met at the base of Mount Saint Helena to ride the vans to the peak of the mountain, which is the highest point in the San Francisco Bay Area. From the site, "We could see all of Northern California and part of Nevada, as well as the Pacific Ocean. It is a majestic silent place," Toni described. "The earth there is solid rock, and Donn and I liked the image of being married on solid rock. We loved that we were in a truly natural and beautiful setting, with the sky, our family, and the earth below us."

BUDGET

Wedding site	$ 0
Reception site	$ 600
Groom's clothing	$ 60
Food, catering, cake	$ 1,500
Beverages	$ 550
Photography	$ 0
Videography	$ 30
Music	$1,000 (country band, $400; rhythm and blues, $600)
Flowers	$ 300
Invitations	$ 30
Minister	$ 0
License	$ 50

Fortune cookies	$ 20
Van rental	$ 790
Total	$4,930

DETAILS

When the van let everyone off at the top of the mountain, Toni and Donn invited their family "to wander around and take in the majesty of the place." After thirty minutes, they took their spots for the ceremony. The ceremony was conducted by a family friend who was also a minister; it was spiritual without religious overtones. Toni and Donn both spoke about why they were there and what led them to this point. They shared vows, stories, poems, and asked for comments from their guests. They exchanged hammered gold rings that had been made by a local goldsmith, out of "old gold from past lives," symbolic of "the molding of our pasts into our present."

APPAREL

Everyone was very casual for both the birthday party and the actual wedding. At the wedding, everyone wore sneakers, and Toni wore an outfit that she already owned: forest green slacks, a white silk blouse, and a long green sweater. She explained, "Green is the color of hope." Donn also dressed casually in a tan shirt and khaki slacks.

MUSIC

There was no music at the ceremony, but plenty at the birthday party. They hired two bands for the event. One was a country band; the other was a seven-piece rhythm-and-blues group, who were lawyers in their day jobs and played great music together on the weekend. The country band came complete with a country dance caller, which helped encourage people of all ages to get up and dance. Toni felt "music was the glue for the party. People are still saying how much fun they had."

FLOWERS AND DECORATIONS

Toni described the flowers at the pre-wedding celebration: "There were beautiful massive country bouquets in a whole range of soft country colors. There were gorgeous roses, Queen Anne's lace, lilies, bright blue and pale violet hollyhocks, and all sorts of wildflowers." They also had long-stemmed sunflowers and raffia wrapped into the arches and beams of the barn.

After the pre-wedding party, Toni took the flowers home and used them to decorate her house. She also made a small bouquet from them to bring to the ceremony.

PHOTOS

At the barn party, several friends, a few of whom were professional photographers, took pictures, which they later sent to Toni and Donn.

At the mountaintop ceremony, Toni's sister shot five rolls of film and later gave the pictures to the newlyweds as a present. Toni brought a camcorder, and another guest taped the ceremony for them.

FOOD AND BEVERAGE

The food at the barn party was catered by a local professional who bartered with Toni for her help as a writer/editor on a cookbook. Included in the $1,200 fee was the cost of the food, three people to help, and all of the rentals, plateware, and linens. Toni cooked some of the dishes herself, and friends (who thought they were going to a birthday party, not a pre-wedding reception) brought several dishes. The menu included marinated olives, cheese platters, *gâteau au fromage*, cayenne-spiced walnuts, hummus with pita bread, guacamole, salsa, chips, chicken with tomatillo mole sauce, lentil salad, tossed green salad, grilled sausages with mustards, miniature tamales, focaccia, brownies, sugar cookies, macaroons, and fresh strawberries. Donn went to Oakland and ordered specially made fortune cookies: the fortune inside read *"Joie de Vivre!"*

At the party, they served bubbly from Domaine Chandon and Schramsberg and Beringer and Mondavi wines, all of which they bought wholesale through the wineries. They also had a pony keg of Sierra Nevada Pale Ale and plenty of drinks for the kids.

After the ceremony was over, everyone present went over to Toni and Donn's house, where they ate leftovers and drank the champagne.

Chapter Eight

FOOD FOR THOUGHT

S oon after you begin to plan the details of your wedding reception, the subject of food is bound to come up. Breaking bread with friends and family after the nuptials is a traditional celebration for newlyweds. But a heavy meal isn't your only option. There are many fashionable alternatives to paying thousands of dollars for a four-course sit-down meal at an expensive hotel.

The information in this chapter will help you make educated money-saving choices when working with a caterer. Chapter 9 will further delve into how to DIY all or part of the food and beverage with the help of friends and family. Chapter 10 includes affordable and easy-to-prepare recipes and menu ideas, many of which can be made in advance.

It is best to start the process of locating a caterer, hotel, or restaurant simultaneously with looking for a wedding location. At this point, you may decide to avoid using a catering company altogether by booking a restaurant, café, inn, winery, or resort to hold the ceremony and host your reception.

By choosing a moderately priced, all-in-one locale, you save money by not having to pay fees for two sites, and you also avoid the confusion of having to direct your guests from one site to another. Many of these establishments have a lawn area or a gazebo that is picture-perfect for the exchange of vows. They also usually have linens, glassware, china, and silverware, so you can avoid the added expense of renting this equipment.

If you already have a ceremony location (such as a church or temple) and you are just scouting reception possibilities, or you know you'd rather celebrate at home or at an outdoor or off-premise location, it's time to start investigating caterers. This chapter will help you ask the questions that you need to choose a caterer or banquet manager, decide on a menu, finalize the details, and negotiate the price.

Whether you decide to hire a caterer, an inn, or a restaurant to provide food for your reception, the following steps will help you get the most mileage out of your money:

1. Decide the style of reception that you want.
2. Investigate caterers, restaurants, hotels, and banquet halls in your area.
3. Call three to five caterers or banquet managers and ask for quotes.
4. Analyze the quotes.
5. Choose a caterer and reception locale.
6. Negotiate the cost and decide on a menu.
7. Finalize all of the details (for example, the contract, beverage service, and the cake).

STEP 1. DECIDE WHAT STYLE OF RECEPTION YOU WANT
The times listed below are general guidelines for each style. Usually the wedding starts one or two hours earlier, depending on the formality and length of the ceremony.

Breakfast 9:00–11:00 a.m.
An early morning or sunrise wedding followed by an omelet station and a juice bar is an innovative money-saving venture. Other a.m. ideas include hosting a full or continental breakfast buffet or a sit-down affair. You will not only cut costs on the food (eggs cost far less than beef), but you'll also reduce costs on the space. Mornings aren't considered prime time in most facilities, so they are apt to give you a price break on the banquet room or a great deal at a restaurant that is usually closed during this time.

Brunch 10:30 a.m.–2:00 p.m.

This is another morning reception alternative that can be hosted as a buffet or a sit-down meal. Options include juice, coffee, eggs Benedict, and luncheon items like chicken salad, mixed greens, or deli trays. Look for good deals at restaurants or hotels that are usually closed for lunch or have private banquet rooms.

A SUBTLE DIRECTIVE

Serving tea, dessert, or hors d'oeuvres instead of a whole meal is a great way to save, but be sure to spell it out on your invitation so your guests don't come expecting to be wined and dined. At the bottom of the invitation, a gentle reminder might read "Light refreshments will be served following the ceremony" or "Join us for tea and canapés following the ceremony." (For more about invitation wording, see chapter 13.)

Luncheon 11:30 a.m.–2:00 p.m.

If you are absolutely set on a sit-down meal, choosing lunch over dinner will definitely save money. Consider a preplated luncheon and/or a limit of one or two courses, such as a soup or salad followed by an entrée, or an entrée followed by cake. A buffet is another alternative, perhaps with premade salads and deli trays. Family-style service, where entrées plus side dishes are passed, is another affordable option. Several well-known Italian restaurants, including national chains such as Buca di Beppo and Maggiano's Little Italy, have affordable options with this style of meal and lots of food at an affordable price.

Tea 2:30–5:00 p.m.

An elegant afternoon tea party can be a formal and traditional alternative to a main-meal reception and one that is bound to cost less. Individual canapés and specialty teas are the mainstay of this style of service. A champagne toast and cake cutting or dessert usually follow right after the tea service.

Cocktail Party 5:00–7:00 p.m.

An open bar can be expensive, but finger food is less costly than serving a sit-down dinner or a full buffet. Rentals are kept to a minimum, and usually a band is not needed for such a quick turnaround party.

Hors d'Oeuvres, Buffet Stations, Tapas, or Sushi 5:00–8:00 p.m.

Pairing this grazing style of food service with wine and coffee can be much less expensive than a traditional open bar and/or a full meal to follow.

Afternoon Dessert Buffet, Champagne and Cake, Punch and Cake, or Cappuccino and Cake 3:30–5:00 p.m. or 9:00–10:30 p.m.

Consider a thrifty alternative to feeding guests savory food. This option lets couples celebrate their wedding with loved ones and have a short and simple reception following the ceremony. This option is best suited for small family weddings that no one has traveled a great distance to attend.

Dinner 5:00–9:00 p.m.

This is usually the most formal and the most expensive reception choice. A buffet as opposed to a sit-down meal can help keep the costs down. Or try choosing a casual dinner theme, such as barbecue or picnic style, that won't require as many rentals or as many upscale food choices. Keeping the guest list small and getting married in a rural area can also make serving a full meal more affordable.

TIPS FOR KEEPING
YOUR FOOD BUDGET LOW

- Decide how formal you want the party to be; usually, the less formal, the less costly.
- Buffets usually cost less than sit-down meals because there is less labor involved.
- Hosting your fete at a restaurant or banquet hall that owns linens, equipment, tables, chairs, and more will cost much less than having to rent everything for a shindig in your own backyard.
- Keep the menu simple, and avoid exotic and expensive ingredients.
- The smaller your guest list, the farther your food dollars go.
- The less alcohol that you serve, the more money you save (e.g., opt for a high tea instead of a three-hour cocktail party).
- Use a caterer for part of your event and go DIY for part. (See the sidebar on page 152.)
- Consider hosting your wedding and reception off the beaten path. Rural locations usually cost much less than those in a big city, up to one-third less, for a similar menu.
- Have the event catered by a local grocery store or deli, or by culinary students instead of an upscale caterer. It could be risky but will save you big budgetwise. If you are using culinary students, check references from other events they have catered, and be sure to run through the menu with them thoroughly ahead of time.

Late Night Reception 9:00–11:00 p.m. or 10:00 p.m.–midnight

This option has couples tie the knot after the normal dinner hour so a full meal is not necessary. Appetizers such as a cheese assortment may be included, or it may be a strictly sweet-tooth buffet. A wedding cake, cookies, petits fours, tartlets, and fresh fruit are often accompanied by a wine and soda bar.

Another option to consider is **drop-off catering.** In this money-saving scenario, you order the food prepared by a caterer but ask friends to pick up the platters on the way to your location. Or you can hire a waitress from a local restaurant or a student from a culinary school to deliver the platters, serve them, and clean up afterward. (If you are considering this option, see chapter 9 for more money-saving and organizational tips.)

STEP 2. INVESTIGATE CATERERS, RESTAURANTS, HOTELS, AND BANQUET HALLS IN YOUR AREA

Put the word out that you are looking for a caterer or wedding location that serves food. Talk to everyone you know, and tell them you are scouting sites and taste-testing for a caterer. Keep your ears open; you never know where your lead might come from. When we were searching for our site, a tourist bureau gave me the number of a B-and-B hotline. The hotline suggested an inn, which was booked. That inn suggested that I try another local inn, which wasn't listed in any of my wedding guides. Although it seemed like a wild goose chase, we just kept making phone calls and eventually found the right spot.

TIP

Consider hiring a caterer for part of the event and going DIY for part. For instance, you can prepare cheese trays or simple appetizers a day ahead, such as Mini Caprese Skewers (see recipe on page 204). A friend or family member could also make a salad and have the caterer plate it for you; then the caterer prepares the remainder of the meal. Or have the caterer be responsible for the meal, and then serve a cake alternative that you made or bought in advance. Offering an assortment of penny candy as a dessert buffet, for instance, could cut $2 to $4 (or more) per person versus an elaborate wedding cake (see box on page 167).

Ask everyone you know about caterers and reception locations:

- Friends, relatives, clergy
- Brides or newlyweds
- The local chamber of commerce
- The tourism bureau
- Other wedding vendors: your bridal dress shop, invitation store, church, etc.

Beyond that, keep looking and leave no stone unturned:

- Surf the Internet, for instance, sites like Yelp, for potential event locations, caterers, restaurant reviews, menu, and serving ideas.
- Google your zip code and "caterer," "wedding reception," "wedding vendors" for local options and ideas.
- Scout local magazines or newspapers for restaurant reviews.
- Also consider your favorite restaurant, deli, bakery, or cooking school.

Avoid locations that require you to choose a caterer from a preapproved list. Often A-list caterers charge more than their competitors. But if you have your heart set on one of these locations, read on and do the best you can to negotiate.

STEP 3. CALL THREE TO FIVE CATERERS OR BANQUET MANAGERS AND ASK FOR QUOTES

By calling around for price estimates or quotes you are asking each caterer or banquet hall, in effect, to bid on your event. The caterer will gather basic information about your requirements (a full bar, rentals, which meal is being served, etc.) and send you a written proposal. The proposal will outline how much they will charge, what you will receive for your money, and why you should choose that specific caterer.

When calling for quotes, have your wedding plans handy:

- Time of day
- Date
- Location
- Theme (if applicable)
- Budget (for food and rentals only)
- Food preferences (vegetarian, chicken, steak, grandma's recipe for biscuits, etc.)
- Number of guests expected to attend

Questions to ask when you're calling around:

- Have they catered at this location before?
- Are they licensed with the city and health department?
- Do they carry liability insurance? In what amount?
- Who will run the event? Will the salesperson you are dealing with be on-site to ensure that everything runs smoothly? Will they stay until the end of the event?
- Do they specialize in certain types of cuisine, such as sushi or pastas?
- Is the food prepared on-site? Is it fresh or frozen? Ask for sample menus to be sent.
- Will they have vegetarian, vegan, and gluten-free choices available?
- Is there a different price and/or menu choice for children? What is the age limit?
- Can they arrange for a lower cost meal for band members or other vendors you may be contracted to feed (e.g., sandwiches in lieu of the $40 per person sit-down)?
- After the menu has been chosen, are there extra charges for last-minute changes?

- Do they have an alcohol license? Do they provide the wine and beverages and trained bartenders, or do they contract out?
- Will there be an adequate number of servers? How does the waitstaff dress?
- How do they figure the labor charges—are they included in the cost or extra? How many hours, price per person, tips?
- Does the caterer own or rent the equipment? (If they own it themselves, it could cost you less.)
- How do they handle the setup and cleanup of the kitchen, dining room, reception area?
- Is the setup and breakdown included in the price quote?
- Will the caterer take care of the trash? (Some locations insist that it is carried off-site.)
- What are the cancellation and postponement policies?
- What other charges or service charges may apply?
- Are there references that you can call?
- Can you attend one of their functions while in progress?
- Do they set up menu tastings?
- Important: Reiterate your budget and stick to it.

Let the caterers you talk to know you are comparison shopping and that you are looking for good food, excellent service, and value for your money.

Before placing your first call, decide how much or how little of the work you want the caterer or banquet manager to bid on (for example, rentals, bar, cake, etc.). Do you want one-stop shopping or do you want to do some of the footwork yourself?

Ask for quotes in writing. Some establishments will have standard menus they can send you, and others won't bid until you have a meeting and work out your menu choices. Realize that the bid is usually going to include taxes and a service charge, but make sure.

Some catering companies charge higher fees for weddings because they often spend more time with brides than with other customers. But if you are planning to book your own band, find your own location, and so on, there is no reason for you to be saddled with this extra charge. Keep in mind that the caterer may have lots of contacts to help you. If they do book a vendor for you, they usually mark up the vendor's fees so they get paid 10 to 20 percent of the charge.

STEP 4. ANALYZE THE QUOTES

Keep the following considerations in mind as you analyze the quotes:

- Be sure the taxes and gratuity are included in the bottom line. Also look to see how the gratuity is split; in some cases it goes to the owner or salesperson, and you are expected to tip on top of it.
- What does the food cost include? Some quotes include the cost of the cooks; some are inclusive of all service. Scout for additional charges on top of your per person charge.
- Are plates, glassware, utensils, and linens included?
- What other rentals will you need and are they included in the bid?
- How many appetizers per person are included?
- If it is a buffet, how long will it run?
- Will anyone be serving the buffet?
- Are the prices guaranteed and, if so, for how long?
- Is there a separate cake-cutting fee?
- Does the price per person fluctuate based on the number of guests?
- When do you have to guarantee the number of guests by?
- What if the number changes after the contract is signed?
- Compare the prices of food, rentals, labor, and so on. How does each caterer stack up?
- How professional does the quote appear to be?
- Are there photos or press clippings about the caterer included in the packet?

- Did the caterer listen to what you said and write a menu that was appropriate for the style of wedding that you intend to have? Did the quote come within your budget?
- Do there appear to be hidden costs, or are all the costs and options pretty straightforward?

Narrow down your caterer choices to the top two and then, if possible, visit a wedding in progress for each. When visiting a catered event, take note of the following:

- How is the staff dressed? Look for professional appearances, including tied-back hair, no tennis shoes or gum, and sincere smiles on the faces of the staff.
- Are the staff members friendly but professional with the guests?
- How is the food handled in the kitchen? Is the hot food hot and the cold food cold? Can you taste an appetizer? Is it flavorful and true to temperature? Is the food displayed nicely?
- Do you observe the staff following good sanitation procedures?
- How organized does the entire event appear? Is the staff calm and friendly, or are they running around frantic?
- How smoothly does the meal service go? Is the food delivered quickly without letting it get cold? Is half of the room finished before the other half has been served?
- Is the serving order logical? The bride's table should be served first, then the guests in the dining room from left to right.
- Does the first plate that leaves the kitchen look as good as the last plate? Or does the staff skimp on portions or serve overcooked or undercooked food at the end?
- Was there enough food (in quantity) for the whole buffet to appear abundant from the beginning of the meal to the end?

- Was a meal of leftovers packed for the newlyweds? (Many couples are so busy or nervous that they don't get to eat much, and this ensures that they will get nourishment later on in the evening.)

A FEW WORDS ON FOOD TASTINGS

In a perfect world, you would attend a wedding of a friend or relative and be so impressed with the caterers that you book them on the spot. Then they send you an estimate that is an incredible value. Unfortunately, the chances of this happening aren't that great. Usually, you are going to hear of caterers by word of mouth and will want an opportunity to taste their recipes before the big day.

Bear in mind that different caterers have different policies concerning tastings. Since it costs the caterer money in labor and food to invite you for a sampling, the caterer may have you rely on references and photographs, unless your reception is large or has a big budget.

Some caterers will allow you to taste food when you visit a wedding in progress. Still others may invite you to their commissary to taste a few samples or perhaps even a full meal. Seldom will a caterer prepare all the food options available to you (especially for a wedding under $5,000). Instead, what they want you to focus on is their style of cooking, how flavorful the food is, and the presentation.

STEP 5. CHOOSE A CATERER OR RECEPTION LOCALE

Before you choose a caterer or get a reliable quote on food and rentals, you'll need to decide on your location. In some cases the choice goes hand in hand. For specifics on location, see chapter 5. Regarding which caterer to entrust with the all-important edibles, the bottom line comes down to professionalism, food quality, and cost.

PROFESSIONALISM. Are the caterers organized, sanitary, and reliable? Do you trust their catering salesperson? Do you feel comfortable enough with them to put the fate of your wedding reception in their hands? Can you speak with references whose wedding they have catered?

FOOD. Does the menu and quality reflect your preferences? Is the food flavorful, prepared with care, and artfully displayed? Is hot food served hot and cold food served cold?

COST. Is the reception within your budget? Does the caterer offer a good value in comparison with the other bids?

Keep in mind what the wedding is really about: love—not food.

STEP 6. NEGOTIATE THE COST AND DECIDE ON A MENU

If you found a caterer that you like and trust, but the quote is out of your budget, it is time to negotiate. Tell the caterer your predicament and ask for suggestions to help keep costs down. Let them know that they are your first choice, but you need their help to stick to your budget and get the most for your money. Sometimes the caterer will throw rentals in for free—they can if they own their own linens or china—or add free appetizers during the cocktail hour. If your wedding is at a hotel, negotiate for the hotel to throw in a changing room, discount room rates, and a reduced price on the honeymoon suite; after all, you are spending a lot of money in one location, usually the largest portion of your budget.

Once you have chosen a caterer and you know that the date you need is available, you can either choose one of the caterer's set menus or have them create one for you. At this point, you are in final negotiation stages, and you want to keep your cost-cutting agenda foremost in your mind.

Here are a few more ideas that will help you lower catering food costs:

- Consider choosing a menu that the caterer is already preparing for someone else on the same day; often they may offer you a price break because it is easier and less expensive for them to prepare the same food for multiple parties.

- Skip having passed appetizers and have crudités or a cheese tray available before the main meal is served.
- Stay clear of exotic ingredients and keep your menu simple. This will not only help your guests recognize and enjoy their selections but it will also keep your costs down.
- Choose lower-priced entrées; skip the beef or salmon and stick with chicken or white fish.
- Having a choice of two or three menu options or hot buffet entrées is ideal, but it usually costs more and may not fit into your budget. Designing your menu to highlight neutral choices, such as pasta or chicken, is a good idea when there are many different guests to please.

GOING GLOBAL

There are many fun ideas to help add life and worldly flavor to your event: Feature an individual country's cuisine or a combination of global options, such as Indian, Portuguese, Brazilian, Mexican, Russian, Polish, Italian, French, and/or Asian food. Tasty ethnic menu items could include tacos, fajitas, raviolis, grilled Cuban sandwiches, panini, barbecue, sushi, teriyaki skewers, empanadas, nachos, spring rolls, papusas, crepes, naan bread, gyros, dim sum, or tapas. The possibilities are endless and can be customized based on your heritage or your favorite foods.

For an avant-garde reception that would be very memorable, hire one or more tried-and-true food trucks to park near your reception locale. From American comfort food to Pan Asian and Mediterranean to creative globally-inspired desserts, a world of foods can arrive at your door reasonably priced.

See page 182 for more foodie themes.

STEP 7. FINALIZE ALL OF THE DETAILS

Once you have chosen a caterer, a location, and a menu, you will probably be asked to put down a deposit to secure the location and the date. Make sure you get a written contract prior to giving the deposit and also insist on a receipt for the deposit and any subsequent payments that you make. If you are utilizing multiple vendors (a caterer, a banquet hall, a bakery, a rental company), be sure to get a contract and receipts from each of them.

Be sure that the following points are included in your contracts:

- Reception date and times
- Number of guests and deadline for a final count
- Price per person for adults', children's, and vendors' meals
- Tax and gratuity fees
- General rules and restrictions
- Terms for payment
- Cancellation and refund policies
- Overtime fees

In addition to the above, the following should be included in the caterer's or banquet hall's contract:

- The menu, including each appetizer and entrée choice selected
- Style of service: buffet, sit-down, or hors d'oeuvres
- How long the food will be served if it's a buffet (e.g., 6:00–8:00 p.m.)
- The number of waitstaff and managers who will be on hand
- The on-site waitstaff/cook hours included in the price
- Waitstaff/cook dress codes
- Liquor/corkage fees
- Beverage service (see pages 162–63)
- Cake service (see pages 164–66)
- Parking information and charges

- Cleanup policies
- An outline of rental equipment that will be provided
- Any special needs, such as a gift table or place cards set per your seating chart

Another option worth considering is to hire a caterer with a cause. Fare-Start in Seattle, for example, are back-to-work cooking certification classes designed for formerly homeless men and women. Cincinnati Cooks! is a similar program based in Ohio. Use the Internet to search for cooking schools and retraining programs near you that cater or have on-site banquets.

FINALIZING YOUR BEVERAGE SERVICE

There are many different options to choose from when deciding what style beverage service you prefer. Once you have decided on the overall style of the reception (high tea, brunch, dinner, or a cocktail party) and how much money you have left to spend, it will become clear whether you can afford to serve alcohol and, if so, what kind.

The traditional open bar is the most expensive drink option available. It usually involves hiring the caterer to provide bartenders, alcohol, drink mixes, beer, wine, and soft drinks for an unlimited amount of time. If you choose this option, the drinks for your reception can cost as much as the food does.

Here are some ways to save money with an open bar:

- Limit the open bar to one to two hours and then go to a cash bar.
- Give out two drink tickets per guests and then go to a cash bar. (Etiquette experts might not approve of these first two suggestions, but you *can* implement them gracefully.)
- Serve wine and beer only.
- Stick with house-brand liquors and domestic wines where available; skip top-shelf liquors and expensive imported wines.

- Skip a bar completely if there is no cocktail hour. Instead, provide a limited number of wine bottles on the tables along with sparkling water or pitchers of iced tea.
- Provide an espresso bar where lattes and specialty Italian flavorings are available.
- Skip the alcohol and consider providing nonalcoholic drinks only with the exception of a champagne (or nonalcoholic champagne) toast.
- Provide champagne for the toast only, limiting the amount to one glass per guest.

If you are buying alcohol through your caterer or reception hall, be sure that you understand how you will be charged: by the bottle, by the glass, or per person by the hour. See if you can negotiate price breaks on any of these charges.

Another money-saving alternative is to provide your own beverages and hire the caterer to serve them, or appoint a family member or friend to do so. (See pages 191–94 for tips on setting up a bar.)

Check to be sure that your caterer or location won't charge a corkage fee if you bring your own beverages. If they do have a fee, calculate if you would still save money over purchasing their wines. Also, some locations have rules or licenses that don't allow the guests to provide their own alcohol; look into the legalities before going this route.

Dry weddings are becoming more accepted as sobriety has become more chic. Some statistics state that up to one-third of the American population does not drink. If you decide to skip the alcohol, sparkling cider and grape juice are excellent, and they make less costly substitutions for the wedding toast. Iced tea, punch, and lemonade are also wonderful nonalcoholic thirst quenchers. In winter, mulled cider and hot chocolate will warm up your guests. Check with your caterer to order the cups, mugs, urns, punch bowl, and/or pitchers needed to serve these drinks.

RESEARCH AND ORDER YOUR DREAM CAKE

The cake table is a mainstay for the traditional wedding celebration. As guests come into the reception area, they all take a peek at the cake in anticipation of eating it later. But start researching wedding cake prices and you'll be shocked to see that they range from $2 to $6 per person and up.

Why do wedding cakes cost so much? Because the pans to bake them in are expensive, as is the cost of top-of-the-line butter, eggs, whipping cream (be sure to ask your baker if he or she uses real butter and cream—this is not the place to skimp). Also, wedding cakes require expert decorators and bakers to design and execute a confection that tastes as good as it looks. There is a wide range of qualities in bakeries. It's a good idea to get referrals and seek out quotes, similar to the process of finding the right caterer. Be sure to taste-test several samples before you sign up with a baker.

The wedding cake consists of four main parts:

1. **The cake** itself is available in many varieties—white, devil's food, banana, hazelnut, carrot, pound cake, and so on. Usually each cake is cut into several layers and filled with icing or a filling.
2. **The icing** or **frosting** traditionally is a buttercream, which comes in a wide range of flavors, from chocolate and lemon to liqueur-flavored (e.g., cherry kirsch or Grand Marnier). Other frostings include fondant, cream cheese, or whipped cream.
3. **The filling** can be any of the above frostings, custard (vanilla, chocolate, lemon curd), preserves (apricot, orange, berry), and/or fresh fruit.
4. **Decorations** can be simple or elaborate: piped borders and flowers, fresh flowers, multiple tiers, figurines for the top of the cake, and cake ornaments such as a bell, a heart, doves, or a gazebo.

So how do you get a cake that looks and tastes great without breaking the bank? Here are a few suggestions to cut the costs without sacrificing style:

- Check with your caterer and local baker first. Usually these are expensive alternatives, but occasionally you will find a good deal. Bakers who aren't wedding-cake specialists usually cost less, and home bakers who don't have the overhead of a bakery often cost the least.
- Ask at your favorite restaurant if its pastry chef would consider baking your cake. Again, double-check the price, but I've heard from many brides that they went this route and saved money while getting an artistic confection that they cherished.
- If your local grocery store has a bakery, get a price quote from it. Oftentimes a supermarket can offer exceptional cakes for much less than a traditional bakery. Check the prices of non-wedding cakes (e.g., sheet cakes) as well, and consider that as an option.
- Investigate prices at a culinary school near you. If students are baking and decorating wedding cakes as part of their curriculum, the per person charge may be greatly reduced.
- Keep the cake simple and avoid labor-intensive decorations. Provide your own cake or ask a friend or relative to buy you one as a present. If you choose a basic cake style instead of one with multiple flavors, icings, fillings, and decorations, the price will be less.
- Skip having multiple tiers with fancy pillars. Either do without and have the cake layers stacked, borrow pillars (if your baker provides this service), or have the baker use disposable pillars instead of the costly crystal ones. Also check with your local rental company to see if it has any available.
- Consider asking for a cake topper as a present. Often friends or relatives will ask what you want or need for a shower and/or wedding present. Let them know what style wedding topper you prefer (e.g., plastic or china). One bride I know received a Lladró figurine couple as a gift.

- Have a small decorated cake for your cake cutting. Then have the caterer serve your guests from sheet cakes that are plated in the back kitchen.
- Buy a multi-tiered cake, but decorate it yourself or have the florist do it for you. Not having extensive decorations on your cake will save the baker time and you money.
- Have a friend or family member bake the cake. (For more tips on this, see page 229.)
- Skip the cake altogether and serve a nontraditional dessert, such as tartlets, cheesecake, or a dessert buffet. See "Desserts Worth Devouring" below.

DESSERTS WORTH DEVOURING

While wedding cakes can be delish and stylish, they are no longer the only end game in town. Here are examples of other flavorful finales appropriate for a wedding reception:

- Old-fashioned penny candy (see box opposite)
- Seasonal pie buffet, with mini tartlets, slices, and squares
- A multi-tiered cupcake tree
- Towers of cream puffs, éclairs, and profiteroles
- Cake pop, gelato, or latte/cappuccino stations, or an ice cream or gelato cart
- State fair theme: popcorn and cotton candy, brownies, lemon squares, ice cream
- A smorgasbord of delightful mini donuts, truffles, cookies, and/or petit fours, perhaps including some gluten-free pastries, such as decadent flourless chocolate tartlets
- Individual wedding cakes on each table that serve a dual purpose as the centerpiece and the edible pièce-de-résistance

Old-Fashioned Candy Station

A wedding I recently attended had catered appetizers and a buffet dinner, then, instead of a cake, there was a buffet of old-fashioned candy. The bride and groom purchased different types of candy themselves and gave it to the caterer to make the impressive after-dinner display. Instead of dessert plates, there were stacks of little penny-candy bags. Each guest took a bag and filled it up with lollipops, hard candies, and old-fashioned favorites like Razzles, super-sour Zotz, salt-water taffy, Smarties, and black and red licorice.

WORKING WELL WITH CATERERS

To ensure the success of your wedding reception, stay in contact with your caterer or banquet manager and keep these final thoughts in mind:

- Make sure you go over your ideal timeline with the event coordinator from the catering company. Tell him or her if you will be having a reception line, how much time you want for any cocktail hour, and what time you want the entrées (if any) served.
- Notify the caterer in advance of any deviations from the agreed-upon menu, such as the need for a vegetarian choice or a guest who can't eat anything cooked with nuts or nut oils. You will eventually want to inform the caterer where these guests will be seated.
- Be sure that the caterer knows what time you need to be out of the reception hall before you incur overtime charges.
- If you make changes at any time after signing the contract, be sure to get them in writing!

A SUMMER TEA PARTY

Rebecca and Dan's Wedding on August 20
130 guests in Eugene, Oregon

PRIORITIES

1. Staying within their budget
2. Making sure that all guests had fun
3. Including both of their large "mixed" families
4. Celebrating the relationship
5. Having a meaningful ceremony focused on the love they share

Rebecca, thirty, met Dan, thirty-one, while working at the registrar's office of their alma mater, the University of Oregon. They had been together for three-and-a-half years when they attended Rebecca's stepbrother's wedding and decided on the car ride home, jokingly, that they needed another excuse to bring the whole family together again. Their discussion turned serious, and they decided to announce their engagement when they arrived home. They wed a year later.

The night before the wedding, Rebecca's stepmom catered a rehearsal dinner at her dad's house, and various other activities were planned over the course of an extended weekend. "It was great to spend time with everyone," Rebecca remarked. "Afterward, we had a lot of people thanking us for hosting a wedding."

LOCATION

Their wedding and reception took place at a completely refurbished Painted Lady Victorian bed-and-breakfast in Eugene, Oregon. The surrounding area was wooded on one side, with lawns and a rose garden on the other. The ceremony was held outside on a small hill in the parklike setting. Rebecca and Dan rented the entire property for the day; the reception took place both inside the common rooms of the inn as well as outdoors, and a rented canopy was set up on the grounds in case of rain.

Rebecca explained their choice: "We decided to spend the bulk of our money on the location. You can either spend on a great place that doesn't need much or spend a lot of money fixing up a place with flowers and decorations."

BUDGET

Wedding site (inclusive of food, china, tables, linen)	$1,800
Dress, alterations, veil, and shoes	$ 400
Groom's clothing	$ 0
Beverages (champagne and tea)	$ 324
Cake	$ 364 ($2.80 per person)
Canopy rental	$ 150
Photography	$ 500
Music	$ 800
Flowers	$ 400
Invitations	$ 120
License, minister	$ 100
Total	$4,958

DETAILS

Spirituality in the ceremony was very important to Rebecca but not that important to Dan. Rebecca felt that guests from many religions would be present. She explained that "even though we don't go to church or practice, I sort of wanted God to be there." In the end, Rebecca and Dan compromised on a ceremony they both were comfortable with.

At the beginning of the ceremony, an ancient Greek passage summoning the gods was read by a friend, followed by a love poem by Rainer Maria Rilke (page 307). Then the minister read a Native American wedding prayer.

The ceremony was similar to that of the Episcopal Church, and their vows were adapted from options given by the minister.

For the photography, they hired a "two for the price of one" husband-and-wife team and had over 120 photos taken. For a set price, they received a wedding album with the 4 x 6-inch proofs, but the reorder pricing was expensive and Rebecca regrets that "we still haven't purchased any more photos."

APPAREL

Rebecca wore a princess-style dress. "It was not what I imagined I would choose. My friend talked me into trying it on. It turns out that I did have that fantasy—but wholesale!" She also wore a pearl-beaded headband with a detachable tulle train that she took off after the ceremony. Dan wore a traditional daytime tuxedo with black pants and coat and a green floral jacquard vest; his groomsmen wore similar attire with a cummerbund in place of the vest. There was no charge for Dan's outfit because the shop included it when he reserved five tuxedos for the groomsmen plus tuxes for the dads.

While on a shopping trip to pick out a dress that was flattering on all five of her bridesmaids, Rebecca became a victim of "bridesmaids' mutiny." Her bridesmaids let her know that they didn't like her choices, and they elected to pick out their own outfits. The only requirements she made were that they all wore hats and that their outfits fit the garden-tea theme. "Somehow it worked," Rebecca stated incredulously. The outfit styles ranged from a tight linen sheath with big red roses to a lavender-and-cream-colored dress worn with a huge silk-flower-adorned hat.

MUSIC

Dan and Rebecca hired a string quartet to serenade their wedding guests during the arrival, ceremony, and reception. During the ceremony, the minister asked all of the guests to pause for a moment of quiet reflection as the quartet softly played in the background. At the reception, the selections were light classical pieces by Handel, Telemann, and Vivaldi.

FLOWERS AND DECORATIONS

Dan's and Rebecca's sisters created the wedding bouquets, corsages, boutonnieres, and buffet table vases out of a mixture of gardenias, white lilies, stephanotis, and ivy. Rebecca's choice of flowers was partially sentimental: "Gardenias were the flowers that my grandpa gave my grandma when they were courting and throughout their marriage." All of the flowers were purchased wholesale at the flower market.

FOOD AND BEVERAGE

For their high tea–style wedding reception, they served specialty teas that were donated by the owner of a tea shop where Rebecca worked. The food and cake were prepared by the staff at the bed-and-breakfast. On each table, as well as on a central buffet table, there were three-tiered silver cake stands that served as both decorative centerpieces and as platters for the finger foods: mini quiches, cucumber sandwiches, smoked salmon canapés, cream puffs, and chocolate-covered strawberries.

Their elaborate wedding cake was styled like a stack of presents and appeared "architectural, like enormous petits fours." Each "package" had its own pastel-shaded icing: blue, pink, green, or white, and every layer was "wrapped" with a contrasting-colored marzipan bow. The bottom layer was a big chocolate cake with raspberry filling, the next layer up was carrot cake, the third layer was white cake with lemon filling, and the miniature box on top was chocolate mousse cake.

Following the cake and champagne toasts, the whole group broke out singing "Happy Birthday" in a baroque style to the many family members who were celebrating their birthdays in the month of August. When asked if there was one thing she would change about her wedding if she could, Rebecca replied, "We should have bought more champagne; we ran out."

The party mode continued on as Rebecca and Dan celebrated their honeymoon with a weeklong trip to New Orleans, which was a present from her grandmother.

Chapter Nine

IF YOU ARE CRAZY ENOUGH TO CATER YOUR OWN WEDDING

○———————○

Most people aren't cut out to handle the details of catering their own wedding. But if you or your betrothed are Food Network junkies, closet chefs, foodies to the bone, maybe kitchen DIY is a given. Can you juggle four thousand things at once? Are you tired of watching *Iron Chef* without getting your hands dirty? Do you feel this is your big chance to show off your catering chops? No doubt it could save you fistfuls of money.

First, a word of warning. If you have never cooked for a crowd or entertained en masse, your wedding reception is probably not the best time to give it a first try. As confident chefs and caterers know, understanding the tricks of timing, being completely at home with cooking techniques, crafting a doable menu, and having the food prepped ahead of time are essential keys for success. If you are game to take all this on, make sure to be maniacally organized long before your wedding day. Even if you don't want to cater your own event, reading this chapter can give you insights that may help you work with the caterer.

As mentioned previously, one strategy to save money even if you have a caterer is to do part of the food yourself, such as cheese trays, sushi, simple appetizers, or a preplated salad. Along that same line of thinking, handling the bar yourself could save big time. Purchase champagne, wine, beer, and/

or alcohol at a warehouse store; then have a friend or two man the bar. Depending on where you are getting married, however, that may not be allowed. It's a good option for smaller at-home venues, where holding a liquor license and event insurance would not be a requirement. Handling all or part of the food and beverage yourself is covered in the following pages. For recipes and additional menus see chapter 10.

Before the big day arrives and it's time to show everyone you invited that all those hours watching the Cooking Channel are paying off, here is my advice for anyone who plans to self-cater all or part of the reception:

- Don't try to do everything yourself.
- Keep the guest list under control—as short and sweet as possible.
- Get friends and family involved in their respective areas of expertise or interest.
- Design the menu and reception to be simple and doable.
- Consider finger foods, mini desserts, a high tea service, snack stations, or breakfast instead of a full sit-down lunch or dinner.
- Prep, prep, prep. Do as much ahead of time as possible without degrading the quality. Some recipes even taste better when made a day ahead.
- Restaurant-quality prepared foods are a shortcut that caterers use to round out the menu. Sushi, deli platters, veggie trays, sliced artisan bread, cut fruit, bakery cookies, and miniatures pastries are examples that will save you work and time.
- Be sure everyone knows his or her roles before the main event: know who is baking; who is making appetizers; who is grilling; who is setting up tables, chairs, place settings, and centerpieces; who will be responsible for reheating and or refilling buffet foods; and who will bus tables and clean up afterward.
- Hire help as needed. Call a caterer or household staffing service to provide a trained waitperson at an hourly rate or ask

waiters at a local restaurant. The least expensive way to go is to hire responsible neighborhood teenagers. Keep this in mind, however: usually the more experienced the help is, the less staff you need.

- Search the web for descriptions of other couples' self-catered weddings. Pay attention to their menus, their preparation and shopping tips, the amounts of food they bought, and their advice on how to pull it off without a hitch.

- Designate a friend or relative to be in charge of the event and keep the timeline on track.

- Consider a potluck or partial potluck. Hire a caterer for some of the food, then add to the menu by making a course or part of the buffet yourself. If you are very adventurous and have many cooks among your friends, a fun (and high risk) option is to host a chili cook-off between ten friends and ask others to bring corn bread, cupcakes, cocktails, and whatever else you want.

- Dessert bars have gained in popularity instead of traditional cake. How about a pie table, or ask each of your friends that bake to make a specific number of their favorite pies, cakes, or tarts? A dessert bar can be your entire food offering, such as a late-night decorate-your-own-cupcake bar, or it can be what follows a main meal or heavy appetizers.

WHAT'S INVOLVED IN DO-IT-YOURSELF?

When I say that I was crazy enough to cater my own wedding, I don't mean that I physically cooked everything myself. I was incredibly fortunate that a friend I had worked with for years offered to prepare the food for me for the cost of the ingredients (which he then purchased wholesale).

As the caterer and event planner, what I did do was write the menu, organize and test the recipes, decide on the ingredient amounts that needed to be purchased, book the location, and hire food servers. I also had to purchase the beverages; walk through the location before the event to decide how to set up the buffet and self-serve bar; buy centerpieces for the buffet and flowers for the cake; order the cake and arrange for a friend to pick it up and deliver it to the wedding; provide platters for all the menu items; provide linens, silverware, cups, plates, and so on; make the cooks and food servers aware of the ceremony and event timelines; and arrange for the cleanup of the facilities.

Here are a few examples from others who catered all or part of their own weddings:

- One couple I know booked a meditation retreat on a cliff overlooking the ocean in Carmel, California. They invited forty close friends and family, and everyone chipped in to cover the cost of renting the site for the weekend. The couple purchased steaks wholesale for everyone through a restaurant they frequented. Each guest signed up to bring a dish for the main event and also something for breakfast and lunch the following day. After the ceremony, they barbecued the steaks on a grill provided by the retreat center and cooked together in the commissary kitchen. The guests I spoke to regarded the weekend as "enchanting" and "a real bonding experience."

- A New York couple rented out a New Jersey summer camp on a preseason camp weekend in May. One hundred guests attended, and they divided up the chores and the cooking. They had a fabulous, albeit rustic, wedding.

- An Illinois couple with strong ties to Italy held a backyard wedding for eighty guests. The family served up a traditional Italian feast: spaghetti and meatballs, vegetable lasagna, garlic bread, cannelloni, focaccia, antipasto (roasted peppers, marinated olives, salami, mortadella, cheese), a garden salad, and lots of Chianti.

- Following their wedding, a couple in Indiana held a formal hors d'oeuvre reception at a local country club for their two hundred guests. It only lasted for two hours, and afterward they invited all of the guests back to the bride's childhood home for a pool party—complete with a full picnic dinner that all of the neighbors had pitched in to make. Sandwiches of all sorts were a mainstay.

- San Francisco foodies wed at City Hall and then held a back-yard feast for 250 guests with globally-inspired foods. They made some of the dishes themselves, but most came from Chinatown and the Latin American districts. Spit-roasted pork and tamales were among the tasty choices.

There is so much stress and expectation, and so many details to take care of, on your wedding day quite aside from food preparation. It is important you decide ahead of time how much of the event you want to plan yourself and how much help you need. Here are some of your options:

- Let friends or family members prepare the wedding feast for you and have them set it up or hire help for the day of the event.
- Prepare the food yourself in advance of your wedding, and hire someone to serve it for you or ask for help from family and friends.
- Hire culinary students to prepare or assist you and your family or friends with cooking and serving for the event.
- Try the potluck approach—prepare or purchase the main en-trée and ask your guests to bring menu items in lieu of gifts.
- Have a caterer prepare and serve the bulk of the meal but pre-pare appetizers, the salad, and/or a dessert bar or the cake to help cut costs. Setting up your own bar can also save a lot of money. (See chapter 10 for more information on setting up the bar and baking the cake.)
- Have a caterer drop-off a self-serve al fresco meal—perhaps a couscous salad and chicken or shrimp kebabs—and make the dessert yourselves.

MENU PLANNING

When overseeing the food preparation, it is important to write a balanced menu that will serve all of your guests' needs while being easy enough to execute successfully.

Keep your menu simple, bearing in mind how many things you have to do on the day of your wedding. Here are some tips to keep in mind:

THE DATE AND TIME OF YOUR WEDDING. Decide if you want to serve breakfast, lunch, dinner, hors d'oeuvres, and/or dessert or cake. The meal or a snacking in-between period will also determine the amount of silverware you need, if any. Some appetizer receptions include finger food only, or they may require a single fork for the buffet, with another fork for the cake. If you skip the cake and serve mini desserts that can be picked up, you can also skip that fork. Finger-food receptions do not mandate seating for each individual guest but rather cocktail tables for small groups. Other menus, such as a dinner buffet or a sit-down meal, may necessitate a full range of silverware, a chair and place setting per person, and a name card preplaced at each table setting.

THE SEASON OF YOUR WEDDING. Write the menu with the weather in mind and choose produce and proteins that are fresh and readily available. For instance, hot soup is an acceptable first course in the winter but not in the heat of August. Whipped cream–frosted wedding cakes are also best avoided in warmer months. Also keep in mind that during the summer months you may need extra refrigeration, cooling boxes, or coolers with ice to safely preserve your prepared foods.

THE KITCHEN FACILITIES ON-SITE. If there is only an outdoor grill and no warming ovens, keep this in mind when writing your menu and plan to serve a grilled entrée and vegetables, or cook the entrées elsewhere and rent hot boxes to bring on-site.

FEEDING A CROWD. Realize that for large groups it is a lot easier to execute a buffet than a sit-down, multiple-course meal. If you are serving over one hundred guests, it is advisable to either design a buffet table so guests can serve themselves from both sides, or put up multiple buffets that mirror each other and serve the same dishes on each buffet. Another option is to set up individual stations around the room or reception site that each have their own theme (e.g., a sushi station, a pasta station, and a beef-carving station). VARY INGREDIENTS, TEXTURE, AND FLAVORS. In other words, design a buffet or each course with foods that complement each other and do not all taste or look the same. For example, avoid serving pureed cauliflower and mashed potatoes. Instead, serve green beans and mashed potatoes.

HOW MUCH FOOD SHOULD I PREPARE?

Long before I went to cooking school or ran a catering company, I attended a wedding buffet that ran out of food before the last two tables were served. This is a bride's worst nightmare! In the catering business, we always add an additional 10 percent to the final guest count to guarantee that this never happens. Also, after pretesting the recipes, you'll get a better feel for how large a portion is indicated. You know your guests and how much they like to eat better than anyone else; fifty athletic football players will eat at least twice as much as fifty ladies who lunch.

Decide ahead of time what you plan to do with leftovers. Options include distributing it among wedding party, guests, and/or staff; donating it to a local charity; or throwing it away because it's been on a buffet and may no longer be safe to eat. If you decide to let people take the food home or to donate the food to a charity, bring gallon freezer bags, plastic wrap, foil, plastic containers, and shopping bags to divvy it up.

The following are standard formulas for portion sizes. Keep in mind I always round up, believing that it's better to have leftovers than to run out of food:

Hors d'oeuvres: 4 to 6 pieces per person for the first hour, to 3 per hour afterward

Lunch: 4 to 6 ounces protein (chicken, fish, etc.) per person *

Dinner: 6 to 8 ounces protein per person*

Vegetables: ¼ pound per person

Starch: ½ to ¾ cup per person*

Rolls: 1 to 2 per person

*If more than one choice is offered, add 2 to 4 ounces per person to your estimate.

If the reception is dessert only and lasts for two to three hours, I'd estimate 10 to 12 bites per person or 1½ to 2 regular-sized items, such as a cupcake or piece of pie. Remember to cut the portions small so people can try a variety of items without wasting a lot.

Ask yourself the following questions before you write your menu:

- Do you want the food to have a theme, or do you want more of a mixed Continental cuisine-style menu? Theme suggestions include a sushi or oyster bar, tapas, a high tea, a clambake, a barbecue, a 1950s-style retro food buffet, or an ethnic or international theme, such as Mexican, Italian, Moroccan, Asian, soul food, Cajun, southern cooking, a luau, California cuisine, or nouvelle French.
- How long do you want the food served for? Passed hors d'oeuvres often last for one hour; an appetizer or main meal buffet usually is out for an hour and a half to two hours; dessert stays out for one to two hours.
- What type of china, glassware, and silverware do you need? Can you get away with upscale paper products purchased online or from a party store, or do you need to rent glassware? Contact a local rental company to see samples and get price quotes. Or buy an eclectic mix of plates, silverware, platters,

and serving utensils from garage sales, flea markets, church rummage sales, and thrift stores.

- Should you use platters or chafing dishes? Silver trays for passing hors d'oeuvres and china platters are understatedly elegant, but you probably will need to rent and/or borrow to have enough to serve all of your guests. Go through the planned menu by item and make a list of all of your needs for serving ware. Consider if you want to keep the hot food hot on the buffet by using chafing dishes or if you prefer to use china serving dishes. If you go the china route, bear in mind that the cooks will have to refill much more often so the food is always hot.

- How many menu items do you want to serve? For a full meal—lunch or dinner—the easiest route is to serve one main dish with a starch, some rolls, and one or two vegetable accompaniments. With one main dish, it is easier to gauge how much to buy, there is less preparation time involved, and it is usually less expensive. On the other hand, the more items you serve, the more confident you can be that your guests will find something they like. If you do offer more than one entrée item, be sure to cut down on the portion sizes for each entrée (e.g., cut a half chicken breast into two pieces so a guest could take a three-ounce piece of chicken and a few slices of ham).

Once you have decided on a menu, it's always advisable to have a dry run cooking all the items in a much smaller quantity prior to the event, testing the recipes to be sure of proper amounts and compatible flavor combinations. This pre-wedding run-through will help you write a to-do list including amounts for the shopping and a timetable for the preparation and cooking of all the dishes. Seeing all of the dishes together will also help you determine how you want to arrange the buffet table. After your run-through, draw a picture of the buffet table to give to your kitchen help. This will enable them to carry out your expectations without interrupting you while you are with your guests.

DESIGNING YOUR OWN WEDDING CAKE

Truth be told, I wasn't crazy enough to bake my own wedding cake. This was partially because I am in awe of the artistry of the pastry chefs with whom I have worked over the years, but mostly it was because of the expense. If I had purchased all of the pans, cake ingredients, pastry tools, and cake separators for tiers, I would have spent almost as much money as I did to pay an expert to bake and decorate the cake. Plus, not every wedding has a wedding cake these days. Consider pies, tarts, cupcakes, and all sorts of other sweets that could finish off your meal.

That said, many brides are adamant they conclude the event with a traditional cake. And a portion of them want to bake it themselves. On pages 229–33 is a luscious lemon cake recipe if you are so inclined. Daria, a bride from Green Bay, Wisconsin, explained her motivation for baking her own cake: "I am not sure that making the cake saved me any money, but I like to cook, and I like to entertain. Since so many people were coming from all over the country [her groom is from Boston, Massachusetts] and we were having our reception at a restaurant, I felt that by baking the cake I had a hand in actually preparing and providing for my guests instead of only paying others to do it.

"I really enjoyed baking my cake. I knew I would be nervous, and I liked the fact that I spent my wedding morning and the days leading up to it buying, preparing, and assembling the cake. It was a lot of work and it took a lot of organization, but I was really happy with the results."

If you are inspired to bake your own cake, one option is to take cake-decorating classes from Wilton Industries. They have several books available to use as guides, and they sell all the baking and decorating supplies you need, including cake stands (so you can avoid the tedious task of doweling and pillaring a wedding cake), cake pans, pastry bags and tips, premade icings, tier separators, pillars, figurines, and a wide range of decorations. The classes are taught around the country in craft and department stores. (For more information on their products or classes, log on to Wilton.com or search online for classes near you.)

Before undertaking the task of baking the cake, look at magazines and pastry books for inspiration and visuals to follow. Then practice, practice, practice everything, including making the icing and using the pastry bag and tips.

George Geary, a traveling pastry teacher and former Walt Disney World executive pastry chef, shared a few suggestions for saving time and money if you plan on making and/or decorating your own wedding cake: "Brides have elaborate expectations because magazines and TV shows feature wedding cakes that cost up to $1,000 or more. But many cakes can be store-bought for as low as $1.50 per person, if you are willing to decorate it yourself.

"Whenever I teach cake decorating, I suggest twenty-five fresh or piped

TIP

One wedding I attended skipped the dessert station and placed a decorated 10-inch round cake on every table as the centerpiece. I've also seen this done with a bottle or two of wine, pitchers of water, a tray of appetizers, or even an entrée, especially Italian foods like pasta. Sharing food at the table in this way—"family style"—is much more interactive than being served. It creates a greater sense of community to pass and share items. Plus, someone usually makes a mess and—hopefully—people relax.

flowers as a good amount for a three-tiered cake serving sixty. Enough to decorate without overwhelming the cake. If using fresh flowers, buy your own flowers or rose petals at a wholesale market, through your florist, or pick them from your backyard. Be sure the flowers are edible, such as pansies or roses grown without pesticides.

"To avoid spending money on cake pans, see if any of the craft stores in your area will rent them to you. Or search on the Internet or in the Yellow Pages under 'cake decorating' for a specialty store and inquire about renting. To avoid the baking altogether (and the price of buying the pans), many bakeries will sell you unfrosted baked cakes at very reasonable prices." To serve up to seventy-five guests, George recommends 9-inch, 10-inch, and 12-inch tiers, each with two layers.

A FABULOUS DESSERT RECEPTION FOR 100

This menu is from a party I helped some friends cater. The San Francisco couple eloped and a month later hosted a late-night reception for one hundred guests in the New York–New Jersey area. They served a few savory items, such as sushi, cheese, crackers, chips and salsa, and lots of desserts purchased from local bakeries. Drinks included a pony keg, champagne, wine, and soft drinks. The party started at 9:00 p.m. and lasted into the wee hours of the morning. Total cost for the reception was $925, including the fee for the waitress, a local culinary school student, who helped serve and clean up.

DESSERT MENU

Petits Fours

Linzer Torte

Fresh Fruit Platter

Chocolate Decadence Brownies

Carrot Cake with Cream Cheese Frosting

Miniature Lemon Meringue Pies

Fresh Fruit Tartlets

White and Dark Chocolate Dipped Strawberries

Sugar Cookies and Almond Florentines

New York Cheesecake

Chocolate Truffles

Salted Caramels

DESIGNING A FABULOUS BUFFET TABLE

To design a gorgeous buffet table, start with pretty serving pieces in the same or similar styles and varying colors and shapes. Cake stands, nice serving utensils, and well-polished chafing dishes (if you are serving hot food) will add to the visual appeal. All of these can be rented, borrowed, or purchased at garage sales or flea markets. If you register for some of this equipment as wedding presents (as I did), you hopefully will receive the platters and serving piece gifts in time to use them on your buffet. Glass blocks, bricks, wicker baskets, pieces of marble, upside-down pots, pans, and boxes can also be used to add height and visual appeal to the table.

If you are buying some of the food already prepared, either drop off your platters ahead of time so the staff or friends can set up or rearrange the finished products onto your serving platters. Paper plateware that appears very upscale is available (although some of it can cost more than renting china or stainless), but the disposable plastic platters that groceries and delis use look fairly cheap. Unless your party is very casual, I would suggest transferring the food to better trays.

If a caterer is dropping off food or you are picking up some of the food from them, ask them to prepare the food on nice platters, mirrors, or baskets for you. They may charge you an extra service charge or insist upon a security deposit to ensure that you return their serving pieces promptly and undamaged.

Stack plates (entrée-, salad-, or cocktail-sized, depending on your menu) wherever you want your guests to start the buffet line: either at a corner of a table, a small table of its own (sometimes a round table adjacent to a rectangular buffet table), or in the middle of a series of tables if you want your guests to get a plate and then go to the right or to the left on "mirrored" buffet tables. Yet another option is to have several different station tables, such as for sushi or carved beef, that each have their own small plates.

Next, decide the order you want to serve your dishes. For a main meal, like lunch or dinner, salads usually go first, then entrées with vegetables, starches, and rolls nearby. I like to vary heights by making pedestals and staircases of sturdy boxes and covering them with additional tablecloths (in a contrasting color to the main tablecloth, often done in the bride's colors, if she has chosen any. Fluff the tablecloth up to appear puffy and arrange the platters at the various heights, making sure that they will not tip or fall when the guests are serving themselves.

Arrange for extra flowers and place them in between platters on your buffet table for added color and beauty. Decide ahead of time if you need to add height or color to your buffet (in addition to the above pedestals), and if so, make or order large bouquets that can either be placed at the center of the buffet or on adjacent tables (e.g., a table with the plateware). If you want to use flowers as a garnish for any of your trays, make sure that they are edible and have not been sprayed with pesticides. Some roses, violets, Johnny-jump-ups, and nasturtiums fall into the edible category.

Here are some affordable buffet and table decoration ideas that you can use in place of, or in addition to, flowers:

- Sprinkle the tables with small candies, such as red cinnamon hearts, or colorful heart-shaped confetti.
- Arrange fresh produce and sturdy herbs (such as rosemary) on the tables in between the serving platters. Lemons; strawberries; red, green, and yellow peppers; zucchini; eggplants; and patty pan squash will all add color and visual appeal to your buffet table.
- Use tulle, ribbons, cloth roses, or flower petals (real or silk) to carry the wedding theme onto your buffet without a lot of added cost.
- Arrange branches of ivy, lemon leaves, cherry blossoms, multicolored autumn leaves, or gold-sprayed leaves on your buffet table before placing the serving trays down for a really polished look.
- Sprinkle multicolored mini-heart foil and paper confetti on the tables. The confetti could be bought from a party store, or handmade ahead of time by cutting it out of paper. Fun paper snowflakes or origami paper, or even just specialty

paper from a paper, craft, or party store, all could be used to spice up your buffet and guest tables.

- For a fun way to decorate the buffet table, intersperse the food items with framed photos of the bride and groom at different times of their lives and their relationship, starting with baby photos and continuing up to and including their engagement. Or make a collage and use it as a backdrop to or the buffet.

- For events with a rustic or old-fashioned theme, many inexpensive vases; antique items like old food cans, boxes, or signs; or even canning jars can be used to create color and character on a buffet or guest table; use them to hold breadsticks, flatbreads, and assorted crackers. Or fill them with water, fresh herbs, sliced or whole fruit, and flowers—for example, rosemary sprigs, lemon slices or mini kumquats, and daisies. Review the chapter 7 for even more do-it-yourself ideas.

HOW DO I STAFF FOR THE PARTY?

These are the guidelines I use when catering a party or special event. If you are using waitstaff that have little or no professional experience, I'd advise staffing a bit on the heavier side.

1 server per 20 guests for a sit-down meal
1 server per 30 to 40 guests for a buffet
1 server per 40 to 50 guests for a cocktail party or hors d'oeuvre reception
1 bartender per 50 to 75 guests; a full bar requires more work and more servers than a beer and wine bar

COST CUTTING AND ORGANIZATION

If you are catering the wedding yourself, review the cost-cutting measures suggested in chapter 8 and ask yourself the questions that are suggested in that chapter for your caterer on pages 154–55. This will help you cover your bases from cook and waitstaff uniforms (ask cooks to wear a chef jacket if they have one, or dress like the waiters in a white buttoned-down or tuxedo shirt and black dress pants and shoes) to who will take out the trash. Make sure to assign all of the tasks or ask the person who is designated to be in charge of the event to review and assign all tasks.

Two ways to save dollars when you are preparing your own food include buying wholesale and bartering for food or services. You can buy wholesale by attending some farmer's markets or seeking out wholesale warehouses such as Sam's Club or Costco. Cash & Carry (smartfoodservice.com) and Food Service Distribution centers, such as Gordon Food Service Stores (gfs. com) in the Midwest, are additional wholesale places that sell to the public. If you live near a produce, poultry, or meat plant, they may let you buy direct, especially if you own your own business and already have a tax identification number. Sam's Club and Costco both have bakeries that make pies, cakes, and prepared entrées on-site. They also sell platters of cheeses, appetizers, smoked meats such as brisket, boiled shrimp with cocktail sauce, and a host of other options. Often they have a brochure that lists foods that they can make if you order ahead of time.

Grocery stores, including Whole Foods and many local markets, also have similar offerings. Just ask at the deli or bakery counter. Although the prices at grocery stores are not wholesale, the fact that you are buying larger quantities may bring the cost down. It definitely saves money versus a caterer. Discount retailers, such as Walmart and Aldi, sell platters and other food items at a reduced rate compared with a full-service grocer.

To barter for products or services, consider all of the items that you need, and think about the contacts you have who can furnish these items. Decide what kind of service you could offer these vendors that would be of benefit to them. For instance, one bride that I know is a writer and traded hours of writing and journalistic coaching with a caterer who was trying to write a book. That caterer also helped further by purchasing all of the products wholesale and not charging the couple any markup. Another bride I know is a publicist who traded hours of work at her traditional fee for 20 percent off of her total bill. Other potential trades include secretarial service for produce, or catering a friend's party if she caters yours.

You may need to rent, borrow, or purchase the following items if you are catering your own reception:

- Flatware: silverware or stainless steel
- Glassware: champagne flutes, rocks glasses, highballs, and so on
- Chairs for ceremony and reception seating
- Tables
- Serving platters
- Warming trays or chafing dishes and serving utensils
- A canopy or tent in case of rain
- A coffeemaker, carafes, cups, and cream and sugar dishes
- Punch bowl and cups
- Champagne buckets or coolers for icing
- Linens: tablecloths, napkins

Additional items that you also may want to rent include candelabras for centerpieces, flower buckets, a wedding arch, a chuppah, a dance floor, and white wooden lattice folding screens. Before you rent, first see if your wedding site has any of these items available for little or no charge. Next, decide if you could buy the items cheaper via garage and rummage sales or the Internet. To me, rentals are a last choice as they can really add a lot to your bottom-line costs.

If you do rent, be aware of the following to get your full deposit back:

- When receiving the rentals, check all items against your order list and the rental company's inventory list.
- Look for chips or cracks.

- Count glasses, silverware, and so on. Be sure that what you need is what you got.
- Report any discrepancies or damages that exist on delivery ASAP so that any changes can be made immediately and overcharges are refunded, and so that the vendor knows you weren't responsible for the damage.
- Find out what condition you need to return the dishes in. Some rental companies just want a light rinsing of dishes, and they do the heavy cleaning back at their facility.

Caterers usually bring along a bag of extra items that will come in handy on location. Some of these are definite necessities, a few are just-in-case. If you are self-catering, consider whether you will need any of these items:

Cutting boards
Knives, scissors, spatulas, spoons
Garbage bags, garbage cans
Paper towels
Matches
Plastic wrap
Aluminum foil
Resalable plastic bags for leftovers
Dish and hand soap
Plastic gloves
Sponges
Safety pins
Tape
Pens, markers

ALCOHOLIC BEVERAGES
Save money on alcohol by limiting the selections:

- Set up a beer, wine, and soda bar.
- Serve one glass of champagne per person for the toast.

- Consider setting up a beer and wine bar and, in addition, offering one type of mixed-liquor beverage that can be made in advance and served from pitchers, such as sangria (see page 235), piña coladas, strawberry margaritas, or mimosas.
- Purchase all your beverage needs wholesale, if possible, through a discount warehouse or superstore or on sale at the liquor or grocery store.

For some couples the full bar is the only option. Here are approximate guidelines to follow if you are setting up a full bar for fifty guests, but keep in mind what and how much your family and friends prefer to drink:

Beer	1 case
Whiskey	1½ liters
Bourbon	1 liter
Gin	2 liters
Scotch	1½ liters
Light rum	1 liter
Vodka	2 liters
Tequila (optional)	½ liter
Champagne	1 case
Red wine	3 to 4 bottles (if for cocktails only)
White wine	1 case (if for cocktails only)
Dry and sweet vermouth	1 750 ml bottle of each

For mixers, stock up on orange juice, Bloody Mary mix, sour mix, tonic, soda water, and garnishes (limes and lemons, as well as cherries for kiddie cocktails).

If you are having one hundred or more guests, you may want to set up more than one bar. If so, repeat the bar setup described above in each location.

The wine and champagne amounts listed above are for a typical cocktail party. The amounts will need to be adjusted if your crowd prefers red wine, if you wish to have a champagne toast, or if you plan on serving wine with your meal. Figure out how many glasses of each you wish to serve per person, and base your calculations on four glasses of wine or champagne per bottle and twelve bottles per case. Realize that you will need additional stemware to accommodate a toast or wine at the meal. Also, bear in mind local laws governing the serving of alcohol and your liability.

Another money-saving option is to choose a primary cocktail or a limited selection of beer and wine in place of champagne and a full bar. For instance, serve craft beer, mojitos, margaritas, Beaujolais or Chilean wines, or White Russians.

Consider, too, a "wine potluck." Ask guests to bring a bottle of wine and a dish to share in lieu of presents. Randomly put a bottle of wine on each table and keep a reserve for when that runs out. In this case you may want to get wine openers made with your names and wedding dates. They would serve a double purpose—guests can open their own wine and take them home as a wedding favor.

NONALCOHOLIC BEVERAGES

As a member of the nondrinking set, I love it when there are a lot of choices that are nonalcoholic. Plus, they are significantly less expensive than top-shelf offerings.

Here are some suggestions:

- Sparkling and still bottled water
- Nonalcoholic champagne, sparkling cider, or grape juice
- Sodas: Cola, lemon-lime, diet drinks, root beer, orange or grape soda
- Lemonade (see the recipe for Minted Raspberry Lemonade on pages 234–35)
- Iced tea and hot tea
- Coffee (plus cream and sugar) or espresso
- Kiddie cocktails
- Italian sodas (Italian flavored syrups mixed with sparkling or soda water)

When setting up your own bar, don't forget to bring these:

- A table, tablecloth, and garbage can
- Bottle openers
- Corkscrews
- Ice buckets (and/or coolers) and tongs
- Pitchers (if needed)
- Bar glasses, glass or plastic (two or three per person)
- Champagne flutes and wine glasses, plastic or glass (one per adult, or more if you are serving wine with dinner)
- Beverage napkins
- Ice: 1 to 2 pounds of cubed ice per person, and crushed ice for chilling wine and champagne
- Stirrers and tumblers for mixing
- Shot glasses or measures

BAREFOOT ON THE BEACH

Alison and Karl's Wedding
60 guests in Manhattan Beach, California

PRIORITIES

1. Privacy and intimacy
2. A certain element of secrecy
3. Speedy planning time—three days
4. Location—on a local beach
5. Personal feeling—they wrote their own vows and played their favorite music

Alison, thirty-one, and Karl, twenty-eight, were both getting married for the second time. They had been together for over four years and had intended to marry for at least a year and a half. They spontaneously decided to "just do it." As Karl says, "Let the record show, Alison asked me."

LOCATION

The wedding was held on Manhattan Beach at sunset. The three-day weather forecast was so favorable that no rain alternative was planned.

BUDGET

Wedding site	$ 0
Bride's clothes	$ 75
Food	$ 125
Cake	$ 95
Champagne	$ 90
Photography	$ 0
Flowers	$ 75
Minister	$ 0
License	$ 60
Total	$520

DETAILS

A friend who was a minister performed the ceremony, and his girlfriend took photographs. They were the only ones who knew that Karl and Alison were getting married. "We knew that we were eliminating family members. We love our families dearly, but they just don't get along well in large groups."

APPAREL

Alison wore a vintage white lace blouse with jeans, and Karl wore a vintage suit that he already owned. They both went barefoot.

MUSIC

The mix that they had prerecorded included love songs performed by a variety of musicians, from Frank Sinatra to the Clash.

FLOWERS AND DECORATIONS

Alison carried a simple bouquet of white tulips. There were no other flowers.

FOOD AND BEVERAGE

After they were married, they stopped and picked up a cake and some Korbel champagne. Then they went home, where Alison had prepared "mountains of food," including a pasta salad with roasted eggplant and feta cheese, a platter of marinated asparagus and peppers, and a Moroccan-influenced chicken dish.

"We just started calling friends to come over and help us celebrate. Somehow, we caught people at the right time; sixty people showed up. We were relaxed but wildly excited that we had just tied the knot. Everyone was happy for us."

Chapter Ten

RECIPES FOR SUCCESS

○————————○

f you are planning to cater your own wedding (or any special event), this chapter will help you decide what to serve your guests and how much.

Included in this chapter you will find this information:

SUREFIRE RECIPES that are grouped by category: appetizers, salads, main dishes, sides, a dessert, and beverages. (See index on pages 198–99.)

PREPARED FOOD ITEMS THAT YOU CAN PURCHASE from your local grocery store, bakery, or deli. Use these convenient edibles to design an entire menu, or purchase a few premade dishes to round out a menu highlighting your own homemade specialties.

MENU IDEAS that will help you design the wedding reception you want.

THE RECIPE FOR CULINARY SUCCESS ON YOUR WEDDING DAY
Before undertaking the task of catering your own wedding, follow the advice in chapter 9 and pay special attention to the following ideals:

Plan a trial run of the entire menu prior to the main event.

Personalize the recipes by changing them to suit your individual tastes.

Prepare as much ahead of time as possible.

Buy ready-made products to save time and round out your menu.

Designate a friend or relative, or hire someone to be in charge at the reception; let all the vendors know to go to that person with any problems they may have.

Index of Recipes and Menus

APPETIZERS

Hors d'oeuvres are often passed at a cocktail hour before dinner or served at a reception in lieu of a main meal. The hors d'oeuvres included here have been chosen because they are easy to assemble and can be made ahead of time.

PROSCIUTTO AND MELON

This appetizer is quick to make and can be assembled a day in advance. Other types of melon can be substituted (e.g., honeydew, casaba), or you can use two types, a green and an orange, and alternate them on the serving tray. You can also serve the prosciutto and melon as a first course by leaving the slices larger and arranging 3 or 4 on a plate with a small amount of mixed greens and a mint vinaigrette.

Makes approximately 40 pieces

1 ripe medium cantaloupe
⅓ pound thinly sliced prosciutto

Cut off the top and the bottom of the melon. Set the melon upright on one of the cut sides. Using a smooth stroking action from the top of the melon to the bottom, let your knife peel off the outer layer. When the entire melon is peeled, quarter the melon by cutting it from top to bottom and cutting each half again from top to bottom. Scoop out the seeds and cut each quarter into 5 slices; cut the slices in half.

Cut each slice of prosciutto crosswise into 3 pieces and wrap the middle of each melon slice with the prosciutto. Arrange on a platter.

STORE-BOUGHT
HORS D'OEUVRE SUGGESTIONS

To save time and add variety to your appetizer buffet, consider purchasing any of the following hors d'oeuvres from a local store, deli, restaurant supply house, or fish market. Another option is to ask a caterer if you can buy these items premade, and then have someone at your reception site cook (if needed), display, and serve:

Artichoke Dip with sliced French
    Bread
Guacamole with Tortilla Chips
Hummus with Mini Pita Breads
Red, Green, and Mango Salsas
    with Tricolored Tortilla Chips
Pico de Gallo with Black-Bean
    Chips and Pita Triangles
Mini Tacos and Taquitos
Miniature Quiches
Assorted Canapés
Savory Tartlets
Phyllo Triangles
Stuffed Mushrooms
Cocktail Shrimp
Crab Claws

Crab Cakes
Chicken Skewers
Chicken Wings
Jalapeño Cheese Poppers
Cheese Tray
Antipasto Tray
Crudités
Miniature Sandwiches
Sushi
Tamales (cheese and/or chicken)
Egg Rolls
Dim Sum Buns
Queso Dip with Tortilla Chips
Fondue with French Bread
Potato Pancakes with Applesauce

SPEED SCRATCH SUGGESTIONS

Start with freshly prepared foods from your local grocer, then slice, top, layer, add, or make a sandwich. Voilà, you have a new creation that looks like homemade but is much easier—speed scratch cooking!

- Pretzel Sandwiches: Spread a sliced pretzel bun or soft roll with whole grain mustard and mayo. Add a filling of your choice, such as honey ham or smoked turkey.
- Quesadillas: Stuff with cheese and salsa and bake. Another filling possibility is sliced chicken, roasted peppers, chopped scallions, and cilantro; serve with salsa.
- Tacos: Use small flour and corn tortillas and a variety of fillings, such as fish, shrimp, shredded pork, or brisket; toss with salsa and cheese, then stuff into the taco shell. Serve warm with sour cream, pico de gallo, and guacamole.
- Tortellini Dippers: Cook tricolored tortellini to al dente, cool, toss with olive oil and pesto, if desired; serve chilled with a dip.
- Flatbread Pizzettas: Start with a pizza crust mix or a canned dough, bake until just undercooked, and top as desired—for instance, with three cheeses, sausage, fresh herbs, sweet peppers, pesto and fresh mozzarella, heirloom tomatoes and basil. Just before serving, finish in the oven. Or cook the crust thoroughly, then top with cool or room-temperature ingredients, such as Caesar salad, or arugula with thinly sliced fennel, lemon juice, dill, olive oil, and shaved Parmesean.
- BLT Bruschetta: Slice a baguette ¼ inch thick on a slight bias, toss with olive oil, bake until golden brown in a 375°F oven. Top with arugula and sliced tomatoes or halved cherry tomatoes. Sprinkle with Italian vinaigrette and crisply cooked bacon pieces.
- Smoked Salmon Crisps: Layer sliced smoked salmon, chive cream cheese, and capers on pita crisps. Add thinly sliced red onion, if desired.

PESTO-CRUSTED BRIE

This appetizer can be assembled in minutes. You can use prepared pesto from the supermarket to save time. For a slightly different flavor profile purchase a sun-dried tomato pesto instead. If you are expecting a large crew, you can purchase a 2-pound cheese round at a specialty cheese or gourmet shop and use ¾ cup of pesto.

Makes approximately 20 slices

¼ cup prepared pesto
1 13.2-ounce baby Brie cheese round

Drain the pesto of any excess oils. Spread the pesto on the top of the Brie, being careful to keep the pesto from spilling over the sides.

Using a hot knife (run it under warm water and then dry it off), slice the cheese in half, then cut each piece in half again, and cut each resulting quarter into 5 pieces: 20 wedges total. Clean the knife after each cut. Arrange on a plate surrounded by crackers, sliced baguette, grapes, and berries.

ENDIVE WITH BLUE CHEESE AND PECANS

Belgium endive is also known as French endive and is a 4- to 6-inch-long, cigar-shaped head of cream-colored leaves. Red endive is also available in some parts of the country; if you can find it, utilizing some of both colors makes a beautifully contrasting platter. If you can't find either type of endive near you, prepare the cheese and nuts on water crackers or celery.

Makes 18 to 20 pieces

½ pound Belgium endive
¼ cup crumbled blue cheese
20 pecan halves, toasted

Cut the bottom off the endive and lay out the individual spears on the cutting board. At the bottom of each spear (near the cut end), place ½ teaspoon of the blue cheese in a small mound, and press a pecan half into it. Arrange on a decorative plate.

MINI CAPRESE SKEWERS

Toothpicks, bamboo skewers, or mini bamboo forks all give a distinctly different look to these easy, delish appetizers. For a super shortcut, skip the olive oil and balsamic-vinegar reduction and just drizzle with a premade balsamic vinaigrette.

Makes 24

24 bocconcini or 48 ciliengine (small balls of fresh mozzarella), drained
24 fresh basil leaves
24 small red, orange, or yellow grape or Sweet 100 tomatoes
Kosher salt and cracked black pepper
Extra-virgin olive oil
Balsamic Glaze (see below) or store-bought vinaigrette

Skewer a bocconcini or a ciliengine of mozzarella, a folded-over basil leaf, then a tomato. If using ciliengine, add one more at the end of the skewer. Cover and chill if not using right away. Just before serving, arrange on a platter, sprinkle with salt and pepper, and drizzle with olive oil and Balsamic Glaze.

Balsamic Glaze

This glaze is addictive! It tastes terrific on the Mini Caprese Skewers, but also consider using it in place of the balsamic vinegar on the Farmer's Market Tomato Salad (page 208), or drizzle it over the Roasted Vegetable Platter (page 211).

Makes ½ cup

1 cup balsamic vinegar

⅓ cup sugar

Pinch of cracked black pepper (optional)

Mix all three ingredients in a nonreactive, heavy-bottomed saucepan. Over medium-high heat, bring to a boil, then lower the heat to medium. Simmer until the glaze reduces by slightly more than half, about 8 to 10 minutes. The result should be a thickened syrup that holds its shape when drizzled. It will continue to cook a little after it is removed from the heat, so do not let it get too thick.

CHEESE AND FRUIT PLATTER

Utilize a variety of three to five types of cheese of different textures, distinct flavors, and contrasting colors. One pound of cheese can serve up to 10 people, depending on how long your party is and what other appetizers you are serving. If you are serving appetizers only, figure on 2 to 3 ounces of cheese per person.

Cut one cheese into cubes (Cheddar and Jack work well). Buy one sliced in the deli, such as smoked Gouda or Swiss, and add a wedge and some crumbles, such as blue cheese. A semisoft cheese like Port Salut can be cut into individual wedges; perfectly ripened Brie also works well, or try the Pesto-Crusted Brie (page 203), or a log of goat cheese.

Garnish your cheese platter with nuts, crackers, baguettes, and fresh or dried fruit: green and red seedless grapes, strawberries, raspberries, or blackberries, dried apricots or dates, toasted almonds or pecans. Sliced apple and pear are a natural accompaniment, but they don't hold well and can't be prepared ahead of time. If there is not room on your cheese tray for bread and crackers, arrange them on a plate or in a napkin-lined basket and place it next to the cheese on the buffet table. Don't forget to put cheese or serving knives near each type of cheese.

CRUDITÉS OF SEASONAL VEGETABLES

To design a beautiful vegetable platter, buy the freshest seasonal produce available; vary the colors, textures, sizes, and flavors of the vegetables; and consider blanching some of the veggies so you can include a greater selection. For every 10 to 12 guests, prepare 2 pounds of raw or blanched vegetables.

Begin with the crudités base. A large flat-bottomed basket works well and looks great on a buffet; a large serving platter can also be used. Cover the surface area with napa cabbage or radicchio leaves, and leave room for the dipping sauce by inserting a bowl where the sauce will eventually go.

Cut the vegetables that will be served raw, such as cauliflower florets, celery sticks, sweet pepper triangles, and green and yellow zucchini coins. Remove the stems from cherry or yellow pear tomatoes.

Blanch the firmer vegetables by cooking them in boiling salted water until al dente, and then quickly cool them under very cold running water. Good choices here are baby carrots, broccoli florets, trimmed asparagus spears, and green beans.

Arrange the vegetables by placing the contrasting colors and shapes in rows that start at the sauce bowl and proceed to the edge of the basket. Fill in the dip (try the Sun-Dried Tomato Dip below) and the basket is ready to serve. Platters like this can be strategically placed at appetizer stations in lieu of or in addition to passed hors d'oeuvres.

SUN-DRIED TOMATO DIP

This dip is my favorite for serving with crudités, chips, and/or cocktail shrimp. It can be prepared and refrigerated several days in advance.
Makes 2½ cups

½ cup marinated sun-dried tomatoes, drained

1 cup mayonnaise

1 cup sour cream

¼ cup milk

½ teaspoon chopped garlic

¾ teaspoon prepared horseradish

1 lemon, juiced

½ teaspoon salt

½ teaspoon black pepper

In a blender or food processor, puree the sun-dried tomatoes, mayonnaise, sour cream, and milk until smooth. Add the remaining ingredients and puree for 1 minute more.

MULTIPLYING RECIPES TO SERVE A CROWD

When figuring out recipe amounts, multiply up, but be aware that you may need to improvise a little. Don't just rely on math. Instead, pay attention to tastes and textures. Check before adding too much salt or seasonings, and correct consistencies (for example, thickness), if needed.

ASIAN-FLAVORED SHIITAKE MUSHROOM SKEWERS

This warm appetizer is great for vegetarians and all mushroom lovers. It works well as a passed hors d'oeuvre and can also be a part of a buffet. For catering, I like to serve the skewers in bamboo baskets that are lined with palm, lemon, or red chard leaves. A small dice of red and yellow peppers sprinkled over the platter adds a lot of color to the dish.

Makes 20 skewers

2 tablespoons olive or peanut oil

2 tablespoons (¼ stick) unsalted butter

1½ tablespoons finely minced ginger

2 teaspoons finely minced garlic

¼ teaspoon black pepper

2 limes, juiced

40 medium shiitake mushrooms (about 8 ounces), stems removed

½ teaspoon salt

20 6-inch bamboo skewers, soaked overnight in water

Preheat the broiler on High.

Heat the oil and butter in a sauté pan over medium heat until the butter begins to melt. Add the ginger and garlic and sauté for 1 minute. Remove from heat and add the black pepper and lime juice.

Secure 2 mushrooms onto each bamboo skewer; arrange the skewers on a cookie sheet and brush them with the oil mixture. Sprinkle the salt over the mushrooms.

Broil the mushrooms under high heat for 5 to 6 minutes, until lightly browned. Remove from the cookie sheet and place on a serving plate. Pour the pan juices over the skewers and serve.

SALADS

A salad can be a component of a plated entrée, a buffet selection, or a meal in itself. From vegetable salads to exotic mixed greens, salads add color, flavor, and excitement that will round out your menu.

FARMER'S MARKET TOMATO SALAD

A selection of perfectly ripe tomatoes from your garden or your local farmer's market will make a fabulous salad for a summer wedding.

Some of my favorite tomato varieties are Green Zebras, Early Girls, Orange Jubilees, Brandywine, Black Crimson, Red Flame, Yellow Pear, Orange Cherry, and red Sweet 100s. If you can't find any of these varieties in your town, you can purchase vine-ripened tomatoes from your local supermarket.

Serves 10 to 12

3 pounds mixed specialty or vine-ripened tomatoes
⅓ cup extra-virgin olive oil
1½ tablespoons balsamic vinegar
Salt and cracked black pepper
2 tablespoons chopped fresh basil
6 ounces crumbled goat's cheese (optional)

Slice the tomatoes into different shapes (wedges, slices, small cubes, etc.) and arrange them on individual plates or a buffet platter. Drizzle with the oil and vinegar. Season with the salt and pepper and sprinkle with the basil. Dot with goat's cheese, if desired.

SPINACH SALAD WITH MANDARIN ORANGES

Fresh mandarin oranges are abundant for an autumn wedding, but canned are available year-round. Baby spinach also works well in this recipe. The dressing can be made up to two days ahead of time. Just reheat, toss, and voilà!

Serves 10 to 12

1 10-ounce bag of spinach, or 2 loose bunches
½ cup extra-virgin olive oil
1 small yellow onion, thinly sliced into rings
½ pound fresh brown mushrooms, sliced
2 teaspoons minced garlic
3 tablespoons red wine vinegar

⅓ cup orange juice

Salt and pepper to taste

3 mandarin oranges, peeled and sectioned, or 2 11-ounce cans, drained

Wash the spinach well and remove the stems. Tear the leaves into pieces the size of a silver dollar. Dry well, place in a large serving bowl, and reserve, lightly covered, in the refrigerator.

In a skillet, heat ¼ cup of the olive oil over medium heat. Add the onion rings and cook until they appear translucent, about 4 minutes. Add the mushrooms; sauté for 5 minutes. Add the garlic and sauté for 1 minute. Stir in the remaining oil, vinegar, juice, and seasonings; remove from heat. Toss with the spinach (the spinach will wilt slightly) and top with the mandarin oranges, or let the dressing cool, cover, and refrigerate for up to 2 days, then warm to a simmer to reheat prior to serving.

Honey Mustard Vinaigrette

This vinaigrette will coat 1 pound of mixed baby greens, which serves 10 to 12 on a buffet. Garnish the salad with your choice of fruit, vegetables, or nuts: cucumber moons, cherry tomatoes, green and red apple slices, red onion julienne, carrot shreds, toasted pecans or walnuts.

Makes 1¼ cups

1½ tablespoons honey

3 tablespoons whole-grain mustard

¼ cup apple juice

¼ cup apple cider vinegar

¼ teaspoon salt

¼ teaspoon pepper

½ cup extra-virgin olive oil

Whisk the honey, mustard, juice, vinegar, and salt and pepper together; slowly add the oil until well blended.

STORE-BOUGHT SALAD SUGGESTIONS

For an easy out-of-the-ordinary green salad, look in your local produce section for prepackaged salad mixes. Each bag will have several varieties of lettuce (Bibb, romaine, radicchio, escarole, etc.) mixed together, thoroughly washed and ready for use. If you are planning to prepare your own salads, check the grocery aisle for a variety of bottled salad dressings that can add panache and save time. The deli case is where you will likely find several of the following premade salad selections:

Potato	Bay Shrimp
Macaroni	Tuna
Pasta	Baby Mixed Green or Spinach
Three Bean	Salad
Asian Noodle	Caesar
Coleslaw	Marinated, Roasted, or Pickled
Shrimp	Vegetables
Chicken	Tabbouleh
Ham	Grain Salads

ROASTED VEGETABLE PLATTER

Choose any combination of your favorite vegetables and roast them at high heat to bring out their natural sugars through carmelization. You can prepare this dish a day ahead, but don't add the vinegar until just before serving. I generally serve this dish at room temperature, but it can be reheated if you prefer. Figure on ¼ pound of raw vegetables per person.

CHOOSE FROM THE FOLLOWING VEGETABLES:

Asparagus, trimmed

Baby squash or patty pan squash, trimmed

Red or yellow peppers, seeded, destemmed, and cut into triangles or strips

Red onion, leek, or scallion, cut into bite-sized pieces

Mushrooms, whole or cut in half

Cauliflower or broccoli florets

Japanese eggplant, yellow squash, or zucchini, sliced ½ inch thick

New potatoes, halved or quartered

Fennel, trimmed and cut into ½-inch slices

Miniature peeled carrots

Garlic cloves

ADD:

Olive oil

Sherry or balsamic vinegar

Salt and cracked black pepper

Fresh chopped basil, tarragon, or rosemary (optional)

Preheat the oven to 450°F.

Coat several baking pans and toss the vegetables lightly in olive oil. Roast each vegetable separately until tender and caramelized, approximately 12 to 18 minutes; cool. Toss with vinegar, salt, pepper, and fresh chopped herbs, if desired.

HEARTS OF ROMAINE WITH SCALLION CILANTRO VINAIGRETTE

I love using chopped hearts of romaine for a buffet or preplated salad. The leaves are hearty yet flavorful and retain their crispness better than other varieties.

Makes 10 to 12 servings

VINAIGRETTE

¼ cup lime juice

¼ cup rice wine vinegar

½ cup chopped scallion, white and green parts

½ cup chopped cilantro

1 tablespoon finely chopped ginger

2 teaspoons low sodium soy sauce

2 teaspoons sugar

½ cup peanut oil

½ cup sesame oil

Salt and pepper to taste

SALAD

1 14- to 16-ounce package of hearts of romaine

Vinaigrette

1 cup thinly sliced radishes

1 cup shredded carrot

½ cup sliced or slivered almonds, toasted

1 cup chow mein noodles

Salt and pepper to taste

Make the vinaigrette: In a medium bowl, whisk the juice, vinegar, scallion, cilantro, ginger, soy sauce, and sugar together; add the oils and blend well. Season with salt and pepper to taste. The dressing can be made to this point and refrigerated for several days.

Make the salad: Cut the lettuce into 1-inch pieces; wash and spin dry. Add lettuce to a large bowl, pour vinaigrette over, and toss. Add in the radishes, carrot, almonds, and chow mein noodles; toss again. Check the seasoning and add more salt or pepper, if needed.

MAIN DISHES

◦──────◦

Whether breakfast, lunch, or dinner, choose an entrée and side dishes that complement each other and appeal to most guests. The following selections are tried-and-true recipes that I have served at many catered functions.

SMOKED SALMON SOUFFLÉ ROULADE

This roulade is a perfect entrée for an elegant brunch or light luncheon. Prepare up to two days in advance and refrigerate until needed. Finish by slicing, reheating, and broiling right before serving.

Serves 10 to 12

½ cup (1 stick) unsalted butter

½ cup all-purpose flour

½ teaspoon cayenne pepper

1 teaspoon salt

1½ cups milk

12 eggs, separated

½ teaspoon cream of tartar

½ pound of smoked salmon, roughly chopped

1 pound cream cheese, room temperature

¼ cup chopped fresh dill

¼ cup grated Parmesan cheese

Preheat the oven to 350°F. Generously butter two 15 x 10 x 1-inch baking (jelly-roll) pans and line them with parchment paper.

In a saucepan over medium heat, melt the butter. Whisk in the flour, cayenne, and salt. Cook 3 to 5 minutes, stirring until the center bubbles. Turn off the heat and stir in the milk. Return to the heat and cook 3 to 5 minutes more, stirring continuously, until the mixture thickens. Remove from heat.

In a large bowl, beat the egg yolks with a wire whisk. Gradually whisk in the flour mixture; beat until smooth.

Using an electric mixer, beat the egg whites and cream of tartar until stiff peaks form. Gently fold the whites into the yolk mixture, being careful not to overmix.

Using a rubber spatula, divide the batter between the two pans and spread it evenly. Bake 15 to 20 minutes, until the roulade springs back when touched in the center. When completely cooled, invert the roulade sheets onto a clean surface and discard the parchment paper.

Whip together the salmon, cream cheese, and dill until light and fluffy. Divide and spread the salmon mixture evenly on the surface of each roulade. Place one of the 15-inch roulade sides in front of you. Carefully roll it up toward the other 15-inch side, until the width of the roulade forms a spiral of egg and filling. Cut each roulade into 10 slices. Refrigerate, covered, if not serving immediately; reheat the refrigerated slices in a preheated 350°F oven for 8 to 10 minutes before proceeding to the next step.

Preheat the broiler.

Spread the roulade slices out on a greased baking tray in a single layer so that a cut side faces up. Sprinkle with Parmesan cheese and broil for 3 to 5 minutes, until lightly browned.

TEQUILA SHRIMP

This is an adaptation of recipe for Drunken Shrimp that Ann Walker had on her tapas and wedding menus when I catered with her in Marin County, California. People loved it and gobbled it up—myself included. For special events, we would just spill a batch onto a platter, then serve it with tiny bamboo forks or toothpicks. To save time when making a large quantity, you can heat an electric griddle and cook directly on it. These shrimp can also be skewered (4 or 5 shrimp per skewer) and grilled, tossed into hot or cold pasta, or used as a shrimp taco filling.

Serves 8 to 10 as an entrée

*2 pounds medium shrimp (approximately 20 to 25 per pound), peeled and
deveined*

MARINADE

2 tablespoons tequila

1 lemon, juiced

1 lime, juiced

1 tablespoon extra-virgin olive oil, plus more for cooking

1 tablespoon plus 1 teaspoon finely minced garlic

1 teaspoon kosher salt

1 teaspoon paprika

1 teaspoon freshly chopped oregano

1 jalapeño, stemmed, seeded, and minced

½ cup cilantro leaves, roughly chopped

Put the cleaned shrimp in a medium metal or plastic bowl and set aside.
Combine the remaining ingredients in a blender and blend until smooth.
Pour over the shrimp and toss with a spoon until coated in the marinade.
Cover with plastic wrap and refrigerate 1 to 2 hours.

Heat a large sauté or nonstick pan over medium-high heat until almost
smoking. Add just enough olive oil to lightly coat the bottom. Add the
shrimp in small batches and sauté. The goal is for the pan to be hot enough
and the shrimp to be dry enough that they sear quickly (versus stewing or
steaming in the marinade). Toss or stir continuously while quickly cooking
for 2 to 3 minutes, making sure the shrimp are cooked on both sides. Serve
immediately with toothpicks.

CAL-ASIAN CHICKEN SALAD

This chicken salad is wonderfully fresh and a perfect lunch entrée. It
works well on a buffet but also could be a part of a preplated luncheon.

Serve it with room-temperature cooked udon or angel hair noodles that have been tossed in a little sesame oil and rice wine vinegar. If you would like the salad to be a bit spicy, add 1 or more tablespoons of chili-garlic paste.

Serves 10

3 pounds boneless, skinless single chicken breasts, cut into 10 pieces

1 cup hoisin sauce

¾ cup orange juice

6 garlic cloves, chopped

3 tablespoons sesame oil

1 pound asparagus

1 pound snow peas, cleaned

½ pound shiitake mushrooms, destemmed and sliced

½ cup rice wine vinegar

1 red bell pepper, julienned

1 8-ounce can sliced water chestnuts, drained

½ cup chopped cilantro

Salt and pepper to taste

Preheat the oven to 425°F.

Combine the chicken breasts with ¼ cup of the hoisin sauce, ¼ cup of the orange juice, and half of the garlic. Coat a baking tray with the oil and place the chicken and their marinade on it. Roast 13 to 15 minutes until done; cool.

Cut off the woody part of the asparagus and cut the remaining portion into 2- to 3-inch pieces. Cook the asparagus in boiling salted water until tender; cool immediately by placing in a colander under cold running water. Repeat the cooking procedure with the snow peas and mushrooms. Drain well.

Mix together the remaining hoisin, orange juice, garlic, and rice wine vinegar. Julienne the chicken and combine with the hoisin mixture, the blanched vegetables, red pepper, water chestnuts, and cilantro. Season with salt and pepper to taste.

Baked Salmon with Yellow Tomato Salsa

This fish preparation is simple yet elegant. The tangy sweetness of the salsa really complements the flavor of the fish. If yellow tomatoes are not available, use vine-ripened or cherry tomatoes instead. In summertime, especially for an outdoor reception, I like to grill the fish instead of baking it.

Serves 10

SALSA

3 cups ripe yellow tomatoes, cut into a medium dice

¼ cup thinly sliced red onions

¼ cup small-diced red pepper

2 tablespoons extra-virgin olive oil

1 tablespoon balsamic vinegar

1 tablespoon chopped fresh oregano

Salt and pepper to taste

SALMON

2 tablespoons extra-virgin olive oil

10 salmon fillets, pin bones removed

¼ cup lemon juice

Salt and pepper to taste

Make the salsa: Combine the tomatoes, onions, red pepper, oil, vinegar, and oregano. Season with salt and pepper to taste and reserve.

Make the salmon: Preheat the oven to 400°F. Grease a cookie sheet with the olive oil and arrange the salmon fillets in rows, being careful that they do not touch. Brush the lemon juice onto the fillets and sprinkle each with salt and pepper. Bake in the oven for 9 to 11 minutes.

Dollop each cooked salmon fillet with 2 heaping tablespoon of the salsa and serve.

Marinated Lamb Chops

Marinated lamb chops that are cooked rare to medium are so juicy that they really don't need a sauce. But bear in mind that die-hard lamb aficionados love mint jelly, so it wouldn't hurt to either have a bowl of it on the buffet or a small dish at each table. Ask your butcher to make sure the chops have no more than a 1-inch tail.

Serves 10

20 1½- to 2-inch-thick lamb T-bone chops
½ cup extra-virgin olive oil
2 teaspoons chopped garlic
2 tablespoons chopped fresh rosemary
Salt and pepper to taste

Marinate the lamb chops by combining the lamb, oil, garlic, and rosemary together several hours or a day before serving; refrigerate.

Season the chops with salt and pepper right before cooking.

Broil the chops under High heat or cook them on a medium-hot grill. Cook to desired doneness, approximately 4 to 6 minutes on each side.

Grilled Chicken Breasts in Corn–Wild Mushroom Ragout

This is one of my favorite recipes for an outdoor summer reception, but it can be made year-round. The ragout can be made several days in advance and reheated just before serving. If you don't have a grill, bake the cider-marinated chicken on an oiled roasting pan at 425°F for 12 to 15 minutes.

Serves 10

RAGOUT

6 tablespoons (¾ stick) unsalted butter

½ cup diced onions

½ pound brown mushrooms, diced

8 ears of corn, cleaned and kernels cut off the cob

2½ cups chicken stock

1½ cups heavy cream

¼ cup chopped fresh tarragon

Salt and pepper to taste

CHICKEN

3 pounds skinless, boneless chicken breasts, cut into 10 pieces

⅓ cup apple cider vinegar

Oil for the grill

To make the ragout, place the butter into a 10-inch sauté pan and melt over medium heat. Add the onions and cook for 2 minutes. Add the mushrooms and cook 4 to 5 minutes more, or until tender but not browned.

Add the corn and the stock. Cook for 15 minutes, or until most of the liquid has evaporated. Stir in the heavy cream and continue cooking until the ragout thickens, approximately 15 minutes. Season with tarragon, salt, and pepper. Set aside. If making in advance, let cool, refrigerate, then reheat prior to serving.

Marinate the chicken breasts by tossing them in a bowl with the apple cider vinegar. Let sit for 5 minutes; do not over-marinate. Shake off any excess vinegar and season with salt and pepper. Lightly oil the grill grates and heat the grill to medium high. Cook the chicken, being careful to retain nice grill markings; turn the breasts over after 4 to 6 minutes on the first side and continue cooking another 4 to 6 minutes, or until no pink juices flow when the breast is cut with a knife.

Spoon warm ragout over the bottom of the platter or chafing dish. Arrange the chicken on top, down the center of the serving dish.

STORE-BOUGHT MAIN DISH SUGGESTIONS

Even if you purchase your entrées premade, you will still save significantly over having the meal catered. The following items are crowd-pleasers and are perfect for a full meal buffet:

Honey Baked Ham

Roast Turkey

Roast Prime Rib or Roast Beef

Smoked Beef Brisket

Leg of Lamb

Glazed Pork Loin

Barbecued Ribs

Lasagna or Baked Pasta

Lemon-Rosemary Chicken

Chicken Parmesan

Poached or Grilled Salmon (served hot or cold)

CHILI LIME-MARINATED FLANK STEAK

Serves 6

1½ pounds flank steak

2 limes, juiced

1½ teaspoons smoked paprika

Salt and freshly ground pepper to taste

Place the flank steak in a shallow, nonreactive 9 x 11-inch baking pan; pour the lime juice over the meat. Season both sides with smoked paprika, salt, and pepper. Let stand at room temperature for 10 minutes or refrigerate 2 to 4 hours.

Preheat the grill or broiler.

Grill or broil 2 to 3 inches from medium-high direct heat, until nicely brown, about 8 minutes. Turn the steak; broil until the desired doneness, about 8 minutes. Cut the beef across the grain at a slight angle into thin slices.

SIDES

○————○

No matter if it's breakfast, lunch, or dinner, it is always a good idea to design the side dishes to be filling enough to make their own meal if a particular guest doesn't care for the entrée. I usually suggest a choice of one or two starches (pasta, potatoes, or rice), and one or two vegetable dishes or a medley of mixed vegetables. The Roasted Vegetable Platter (page 211) also works well as a side dish.

To serve a warm seasonal medley, blanch two or three varieties of prepped vegetables separately, drain, cool, and reserve. Prior to serving, reheat the vegetables by sautéing them in butter or olive oil and fresh chopped herbs; season with salt and pepper. Consider these vegetables: zucchini and yellow squash (cut into half-moons or julienned), baby carrots, quartered mushrooms, pearl onions, broccoli or cauliflower florets, and sweet pepper julienne.

YUKON GOLD MASHED POTATOES

Whenever I serve these mashed potatoes, I always get compliments. I use the creamy Yukon Gold new potatoes, and I do not peel them. I usually prepare the dish a day in advance, up to the point they are covered with tin foil. The next day, I bake the potatoes in a 375°F oven for 40 to 50 minutes, until they are warmed through.

Serves 8 to 10

3 pounds medium Yukon Gold potatoes

1½ teaspoons salt

½ cup (1 stick) unsalted butter at room temperature

8 ounces cream cheese at room temperature

1 tablespoon minced garlic

1½ cups milk

¼ teaspoon black pepper

Wash the potatoes, lightly scrubbing off any dirt spots and cut off any visible "eyes." Place the potatoes in a 1-gallon pot, covering them with cold water and ¼ teaspoon of salt; bring to a boil and reduce to a simmer. Continue cooking until the potatoes are tender, approximately 25 to 30 minutes. Drain.

Preheat the oven to 375°F.

While the potatoes are still warm, add 5 tablespoons of the butter and the cream cheese, and whip until most of the lumps are broken up. Add the garlic, milk, remaining salt, and pepper, and whip until the potatoes are creamy. Using a spatula, evenly spread the potatoes in a greased 3-quart casserole dish or a chafing dish insert. Cut the remaining 3 tablespoons of butter into small cubes and dot the potatoes. Cover the dish with tin foil.

Bake for 30 to 40 minutes, removing the foil halfway through baking. If additional color is needed on the top, place the potatoes under the broiler for a few minutes before serving.

STORE-BOUGHT
SIDES SUGGESTIONS

Whether you want to purchase prepackaged convenience foods (like a boxed blend of wild and white rice, refrigerated bread doughs, or frozen lasagna) and bake them yourself, or ask your local grocery store, gourmet shop, restaurant, or bakery to prepare them for you, there are a lot of options to choose from. Or buy a basic food, such as wild rice, and spruce it up by adding fresh herbs, dried cherries, and chopped dried apricots. The steam-in-the-bag vegetables can also be prepped ahead of time and held warm or reheated right before meal time. Here are several suggestions to start with:

Bread, Rolls, Corn Bread,
    Focaccia, Croissants
Green Beans with Pecans or
    Almonds
Vegetable Medley
Roasted Potatoes
Potato Gratin
Twice-Baked Potatoes
Mashed Potatoes
Fingerling Potato Medley
Sweet Potatoes
Rice Pilaf or Rice Medley with
    Lentils
Wild Rice

Wehani or Brown Rice
Couscous
Polenta or Cheddar Grits
Quinoa
Risotto
Tortellini, Ravioli, Lasagna, or
    Fettuccine
Stuffing
Roasted Cauliflower or Broccoli
Brussels Sprouts with Bacon
Stuffed Tomatoes with Spinach
    and Cheese
Zucchini, Yellow Squash, and
    Carrot "Noodles"

Lemon-Zested Orzo Pilaf

Orzo is small rice-shaped pasta that is available at most large grocery stores. The pasta can be cooked in advance and refrigerated. Before serving, mix together the ingredients, place in a 9 x 13-inch casserole dish, and bake for 20 to 30 minutes.

Serves 10

1 pound orzo pasta
1 tablespoon extra-virgin olive oil
¾ cup chicken stock
3 tablespoons prepared pesto
Zest of 2 lemons, chopped
Salt and pepper to taste

Preheat the oven to 400°F.

Cook the pasta in boiling salted water, following the instructions on the package, approximately 8 to 10 minutes. Drain into a colander and rinse with cold water. Let drain completely.

Grease the bottom of a casserole dish with the olive oil. Combine the orzo and all of the remaining ingredients in a bowl and transfer them to the greased dish. Cover with foil and bake until thoroughly heated, about 20 to 30 minutes. Stir and serve.

Asparagus with Buttered Bread Crumbs

This dish is an updated version of the asparagus I was served as a child. Asparagus is a popular catering vegetable because it tastes great and is also visually appealing.

Serves 10

¾ teaspoon salt
3 pounds asparagus

4 tablespoons (½ stick) unsalted butter

½ teaspoon finely minced garlic

½ lemon, juiced

½ cup bread crumbs

Lemon slices for garnish (optional)

Bring 3 quarts of water to a boil and add ½ teaspoon of salt to the water. Trim off the woody ends of the asparagus, usually 2½ to 3 inches. Cook the asparagus in the boiling water until al dente (cooked through with a slight bite to the tooth), approximately 6 to 9 minutes depending on the thickness of the asparagus. Drain the asparagus into a colander, running cold water over it until completely cooled. Dry and set aside.

Preheat the oven to 375°F.

Melt the butter in a sauté pan. Add the garlic and cook for 2 minutes. Add the lemon juice, bread crumbs, and remaining ¼ teaspoon of salt. Place the asparagus in a greased ovenproof serving dish, making sure all of the tips face in the same direction. Spoon the bread-crumb mixture over the stem ends of the asparagus and bake in the oven until warmed through, 15 to 20 minutes.

Maple-Glazed Carrots

These carrots are a winner year-round. If you love maple flavor and want it to be a little stronger, add an extra tablespoon to the finished carrot glaze.

Serves 10

2 tablespoons (¼ stick) unsalted butter

1 pound peeled baby carrots

½ cup low-sodium chicken broth

2 tablespoons maple syrup

Salt and pepper to taste

2 tablespoons fresh chopped parsley or dill (optional)

Melt the butter in a saucepan; add the carrots and sauté over medium heat for 2 minutes. Add the broth and syrup and bring to a boil. Cover and reduce heat to low. Cook for 10 minutes or until carrots are tender.

Remove the carrots with a slotted spoon and reduce the remaining liquid to a glaze, approximately 12 to 15 minutes. Pour over the carrots and season to taste. Garnish with 2 tablespoons fresh chopped parsley or dill, if desired.

EDIBLE IDEAS: A WEDDING WITH NO CAKE

One of the biggest trends in weddings today is a buffet of alternative desserts with no wedding cake in sight. Donut displays, lots of old-fashioned candy, large and small pies, tarts, sweet comfort foods, bite-sized desserts in shot glasses—you name it, anything goes. Check out Pinterest and wedding blogs and see what other brides and caterers are up to. In the meantime, here's how to make a DIY cupcake table that will wow your guests:

- Purchase "naked" cupcakes from a local baker or make them using cake mixes.
- Vary the sizes, making mini and standard-sized cupcakes. You can also make cake pops, mini Bundt cakes, or bake a sheet cake and use cutters to cut out shapes.
- Make several different flavors of cake, for example, dark chocolate, vanilla bean, confetti, angel cake, carrot cake, German chocolate, marble, and red velvet. You could also make brownies in a cupcake size, little cheesecakes, and crisped rice treats. Or make a basic cake flavor, such as vanilla, poke a hole in the middle, and fill it with pudding, liqueur, or candy.
- Decorate with flair. One option is to match the event's color scheme or theme. Or decorate with edibles that look professional, such as crushed rock

candy, sprinkles, colored sugar, candied violets, halved strawberries, metallic sprinkles, edible colored spray paint, edible flowers such as nasturtiums, candied fruit, drizzled sauce (e.g., caramel, melted white chocolate), and fresh mint.

- You can decorate a cake or cupcakes beforehand, or serve plain cupcakes and set up a station where guests can decorate them. Meringue, cookies, and crushed candy (for instance, candy canes or toffee) are a few more ideas that will add flavor, texture, and visual intrigue to your cupcakes or DIY topping station.
- Consider these topping combinations: trail mix; s'mores (mini marshmallows, chopped graham crackers, and chocolate pieces); mini candy of any type, including little Reese's cups, M&Ms (especially if they have the couple's initials on them), SweeTart Hearts with messages on them, cinnamon Red Hots; and glazed fruits.
- To make your display *pop*, vary the heights of the trays, platters, and cake stands; for instance, try different-sized multi-tiered cupcake trees, some plain cupcake stands, flat and multi-tiered platters in different shapes, and/or wrap boxes of varying heights in different-colored tissue papers or napkins and place items on them. Vary the colors, textures, and flavors to make the display stand out.

For more cake alternatives, see pages 166–67, 185, 233–34.

DESSERT: THE WEDDING CAKE

As I mentioned in an earlier chapter, I did not bake my own wedding cake. So when it came time to create a cake for this book, I felt the need to ask the advice of several baking experts and consult the pages of multiple wedding-cake books. One suggestion I was given is that if you want to make your own cake, but don't want to bake from scratch, use a cake mix instead. With today's pudding-moist box mixes, it is likely that no one will even notice. Each mix makes 4 to 6 cups of batter, and you will need five or six boxes to fill the 6-, 10- and 12-inch cake pans twice.

For ambitious bakers who want a traditional genoise cake with butter-cream frosting or a more advanced style of cake, consult *The Cake Bible* by Rose Levy Birnbaum. Complete with decorating tips, *The Cake Bible* features hundreds of cake, filling, and frosting recipes serving anywhere from 6 guests to 250. Other books to browse include *The Wedding Cake Book* by Dede Wilson, *The Buffet Book* by Carole Peck and Carolyn Hart Bryant, *Martha Stewart's Weddings*, and *Wilton Weddings*. (See pages 182–84 for more advice on designing your own wedding cake.)

BUTTERMILK POUND CAKE WITH LEMON CURD, MIXED BERRIES, AND CREAM CHEESE FROSTING

Pastry chef Gina DeLeone creates fabulous wedding cakes for lucky couples in southern Oregon. When we worked together in California, I fell in love with her Buttermilk Pound Cake. Gina happily shared the recipe and much advice on how to put together a wedding cake in a home kitchen.

To make this delicious three-tiered cake, you will need an electric mixer with a 5-quart bowl; 6-, 10-, and 12-inch cake pans; 6- and 10-inch cardboard rounds; a cake-decorating turntable; a cake-decorating spatula; parchment paper; plastic drinking straws; toothpicks; a 6-inch cake tier separator set; and a decorative cake stand or cake base. This equipment is available at your local craft or cooking store. (Mail order or online shoppers can purchase their wares from Wilton Industries by calling 800-794-5866 or going to Wilton.com.)

BUTTERMILK POUND CAKE

Each tier of this assembled cake requires two layers, so purchase enough ingredients to make the recipe twice.

This versatile cake is also a delicious base for a fresh berry trifle. Just cut the baked cake into bite-sized pieces, then layer them with mixed berries and whipped cream. I also have used it for a scrumptious bread pudding.

Serves 60

PER BATCH

1½ cups (3 sticks) unsalted butter, room temperature

3 cups sugar

6 eggs, separated

1 tablespoon vanilla extract

3¾ cups all-purpose flour

1½ teaspoons baking powder

¾ teaspoon baking soda

½ teaspoon salt

2¼ cups buttermilk

½ cup 2% milk

Preheat the oven to 325°F. Cut two circles of parchment paper to fit the bottom of each cake pan. Line each pan with one of the circles (be sure it lies flat), then grease and flour the sides of the pans.

Cream the butter and sugar together until light; add the egg yolks and vanilla, mixing until well incorporated. In a separate bowl, sift together the flour, baking powder, baking soda, and salt.

Mix the buttermilk and milk together. Add half of the milk mixture into the butter mixture and mix on low speed until barely incorporated; add half of the dry ingredients. Alternate wet and dry ingredients again, being careful not to overmix.

Whip the egg whites until they form stiff peaks. Gently fold the whites into the cake batter and distribute the batter in the prepared pans. The pans should be about half full. Bake the cakes 35 to 50 minutes, until the center of the cake springs back when touched or a toothpick inserted comes out clean.

Cool on wire racks and wrap in plastic until ready to use (up to 2 days) or freeze for up to 3 weeks. Wash and prepare pans and repeat the entire recipe to make the second layer for each tier.

LEMON CURD FILLING

Lemon curd and mixed berries add flavor, color, and texture in between the layers of this multi-tiered confection.

Makes 6 cups

2½ cups sugar
7 eggs
9 lemons, juiced
1 cup (2 sticks) unsalted butter, room temperature

Using an electric mixer, whisk the sugar and eggs together until light and fluffy, about 5 minutes; add lemon juice and whisk until well blended.

Pour the lemon mixture into the top of a double boiler. Using a wire whisk, stir constantly over simmering water until very thick, 15 to 20 minutes.

Remove from the heat and stir in the butter. Let the curd cool to room temperature and refrigerate until needed, up to 4 days.

CREAM CHEESE FROSTING

This cream cheese frosting is best made 30 minutes before frosting the cake. Two batches are needed to frost all of the layers. If you prefer to omit the lemon curd, you could make a third batch to use as an alternate filling. After making each batch, refrigerate it for 15 to 20 minutes before using.

ONE BATCH

12 ounces cream cheese, softened

7 cups sifted confectioners' sugar

1 tablespoon vanilla extract

1 tablespoon heavy whipping cream

6 cups berries—raspberries, blueberries, and blackberries, washed

2 cups edible flowers or rose petals

Using an electric mixer and wire beaters, whisk together the cream cheese and confectioners' sugar until all of the lumps are gone and the mixture is creamed, about 5 minutes. Add in the vanilla and whipping cream until well blended.

When assembling, work quickly and regulate the temperature of the room you are in to around 70°F. Keep all layers, curd, and frosting that you are not using refrigerated until needed. In hot weather, be sure to leave the finished cake in the refrigerator until right before cake-cutting time.

Start with the cake base: Place a 12-inch cake layer on the cake foundation and place the foundation on the turntable. Spread with a thin layer of the lemon curd (about 1 cup) and arrange berries to cover the top of the cake. Spread 1½ to 2 cups of filling on top of the berries, leaving about 1 inch uncovered near the sides of the cake.

Place the second 12-inch cake layer on top, and frost the layers and sides with a thin coating of Cream Cheese Frosting using an offset icing spatula. Refrigerate the base layer. Repeat the filling and frosting procedure on both the 6- and 10-inch cake tiers, placing a cardboard cake circle under each tier before beginning. Refrigerate before applying a second layer of frosting.

Using more frosting this time, frost each tier again. Fluff and swirl the frosting to create a cloudlike effect. If you prefer more of a shine, continuously dip your spatula in hot water while frosting the cake. Refrigerate each tier while frosting the others.

Center the 10-inch cake pan on top of the 12-inch base and outline it with a toothpick. Cut four plastic straws to the height of the cake tier and insert them inside the traced circle. The straws will serve as added support for each layer. Place the frosted 10-inch cake tier onto the traced circle and straw supporters.

Center and trace the bottom of the separator set for the 6-inch tier. Cut straws as described above or utilize the cake pegs that come in the set; insert them inside the traced circle. Place the bottom of the separators onto the circle. Put columns and the top of the separators in place. Put a dollop of frosting on the top separator to help the 6-inch cake round stick. Place the final cake round on top.

Decorate the top of the cake and in between the layers with fresh flowers similar to those in your wedding bouquet. Sprinkle roses or other edible flower petals in the creases between the 10- and 12-inch layers to hide any imperfections. Refrigerate until showtime!

STORE-BOUGHT DESSERT SUGGESTIONS

n addition to (or instead of) purchasing or making a cake, consider offering a selection of individual tartlets, bakery-made butter cookies, florentines, or Peruvian wedding cookies.

Here are more suggestions:

Bread Pudding
Donuts and/or Mini Donuts
Cake Pops (you can buy a kit to make them or use a simple recipe)
Fresh Fruit or Berries

Fruit or Cream Pies

Fruit Crisps or Cobblers

Brownies and Bars

Chocolate Fondue

Ice Cream or Ice Cream Cake

Cheesecake

Lemon Squares

Petits Fours

Layered Fruit or Chocolate Trifle

Tiramisu

Individual Parfaits

Chocolate Truffles

After-Dinner Mints

BEVERAGES

MINTED RASPBERRY LEMONADE

An electric juicer will come in handy for this tasty treat. Squeeze the lemons several days in advance and finish the lemonade the day before serving. To save time, use store-bought lemonade instead of squeezing your own; just add the pureed raspberries and chopped mint.

Makes 1 gallon

3 cups freshly squeezed lemon juice (12 to 15 lemons)

2 teaspoons finely chopped fresh mint

1 cup fresh raspberries, mashed with a fork

1½ cups sugar

12 cups water

Whole fresh raspberries, sliced lemons, and mint leaves, for garnish (optional)

Stir together the lemon juice, mint, raspberries, sugar, and water until the sugar dissolves. Pour into pitchers and garnish with fresh whole raspberries, sliced lemons, and mint leaves, if desired. Serve well chilled or over ice.

ITALIAN SODAS AND SODA SPRITZERS

Signature alcoholic cocktails are all the rage. But what about nonalcoholic options, sometimes referred to as "mocktails"? Consider setting up a self-serve Italian soda bar for your flavor lovers and kids of all ages. Include a variety of different syrups, plus club soda, to make spritzers. Top off the fun with playful garnishes, such as mini umbrellas, maraschino cherries, and lime or pineapple wedges; even sour gummy worms or Skittles would work.

Makes 1 10-ounce glass

1 cup crushed or 1½ cups cubed ice

2 tablespoons (1 ounce) flavored Italian soda syrup, such as blue raspberry, strawberry, watermelon, or blackberry

8 ounces of club soda (for an Italian soda) or Sprite or 7-Up (for a spritzer)

Place ice in the glass, pour the Italian soda syrup over it, top it with club soda, 7-Up, or Sprite.

JUICY-FRUITY SANGRIA

Wine, fresh fruit, and carbonated soda are key ingredients in this cravable "punch." For added zip, try it with the rum.

Makes 1 pitcher

1 bottle red wine

¼ cup lime juice

1 cup fresh orange juice

1 cup pineapple juice

2 cups lemon-lime soda

¾ cup rum (optional)

1 cup diced pineapple

1 lemon, thinly sliced

1 lime, thinly sliced

1 orange, washed, sliced into thin rounds

Fresh mint leaves, for garnish (optional)

Mix the wine, juices, soda, rum (if desired), and diced pineapple together in a large pitcher with ice. Let the flavors marry for 2 to 4 hours. Stir in the sliced fruit, top with mint leaves, and serve.

STORE-BOUGHT BEVERAGE SUGGESTIONS

When purchasing ready-made beverages for your reception, decide if you want to put out coolers with individual drinks or have a beverage bar with pitchers of drinks—or both. (See pages 191–94 for advice on setting up a bar and page 235 for Italian Sodas and Soda Spritzers.) The following nonalcoholic drinks are available at your grocery store:

Homemade or Store-Bought Iced Tea or Latte Drinks

Arnold Palmers (½ iced tea, ½ lemonade)

Fruit Punch, Lemonade, Sunny D

Orange, Apple, and Grape Juices

Juice Blends

Smoothies

Soft Drinks: Coke, 7-Up, Root Beer, Orange Soda

A Pony Keg of Root Beer or Green River (lime soda)

Root Beer Floats

Regular or Chocolate Milk

Kool-Aid

Iced Coffee

MENU IDEAS

○————————○

The following menu suggestions were designed to help you plan a wedding reception for breakfast, lunch, dinner, hors d'oeuvres, or dessert. The menus consist of recipes from this chapter, interspersed with store-bought suggestions (marked with an asterisk) and recipes from your favorite cook (marked with a ~).

EASY HORS D'OEUVRE BUFFET

This hors d'oeuvre buffet is perfect following an early afternoon wedding. It could all be placed on one buffet table or broken up between two tables. If you'd like a bit more variety, add store-bought canapés, cocktail prawns, and/or bowls of chips and salsa to this menu.

Prosciutto and Melon (page 200)
Endive with Blue Cheese and Pecans (page 203)
Cheese and Fruit Platter (page 205) with Crackers* and Sliced Baguette*
Vegetable Crudités with Sun-Dried Tomato Dip (page 206)
Miniature Quiches*

HEARTY APPETIZER MENU

This appetizer menu could be partially passed, with buffet stations around the room. It is considered a little heavier because it has more menu items, plus a fair amount of bread, crackers, cheese, and dessert to help guests fill up.

Mini Caprese Skewers (page 204)
Warm Artichoke Dip* with Focaccia*
Asian-Flavored Shiitake Mushroom Skewers (page 207)
Soft Pretzel Rolls* with Honey Ham* and Whole Grain Mustard*
Cheese and Fruit Platter (page 205)
with Sliced Salami*, Crackers*, and Baguette*
Roasted Vegetable Platter (page 211) with Balsamic Glaze (page 204)
Tricolored Tortellini* with Sun-Dried Tomato Dip (page 206)
Cookies, Mini Tartlets, Fresh Strawberries, and Dried Apricots*
Mini Assorted Cake Pops* or a Cupcake Display (pages 227–28)

CONTINENTAL BREAKFAST BUFFET

This is a relatively low-stress menu. The donut holes, mini quiche, and bagels can be bought the day before from a local bakery or the grocery store. The smoked salmon, miniature quiche, cream cheese, fresh juice, half and half, sugar, and coffee could all be purchased at a wholesale store (e.g., Costco or Sam's Club).

Smoked Salmon*
Chive Cream Cheese*
Miniature Bagels*
Miniature Quiche*
Donut Holes* or Coffee Cake*
Fruit Salad*
Orange and Grapefruit Juices*
Coffee and Tea

TRADITIONAL BREAKFAST

Have a friend or family member prepare your favorite scrambled egg and home-fried potato recipes, and serve them in chafing dishes for an elegant hot breakfast following early morning nuptials.

Scrambled Eggs with Chives*
Home-Style Fried Potatoes*
Ham, Bacon, and/or Sausage*
Miniature Muffins and Croissants*
Sliced Melon and Berries* (or prepare them yourself)
Juice, Coffee, and Tea

AN ELEGANT BRUNCH

After a mid- to late-morning wedding, this breakfast-lunch combination will appeal to your hungry guests.

Smoked Salmon Soufflé Roulade (page 214)
Prosciutto and Melon (page 200)
Spinach Salad with Mandarin Oranges (page 209)
Farmer's Market Tomato Salad (page 208)
Crusty French Bread*
Carrot Cake with Cream Cheese Frosting*~
Minted Raspberry Lemonade (page 234), Iced Tea, and Coffee

AL FRESCO LUNCHEON BUFFET

*This selection of salad and sandwich fixings makes
a great informal luncheon buffet.*

Cheese and Fruit Platter (page 205) with Sliced Baguettes*
Roasted Vegetable Platter (page 211)
Farmer's Market Tomato Salad (page 208)
Mixed Greens with Honey Mustard Vinaigrette (page 210)
Cal-Asian Chicken Salad (page 216)
Assorted Cold Cut Platter Served with Miniature Rolls*
Condiment Tray with Sandwich Spreads, Lettuce,
Onions, Olives, and Hot Peppers*

PREPLATED LUNCHEON

*For a festive sit-down luncheon, have your cook arrange a portion of each
salad along with a triangle of focaccia on each individual plate. Twenty
minutes before the luncheon begins, have the waiters set a plate at each place
setting. Also put a pitcher of iced tea, bottled water, and glasses with ice on
each table. After the guests sit down and eat lunch, the waitstaff will remove
the plate and serve your wedding cake and hot coffee.*

Cal-Asian Chicken Salad (page 216)
Hearts of Romaine with Scallion Cilantro Vinaigrette (page 212)
Asian Sesame Noodles*
Scallion Focaccia*

Try a Latin twist on traditional surf and turf for a delicious buffet that will appeal to many palates. The steak can be presliced and arranged in a chafing dish. For an added touch have an extra waiter or cook carve them to order on a (rented) wooden cutting board. (Be sure the knife is sharp.)

Seven-Layer Dip* with Vegetables and Chips*
Queso* with Crispy Tortilla Chips*
Pork and Cheese Tamales*~
Beef Taquitos*
Tequila Shrimp (page 215)
Chili Lime–Marinated Flank Steak (page 221)
Rice and Beans*~
Warm Tortillas*
Assorted Salsas*~ and Guacamole*~
Mixed Green Salad*
Dinner Rolls*
Signature Cocktail: Juicy, Fruity Sangria (page 235)

SEASONAL DINNER BUFFET MENU SUGGESTIONS

These menus are based on the recipes in this chapter, with a few classic additions that work well for a crowd, like potatoes gratin. Serve each menu with freshly baked bread and rolls purchased from a local bakery.

SPRING

Crudités of Seasonal Vegetables with
Sun-Dried Tomato Dip (page 206)
Pesto-Crusted Brie (page 203) with Crackers* and Baguettes*
Mixed Spring Greens* with Raspberry Vinaigrette*
Marinated Lamb Chops (page 219)
Yukon Gold Mashed Potatoes (page 223)
Asparagus with Buttered Bread Crumbs (page 225)

SUMMER

Endive with Blue Cheese and Pecans (page 203)
Prosciutto and Melon (page 200)
Hearts of Romaine with Scallion Cilantro Vinaigrette (page 212)
Baked Salmon with Yellow Tomato Salsa (page 218)
Wild Rice with Scallions~
Zucchini and Yellow Squash "Noodles"~

AUTUMN

Tequila Shrimp (page 215)

Cheese and Fruit Platter (page 205)

Farmer's Market Tomato Salad (page 208)

Roasted Vegetable Platter (page 211)

Grilled Chicken Breasts in Corn–Wild Mushroom Ragout (page 219)

Bowtie Pasta Tossed with Extra Virgin Olive Oil and Parmesan Shreds~

Ciabatta Rolls*

WINTER

Crudités of Seasonal Vegetables (page 206) with Spinach Dip*

Cheese and Fruit Platter (page 205)

Spinach Salad with Mandarin Oranges (page 209)

Honey Baked Ham*~ with Assorted Mustards*~ and Small Rolls*

Potatoes Gratin*~

DESSERT BUFFET EXTRAORDINAIRE

Saltwater Taffy*

Hard Candy*

Penny Candy*

Licorice Laces*

Assorted Cream Pies*~

Fresh Fruit Cobbler*~

Cookie Platters*~

Cupcake Display (pages 227–28)

A COUNTRY WEDDING WITH KIDS

Ann and Pat's Wedding on April 18
18 guests in Galena, Illinois

PRIORITIES

1. Intimacy
2. Inclusion of their children and new baby
3. Affordability
4. A sense of elegance
5. Personal to them, reflecting who they are

This wedding was a second marriage for both Ann, forty-one, and Pat, twenty-nine. Together, they have four children, whom they wanted to be a part of the celebration: a newborn boy, Matthew; Ann's two girls, Sarah, ten, and Laura, seven; and Pat's daughter, Stephanie, who was six. They decided to get married in a town called Galena, which is a few hours from their home in Chicago. Eleven additional family members joined them for the wedding weekend in the historic town and sprawling countryside.

LOCATION

The wedding took place in a small white chapel with a traditional steepled roof and stained-glass windows. It was situated amid rolling hills and surrounded by trees that were in full bloom. Inside, the charming small space was decorated with dried and silk flowers. An ivy-covered table in the front of the room held an easel with a hand-painted picture of two rings intertwined.

Following the ceremony, the celebration took place in a comfortable five-bedroom country house that Ann's brother rented for the weekend (the kids stayed there with their uncles after the ceremony). It had a Jacuzzi, acres of greenery, a babbling brook, and a lake. Ann and Pat brought their dog, and Ann's brother, Danny, also had his two dogs on the estate for the weekend.

BUDGET

Wedding site (including minister)	$ 250
Reception site	$ 0
Dress, alterations, veil, and shoes	$ 250
Groom's clothing	$ 190
Outfits for the kids	$ 250
Food and beverage	$ 0 (gift from Ann's brother)
Cake	$ 0 (gift from Ann's dad)
Photography/video	$ 275
Flowers	$ 140
License	$ 60
Total	$ 1,415

DETAILS

Pat and Ann originally met a few years earlier when Pat, a professional violin teacher, was giving lessons to Ann's oldest daughter. They maintained a five-year friendship before they started dating. After they became a couple and dated for six months, they decided to get married. They spent their engagement period, also six months, planning the wedding and integrating households.

Their ceremony consisted of a basic wedding-chapel package, including a minister, readings from Corinthians, and a prayer for couples. Ann explained, "There was a strong spiritual element present. We invited God to share in our day, and we definitely felt it." According to Ann, "The best moment of the wedding was walking down the aisle toward Pat, who was holding the baby and surrounded by all three girls."

APPAREL

Ann rented a beaded silk dress (that retailed for more than $1,000) with a V-neck and low back. It had a fitted bodice, puffy sleeves, and an A-line skirt with a slit in the back. Alterations were included in the price of the rental. Ann declined to wear the matching train or a veil, and instead she wore her hair up with a beaded comb holding it in place. She already owned the low-heeled white leather pumps she wore.

Pat had on a black suit from Marshall Field's with a yellow and black tie. Sarah, the oldest girl ("our tomboy"), wore a pale pink silk vest with silk pants, and the younger girls wore lacy pink dresses. The baby had on a white buttoned-down shirt with a black bow tie, black knickers, and suspenders.

MUSIC
Ann walked down the aisle to Celine Dion's rendition of "My Heart Will Go On." They brought a CD player with them, and an attendant in the chapel played the aisle songs for them as well as the recessional music by Yo-Yo Ma. During the reception, they played more of their favorites, including the music of Sting and Patsy Cline, along with the soundtrack from *Leaving Las Vegas*.

FLOWERS
Ann carried a spring bouquet with tiger lilies, blue wildflowers, white tulips, and yellow snapdragons. Pat and Ann's fathers wore white rose boutonnieres, and all of the girls carried small bunches of yellow tulips with baby's breath.

PHOTOS
The chapel photographer took formal shots on-site. Photo proofs and video of the ceremony were part of their package. The whole family took candid pictures back at the house.

FOOD AND BEVERAGE
When the wedding party arrived back at the house, everyone changed into jeans and casual clothes. Ann's brother, Danny, and his partner, Jim, both avid cooks who love to entertain, prepared most of the food, but everyone who came helped in some way. Wedding guests feasted on an array of appetizers:

grilled Italian sausages, spicy chicken wings, assorted cheese and crackers, pistachios, cashews, and roasted eggplant caviar on herbed pita chips.

The dining room table was set buffet-style for the main meal. For a table centerpiece, Jim cut apple and cherry blossoms from trees in the yard and mixed them with store-bought white mums and roses. The menu included grilled beef tenderloin with horseradish cream sauce and miniature rolls, herb-crusted chicken breast strips, grilled vegetables, marinated broccoli salad with almonds, and mixed baby greens. Lemonade, iced tea, sodas, bottled water, and gourmet coffee were served as beverages. Jim estimated the cost of the wedding food, beverages, and disposable paper products to be approximately $575. Ann's dad brought the wedding cake, a traditional three-tiered white genoise cake with vanilla custard filling and buttercream icing (cost $125).

Chapter Eleven

SO YOU WANT TO BE
IN PICTURES

○————————○

Weddings tend to go by so quickly, and each moment is so precious that having a photographer chronicle the event with a still or video camera is the only way to really capture the moment for posterity. But there is a wide range of choices (and prices) when you sit down to make some decisions. This chapter will discuss the advantages of using a professional photographer and the advantages of using an amateur photographer, buying a package or à la carte photos, how to find a great cut-rate photographer, and more.

WEDDING PHOTOGRAPHY

Let's start out by envisioning what most couples want from their wedding photographs: in general, the goal is to have the photographer tell a story that begins when the bride and groom are getting dressed; chronicles the ceremony, reception, family, and guests in attendance; and ends with the cutting of the cake or the couple leaving for their honeymoon. The photographs (and video) should capture the feelings, moments, and expressions of the day.

Next, it's time to revisit the priority list from pages 26–28 to look at how important photographs are to you as a couple. It would be a good idea to take an inventory of what you have spent money on so far, and what you know you are still going to spend money on. What I am getting at here is that there is a really wide range of pricing for photos and video; the bill for photos alone could run into the thousands. Or you could choose the least expensive option and stick with amateur photography. By taking stock of where you are financially in this project and where you still need to go (like paying for a band, flowers, decorations), you can determine what level of photographic coverage you can afford.

In interviewing couples for this book, I found that using a professional photographer was very important to some, while to others having family members or friends shoot the photographs and videos worked out really well. Either way, most couples aspire for their photographs to be sharable via social media, printable in a variety of sizes, and stored on an SD card or thumb drive. Budget-conscious brides and grooms can negotiate to own the copyright so they can reproduce the photos themselves without having to buy everything through the photographer.

The following are the pros and cons of hiring an amateur. These insights are based on interviews with dozens of newlyweds and several professional photographers.

PROS AND CONS OF USING AN AMATEUR

PROS

- Although it obviously saves money, the cost can vary from nothing (if the photos are a wedding gift) to a few hundred dollars for possible equipment rental, printing, and perhaps an hourly fee.
- You will get to keep the negatives, and you won't be overcharged for reprints.

- The person you choose will hopefully have a fresh take on weddings and an enthusiasm that a seasoned photographer may not have on his or her fourth wedding of the week.
- If you use a friend or family member as your photographer, many of the guests will already know him or her, and he or she will seem like less of an intrusion.

CONS

- There is a higher chance that the photographs may not turn out—and the moment will be lost forever. Also, cameras can break or malfunction, and the battery can discharge. Nonprofessionals may not have a backup on hand.
- It can be hard to find someone you trust, who is responsible and committed to doing an excellent job. There is a risk that he or she may not understand how a wedding functions, which shots to take, or he or she could miss key memories that you may wish to have documented.
- Lack of technical equipment and expertise could be a problem. For example, an amateur is less accustomed to lighting and shadows, and he or she may not have access to or the know-how to deploy multiple lenses.
- He or she may not know the ins and outs of using a manual flash, managing indoor lighting in a church setting, compensating for bad weather, or balancing flash output with a sunset.

If you decide to go the amateur route (as many brides I interviewed did), first determine if there are any artistic family members or friends that you would like to ask to be in charge of the photos. If no one comes to mind and you need to track down your own cut-rate photographer, check out local colleges, especially a school of visual arts, photography, or film school. Post a note on their employment board, if possible. Oftentimes, aspiring photographers, or art students in general, will shoot weddings to help build their portfolio.

When you meet with potential candidates, ask how many weddings they have been to, and whether they have ever shot a wedding before. Look at photographs that they have taken and talk to them about how they would approach shooting your wedding. Find out what their fees are, what kind of camera they have, how long they will stay at your wedding (arrival and departure times), how many pictures they will take, the number of prints they will include, as well as the sizes and the quality of the printing and paper; plus will a wedding album be part of the package? Also explore any extras that are important to you, for instance uploading to your website and retouching a certain percentage of shots. Be sure to get any agreed-upon points in writing. It's especially important that the contract states you own the copyright, but there are still some photographers who insist on keeping the copyright. My suggestion for couples on a budget is to keep looking until you find someone who will include all rights.

When we got married, I asked an acquaintance who was a mortgage broker by day and an artist on the weekends to take our pictures. Unbeknownst to me, she had apprenticed with a well-known wedding photographer while she was in graphic arts school. The day of the wedding, she moved in and out of the crowd and got along with everyone really well. Since we married before the digital technology explosion, we used film, both color as well as black and white. Shots ranged from portraits to candids, and they covered all of the main events up to the throwing of the bouquet. The charge—including a wonderful wedding album with 110 pictures, 4 x 6-inch prints, and the negatives—was $325. Above all, we really loved the pictures!

These days, bargain photo packages are closer to $500 and up, but for that amount you should get more for your money. The fee covers the photographer's time, expertise, equipment, and creative abilities. There are websites that specialize in deals starting at $595, such as Weddingbug.com. Keep in mind that well-known photographers may charge ten or twenty times that. Packages of $5,000 to $10,000—even upward of $20,000—are not unheard of with large upscale weddings.

David Slaughter, an Ohio-based wedding and portrait photographer, offers the following suggestions for aspiring amateur photographers:

- Preplan by going to the wedding site a week or two in advance at the same time of day that the wedding will take place. Doing so will give you a good sense of the lighting. Further, you can decide on ideal locations to take traditional formal shots of the wedding party, extended families, newlyweds, and friends. Plus you can determine where to place a tripod during the nuptials and test angles from different vantage points (which is much easier to accomplish before all the guests are on-site).

- The day of the wedding: arrive two to three hours before hand. Take photos of the bride's dress, veil, shoes, and jewelry. Consider shooting the reception space before and during setup. A wide-angle establishing shot of the location is another basic that can be taken before the festivities start. Time permitting, pictures of the bridal party and grooms-men, plus key family members with the bride and separately with the groom, can also be taken beforehand.

- Lighting is the key to professional-looking photographs and is especially difficult indoors in a church or outdoors in direct sunlight. If possible, use a fill flash bracketed above the camera. This will eliminate red-eye and dark circles under the eyes.

- Consider renting a professional camera setup for the day. For $200 and up you can rent a professional Nikon or Canon camera with a high flash. Be sure to try the camera out on another occasion first. Both Borrowlenses.com and Lensrental.com have customizable equipment-rental packages for photography and video. The quoted price includes shipping, handling, insurance, professional cameras, flash, lenses, brackets, cords, and SD cards.

- If you plan to save money by going to a discount store for printing, make sure it is using archival quality paper rated 15 years or higher. It would be pennywise and pound foolish to cut costs in this area, only to discover many years in the future that your photos did not hold up.
- Ascertain that the printer for the photos has at least six cartridges so its clarity and a better range of color variation will add contrast and quality. The photography-processing labs that professionals have used for decades are now open to amateur photographers also. One such lab is Mpix.com, which features high-quality printing in twenty-nine different sizes starting at 19 cents a print.
- Mpix.com also offers framing, retouching, and printing of coffee-table books or soft-covered assembled photo albums. Drag-and-drop design will help you make one-of-a-kind keepsakes, gifts, and thank-you cards. Choices of luxurious paper, including metallic, textured, or canvas, with or without framing, are all options.

SNAPSHOTS AND MEMORIES

If you are having a rehearsal dinner party, ask an attendee or family member to chronicle the event for you with a camera. Likewise, if your wedding is taking place over the course of a weekend, and several events are planned, be sure that at least one person agrees to bring a camera and take pictures for you at each function.

Photos taken by guests using their phones are a terrific adjunct and may catch very special moments a single photographer might not be privy to.

Bear in mind that while the pixel count on a handheld phone may be high, the photos will still not compare to using a freestanding camera with the same number of pixels. That is because the sensor that takes the photos on a phone or tablet is much smaller, or not as wide as is needed, so the brightness does not come through.

Another recent trend is photo-booth rental. Several friends or family members can crowd in together, sometimes wearing props or silly costumes. A camera setup takes three or four quick shots that later print out in an old school style photo strip. If you set it up yourselves with a laptop and camera, and possibly a printer, it may be worth it. Otherwise, for the price of $300 and up, I suggest you save your money. If money is no object, having a photo-booth setup can be a fun add-on. For frugalista weddings—where every dollar needs to stretch—getting a stack of photos of your (sometimes drunk) friends and family may not be a memory worth shelling out part of your budget for.

HIRING A PROFESSIONAL PHOTOGRAPHER

If using an amateur just seems too risky to you, or having professional pictures taken is high on your priority list, then finding the right photographer is the next step for you to take. A good photographer will be booked far in advance, so it's best to start your search six to eight months before the wedding. Get some referrals from friends, other vendors you might be using (caterer, florist, church staff, etc.), or your site coordinator; check online sources such as Yelp.com for ratings or your local chamber of commerce's site; and visit wedding shows.

ADD A TOUCH OF SENTIMENT

I f you are designing your own wedding album, personalize it by inserting a copy of your wedding invitation, wedding program, some dried flowers from your bouquet, and your menu.

If you can find fabric that matches your dress, for example matching silk or lace, create a custom wedding album cover by sewing or gluing the fabric on. Decorate with ribbon from your bouquet, headpiece, or presents you received.

When considering what photographer to use, meet with more than one to see what style you like and always look at their wedding portfolio. When you view the albums, keep in mind that you are seeing their best work ever, and probably a very expensive and comprehensive shoot (they are setting you up for the up-sell). Ask yourself these questions:

- Do the pictures in the album build on each other to tell a story?
- Is there a sense of uniqueness about each wedding photo-graphed? Do the photos have good color, lighting, and clarity? Or are they cookie-cutter, all looking similar?
- Did he or she capture the emotions and feelings of everyone present?
- Are the pictures interesting and varied in approach—a mix of black and whites, candids, and portraits?

When you find a photographer whose work you like, begin asking more detailed questions:

- Is the photographer available on the date of your wedding?
- What will the total charges be?

- Will he or she be working alone or bringing an assistant? (An assistant helps handle the lighting and carries the extra cameras and film.)
- How will they dress? (This is important at a formal wedding.)
- Are packaged plans available? What is included?

PACKAGED PLANS VERSUS À LA CARTE PHOTOGRAPHY

Comparing the pricing of various wedding photographers can be confusing. Every photographer seems to have his or her own pricing system, as well as convincing reasons why it is superior to the others. It is important to know what you want and not get talked into an extravagant package that you can't afford. Compare the plan prices with buying individual photographs. Then compare to local competition. Be sure to check that their reprint prices are competitive.

Make sure you feel comfortable with the photographer before you book him or her. Ask yourself: Would I want to have this person at my wedding, interacting with my guests? If the answer is no, find someone else. Before you put down a deposit, compare prices with other photographers in your area.

It is important to understand exactly what you are getting for your money and to have it in writing. The contract should spell out the following:

- Who the photographer will be and his or her arrival and departure times
- How many shots will be taken with what type of cameras and lenses
- What you are getting in your package, for example, an album with eighty 4 x 6-inch proofs and three 8 x 10s, HD CD, copyrights for all photos
- The date the proofs will be ready, how long a

photograph order will take to process, what reprint charges are, and any other charges you may incur (overtime, travel expenses)
- Whether or not it is your responsibility to feed the photographer (and possibly an assistant) at the wedding

More Money-Saving Tips

- Photographers who work out of their homes can cost a lot less than photographers who have to maintain the overhead of a studio. Also consider the money-saving possibility of using a photographer who has a regular day job (e.g., a staff photographer for a newspaper or a graphic artist) and does weddings on the side.
- Avoid paying for a photographer's assistant. In some cases, the photographer will bring a spouse or a student as an assistant without charging you extra.
- One way to cut costs is to book the professional for the ceremony only, and then ask friends to chronicle the reception for you. The less time the pro has to be on-site, the more money you save.
- Consider asking for 4 x 6-inch photographs to be used in your proof album instead of the customary 3 x 5 inches. They only cost a little bit more, but photographers won't automatically give them to you (because they think if you have 4 x 6-inch prints, you will be less likely to order 5 x 7-inch reprints).

VIDEO OPTIONS

I highly recommend having someone videotape your wedding. At our wedding, two different friends took video footage, one with a rented camera and one with a home camera. Both tapes were given to us as gifts. The videos

A SAMPLE SHOT LIST

Whether you are using an amateur or professional, it is a good idea to write out a shot list and give it to the photographer ahead of time. Then ask a family member or friend to point out the people on the list to your photographer. Not having to deal with the photo details like this on your wedding day will make the event more stress-free.

Here is the shot list we gave our photographer before the wedding:

Bride with matron of honor

Bride with mom

Bride's family

Bride with brother

Bride's brother's family

Groom and best man

Groom and dad

Groom and mom

Groom and sister

Groom's family

Groom's sister's family

Bride, groom, and groom's family

Bride, groom, and bride's family

Bridal processional

Attendants and children in processional

Lots of ceremony shots

Ministers

Toasts

Individual family shots of all those invited

Bride and groom's first dance

Cake cutting

Throwing the bridal bouquet

Bride and groom exiting the venue

were entertaining, comprehensive, and a great recording that we watch every year on our anniversary.

If having a professional videotape your wedding is high on your priority list, use the same methods described earlier in the chapter to find a good videographer at a price you can afford. Some pros charge as little as $500, while most charge $1,000 and up; with an overall budget of $5,000, you likely do not have the funds to spend more than $1,000. Keep in mind that high-end photographers and videographers charge ten or twenty times that amount, so you may have to do a fair amount of research to find someone you can afford, or you may decide to ask a friend or family member to help here if it is not on your priority list.

In some cases, the photography studio (or wedding chapel, if you are marrying in one) will have a discount package if you buy both services from the one company. Also consider hiring the pro for the ceremony alone (versus the entire event), to keep your costs to a minimum.

When considering professionals, a lot of what you are paying for is video quality and editing options. The least expensive editing option is to purchase raw footage only, for the fixed number of hours you commissioned the coverage at your wedding. The problem with this is that most folks don't want to sit down and watch a raw, uncut tape. Although you could always choose later to have it edited, it might be worth your while to choose a package that includes some editing. For example, if the videographer edits while shooting, called in-camera editing, you will end up with a more concise tape and a more moderate price tag. This option is best done by a professional and is not suggested for amateurs (because you wouldn't want them to lose any valuable audio).

The most expensive editing option is a post-edited tape to which the videographer can add graphics, still photos (for example, baby pictures of the couple), and blend tapes from multiple cameras. One way to save money is to have an amateur (or two) videotape the entire wedding and, later, pay a professional to edit the tape and add in the extras (a music track, titles, and dates) to personalize it. Or you can do it yourself, using iMovie or Final Cut Pro software.

When looking at videographers' sample tapes, ask yourself the following questions:

- Does the video tell a story? Is it interesting to watch?
- Does the tape seem professional, smooth running, and clear?
- How is the lighting? Do the indoor pictures seem bright

enough? Has external lighting (floodlights) been used, or is the camera equipped with a light sensor?

- Pay close attention to the audio: Is the sound clear and vibrant? Can you hear the vows word for word? Is the audio in sync with the videotape?
- Are there several different camera angles and a variety of shots from establishing shots to close-ups? (Ask to see complete wedding videos, including unedited footage.)

To narrow the search, ask more detailed questions:

- Is the videographer available on the date of your wedding?
- What would the total charges be? Find out exactly what you get for the fee, for example, three hours of shooting time and two hours of editing. Look for hidden costs (overtime, editing charges) and compare prices. Stipulate in writing that the bride and groom own the copyrights.
- How will they dress? Requiring the production crew to dress in black head to toe is a classic option that works well for casual or formal events.
- Be sure that you meet the actual person who will be shooting your wedding. Decide if you feel comfortable with that person and be sure to check his or her references.
- Be sure to get everything in writing: the time, date, amount of coverage, and payment plan.

The quality of home video cameras keeps improving, and many of the couples I interviewed relied on family or friends to be videographer for their wedding day—with no regrets. Ask around to see if anyone already owns a home-video setup and if they would help you by shooting your wedding. Another option to consider is to rent a professional video camera for a day and ask a reliable artistic friend to run it. The rental, at $100 a day and up, could be well worth it in the long run.

The following tips for amateur videographers were supplied by Julie

McGlone, a television producer in Avon, Connecticut. Julie explained that "the key to success here is to know you don't get a second take."

- Before the wedding: be sure the videographer does a walk-through at the location of the ceremony and reception. The walk-through should take place at the same time of day as your ceremony. This will enable the videographer to decide where to set up and help to identify potential lighting problems.
- The day of the wedding: have someone point out who the important people in the family are (so they can be sure to get footage of your favorite uncle instead of your mom's boss).
- Be sure to have a new battery in the camera, an extra battery just in case, plus a brand-new SD Card and a backup. Make sure that the projected amount of time and quality will work with the SD cards chosen, and bring extras just in case.
- From the beginning to the end of the ceremony: do not stop rolling, even if your view gets obstructed! You can edit the video later, but it is important to get every word on audio!
- Take pictures of everything—from the whole location to close-ups of the bouquet, the buffet table, stained glass at the church, people arriving at the ceremony, people dancing, the toasts, cake cutting, general interaction, reception tables, and the rings. While in the editing phase these pictures can be used as cutaways to replace low-quality footage (for example, a shot of the back of someone's head).
- Find out what about this wedding is unique and sentimental to the bride and groom, and make sure it gets plenty of footage. The bride might be wearing her mother's dress, or the flowers might be magnificent, or the sun might be setting over majestic purple mountains.
- Ask friends and well-wishers to say a few words of encouragement on tape and later edit this into a montage at the end of the tape.

- Edit the tape chronologically, from people entering, the ceremony, the reception, and the bride and groom leaving on their honeymoon, followed by the encouragement montage.
- Consider setting up a fixed GoPro camera on a tripod to shoot from a second camera angle continuously during the ceremony. If planning to stream live on the web, it can be the same camera. It's a gamble, but test-shoot beforehand to make sure where the couple is supposed to stand will be well framed. Later you can use Photoshop to add in pictures from the GoPro camera. Julie insists it's critical to shoot with a higher quality camera and only use the GoPro as a cost-effective backup.

HOME IS WHERE THE HEART IS

Ann and John's Wedding on April 17
65 guests in Providence, Rhode Island

PRIORITIES

1. Having their close friends and family present
2. Avoiding family conflicts
3. Having the ceremony and reception at home, not in a church
4. Making the wedding fun
5. Keeping the expense low

John, forty-four, and Ann, twenty-nine, had been living together for three-and-a-half years when they decided to get married. John popped the question on Valentine's Day, and Ann accepted his engagement offering: a pink-gold wedding band that originally belonged to John's grandmother, inscribed with her 1908 wedding date. They got married fourteen months later in their apartment in Providence, Rhode Island.

LOCATION

Ann had just completed her bachelor of fine arts at the Rhode Island School of Design and was on an internship in Boston. John was a writer, working on his second novel. They lived on the second floor of a bright and sunny restored Victorian house that had ornamental stained glass. "We loved the place and wanted our friends to see our home and be a part of our family." The long and narrow rooms of their apartment were decorated with Ann's artwork, printmaking equipment, and all sorts of bright-colored bowls, pitchers, goblets, and giant two- to three-foot handmade vessels.

BUDGET

Wedding, reception site	$ 0
Dress, alterations, veil, and shoes	$ 300
Groom's tuxedo	$ 140
Food	$ 495
Waitstaff	$ 350
Beverages	$ 420
Cake	$ 125
Rentals (chairs and a coat rack)	$ 125
Photography	$ 0
Music	$ 0
Flowers	$ 390
Invitations	$ 65
Minister	$ 95
License	$ 70
Decorations	$ 105
Makeup	$ 50
Total	$ 2,730

DETAILS

Friends—"a mix of lawyers, artists, and psychiatrists"—and family came from all over the country to witness John and Ann's nuptials: sixty-five in all, from Colorado, California, Kentucky, New York, and Virginia. A friend who was also a judge performed the 3 p.m. nondenominational ceremony. John described their self-written vows: "We spoke of the nature of love, the bonding of rings, happiness, and commitment."

When asked what their favorite wedding memory was, John answered, "It was the collective laughter at certain parts of the ceremony, and watching the outpouring of emotions, the tears, and the unrestrained joy."

APPAREL

Ann wore a 1913 Belgian lace full-length wedding gown that she purchased from a vintage shop. The lace was a slightly sheer, fine-netted floral. The dress had puffy elbow-length sleeves, a fitted waist, and a satin underslip. On her feet, she wore off-white leather pumps.

Ann's hair was set into curls that cascaded out of a tiara of flowers with a very traditional tulle veil in the back. A friend of hers, "an incredible makeup artist," made her up and helped her get ready (Ann had previously purchased makeup, with the help of her friend, from Filene's Basement). She had on pearl earrings that she had received as a gift; she borrowed an antique sea pearl necklace-and-brooch set to complete the outfit.

John researched period costume books to find out what was worn for weddings around 1910. Then he searched vintage shops until he found the perfect match to Ann's dress: a black cutaway tuxedo with a gray vest and a gray-and-black ascot. With it, he wore a white shirt and black leather shoes.

Ann and John let their attendants, a maid of honor and a best man, choose their own attire.

MUSIC

There was a constant mixture of music throughout the whole event. Several of John's friends were in bands and brought their musical instruments, including a harp and a banjo. The music ranged from the traditional "Here Comes the Bride" processional to Irish music and lively bluegrass during the reception.

FLOWERS AND DECORATIONS

Ann's bouquet was a mixture of off-white roses with subtle pink highlights, lilies of the valley, wildflowers, daisies, and stephanotis. The groom wore a rose and lily of the valley boutonniere, while the maid of honor and best man wore plain roses. Ann arranged her own flowers and decorations, but she purchased the bouquet and boutonnieres already made. There were vases of pink tulips all over the apartment, and a coarse tulle was used to decorate the windows, creating a cloudlike effect.

PHOTOS

A friend of John's who was also a student at the Rhode Island School of Design took photographs at the wedding and gave them to the couple as a gift. He shot large-format black-and-white pictures that Ann later made into a wedding album.

FOOD AND BEVERAGE

To help at the reception, Ann and John recruited friends and hired three students from Rhode Island School of Design, including a bartender and serving help. Some of their friends who were enthusiastic cooks brought dishes in lieu of presents.

Their menu consisted of wafer-thin-sliced Smithfield ham with home-made butter biscuits, roast turkey, mountains of jumbo shrimp, salads, assorted cheeses, baked Brie, spanakopita, and chips. They served champagne and sodas and had two kegs of Hope Lager. Paper products and plastic champagne flutes were used for ease of cleanup.

Their wedding cake was a yellow layer cake with chocolate cream filling that was bought from a French bakery they frequented. "It was decorated to look like a gingerbread-style Painted Lady Victorian with four tiers of pastel icings, and white and pink roses." In addition to the wedding cake, a mint-chocolate-chip ice cream cake was served in honor of Ann's and her brother's birthday.

Chapter Twelve

CRAZY GOOD TUNES:

THE WORLD IS YOUR PLAYLIST

○———————————○

One of the most memorable aspects of your wedding will be the music. This does not mean it has to be the most expensive. As with other areas in your wedding, first look at where it sits on your priority list and what you have budgeted for it. Especially for the DIY crowd, consider what resources you may have in your circle of friends and family. Are there singers, musicians, DJs, or instrumentalists who you may have a connection to? Or do you and your betrothed—or maybe a few friends—enjoy downloading music and have great iTunes collections? That may be all you need to create low-cost—or even no-cost—ambience with music. This chapter will delve into inspired musical ideas for your ceremony and reception.

Whatever your preferences are in music and in the medium through which it's delivered, selecting the music for your wedding depends a lot on personal taste, what you think your family and friends would enjoy, and how deep your pocketbook is. If you are reading this book, it is fairly unlikely that you are planning to hire an orchestra to play at your wedding. Nevertheless, live music may rank high on your priority list. If so, or if you know you absolutely must hire a DJ, then finding the right people, getting a great price, and picking out appropriate songs are your next steps.

CEREMONY MUSIC VERSUS RECEPTION MUSIC

Wedding music is typically played at two different times during the event: for the ceremony and for the reception. Sometimes the same musicians play at both, especially if the whole event takes place in one locale. But generally speaking, the music is distinctive for each part and requires two sets of musicians, or musicians at one and recorded music at the other. If all of your music is recorded music, you are likely to want a different style at the ceremony and at the reception.

Categories of Music for the Ceremony

Whether making your own CDs or playlists or hiring professional musicians, when thinking about the music for your big day, break down the stages of your wedding into the following categories:

PRE-CEREMONY. Background music plays while guests are congregating. Prerecorded love songs work well for this purpose. An instrumentalist, playing exquisite soft melodies on a harp, acoustic guitar, viola, or even softly on a piano, is another fine way to welcome guests.

PROCESSIONAL. This is what you walk down the aisle to. Classical, Christian rock, and folk music, live or recorded, all offer memorable possibilities.

CEREMONY. Hymns, classical pieces, or spiritual selections are usually played or performed during the ceremony. A soloist or vocalist with a piano, organ, or guitar accompanying could also be apropos. If you are going to have a wedding program, possibly put the words and music into the program so guests can sing along.

RECESSIONAL. Make this a triumphant exit song with an upbeat tempo!

Categories of Music for the Reception

From love songs to dance music, the tempo builds throughout the reception.

COCKTAIL MUSIC. This lasts thirty minutes

TIP

Keep in mind that it is best to make decisions about what you want musically at least four to six months out. DJs and good dance bands tend to book far in advance, and the sooner you choose one, the better your chances are that they'll have the date available.

to one-and-a-half hours in length, depending on how much time you allot for cocktails and hors d'oeuvres. Classical, symphony, individual instruments, love songs, or a soloist are appropriate here. If you want more upbeat music, consider rock and roll, alternative, or fast country tunes.

DINNER MUSIC. Choose wonderful romantic background music, picking up the tempo a little bit—up to the time dancing begins.

RECEPTION AND DANCING MUSIC. This includes the couple's first dance and dances with the parents. The pace will pick up after the main meal. Look to get everyone up on their feet dancing. Don't forget to add a few slow dances for the hopeless romantics in the audience. You may want to have specific songs designated for the cake cutting, garter toss, and throwing of the bouquet, if those traditions will be included in the reception.

ARE MUSIC AND DANCING A PRIORITY IN YOUR WORLD?

If so, *and* you have a great voice, consider singing down the aisle or having a flash-mob dancing spree as a memorable highlight of the festivities.

To garner ideas, log onto YouTube and peruse wedding videos that feature singing, dancing, gymnastics, and flash mobs—as part of the ceremony or reception. You can find brides, grooms, officiants, and entire wedding parties that sing or dance their way down the aisle. Type in "JK Wedding Entrance Dance" and see for yourselves the wedding processional video that went viral and has been watched by over eighty-five million viewers.

THE WHO, WHAT, WHERE, AND WHEN OF YOUR MUSIC PLAN
Ask yourselves the following to determine what type of music (if any) you want at your ceremony and reception, and who is going to play it.

Is music at the ceremony and reception essential?

If the answer is no, you are not alone. Several couples I interviewed elected to have no music whatsoever during the ceremony. One bride explained, "We really wanted to keep the ceremony simple and keep the focus on the vows." Other couples who were getting married in natural settings said that they preferred to hear the wind or the crash of the waves as the backdrop for their ceremony. For a brunch, luncheon, or tea reception, music is not a mandatory expectation.

What if the answer is yes, music is essential, but it is not a top-five priority?

Then this is a place to make budget cuts. There are plenty of prerecorded versions of Mendelssohn's "Wedding March" to choose from. From a reception point of view, hiring a DJ is usually less expensive than hiring a live band but costs more than a DIY playlist, of course.

What if live music is essential and a priority?

- Earmark part of your budget to cover the costs. How much of the budget depends on where and when you want the music, and what you have in mind.
- Find out if the ceremony location has anyone that they normally use for such an occasion. Churches, synagogues, and wedding chapels often have either staff musicians or members of their congregation who perform at very reasonable rates. Ask your officiant for suggestions or referrals for anyone from a soloist to an organist.
- Also consider if there is anyone musically inclined in your family or your circle of friends who could do the honors. Does anyone play guitar, flute, harp, or piano, or have an incredible singing voice? Brainstorm with family and friends to see if there is anyone who fits the bill. It can be very meaningful to have people you know involved in your ceremony or preforming at your reception. Or does a friend or family member have an amazing iTunes or CD collection and

amplifier system? Can friends recommend someone, for instance a college student, who can DJ at a fair price?

CELESTIAL SINGING

A New York bride offered this advice: "The church staff can really help. All you have to do is ask. We hired a woman from our church's choir to sing a pre-ceremony solo and another solo at the end of the ceremony. She was superb and charged us all of $50! The church organist was also excellent and likewise cheap."

Does your location(s) have restrictions on or requirements for the music that can be performed?

- Before you get ahead of yourself hiring a band or picking out specific songs that you want played, check with your officiant to clarify the rules and regulations on what can and can't be included musically in your ceremony. For example, the well-known march "Bridal Chorus," by Wagner, better known as "Here Comes the Bride," is not allowed in many synagogues (because Wagner was a well-known anti-Semite). Often Catholic churches do not allow secular songs. Instead, they have their own list of approved songs. If you are working with a wedding coordinator from your house of worship, he or she should be able to steer you toward what is allowable at your site.
- Before getting quotes, find out the rules and regulations governing live or amplified music at your reception site. Some

sites don't permit it at all, while others give specific decibel levels to stay within and a curfew time for the music to stop. If you are having an at-home wedding, check with your local town or city hall to see what your neighborhood requirements are (i.e., whether any permits are required or what the ordinances regarding loud music are). If there is room in your budget, consider inviting the neighbors to keep complaints to a minimum.

DANCING TILL DAWN

Whether you are recording your own iTunes mix, playing CDs, or hiring a band or DJ, consider these music styles for your reception:

Big band sounds
Christian rock
Classical: string quartet, chamber music, opera, or symphonic music
Country music, complete with line or square dancing
Disco
Ethnic rhythms, such as the hora (Jewish) or polka (Polish)
Hip hop or rap
Irish music
Jazz
Reggae or calypso
Rhythm and blues
Rock and roll
Salsa
Spanish guitar or mariachi
Spiritual or gospel
Swing

LET THE MUSIC MOVE YOU

Angela Muchmore, a soloist and church music ministry leader from Cincinnati, Ohio, shared the following advice for couples working with church singers and musicians:

- "Ave Maria," "Amazing Grace," and "Somewhere Over the Rainbow" are beautiful choices a cappella or with live or recorded instruments as an accompaniment.
- To save money, instead of having multiple instrumentalists or a band, prerecorded background music (piano, guitar, flute, or horn) works well. Most churches these days have sound systems that you can plug into and are designed especially for the acoustics of your locale.
- Arranging singers and instrumentalists through your location is a lot more affordable than going through a wedding planner or finding someone at a wedding show. You can save several hundred dollars.
- Songs custom written by a songwriter or musician friend specifically for your wedding are a very sentimental addition to the ceremony. They can vary greatly in price, so Angela recommends asking up front what the fees would be and if you would own the song. If so, it would likely be cost prohibitive. If the writer is a close personal friend, perhaps he or she would be interested in giving the song as your gift. Another cost-effective option is to barter for your time and talent; that is, exchange a song for helping with website design, or for writing and distributing a press release to local media outlets on the songwriter's behalf.

PROS AND CONS OF
DJ VERSUS LIVE MUSIC

PROS

- Hiring a DJ will cost much less, on average less than half the price of a professional band.
- DJs require less room to set up.
- Usually a DJ can play a combination of styles of music, while a band may not have as wide a repertoire. (For example, a rock band might not play love songs.)
- DJs play the popular songs by the artists who recorded them.
- Recorded music is less risky than hiring a live band that might turn out to be a dud.
- When the DJ goes on a break, the music keeps going. When a band takes a break, everybody stops dancing (unless you arrange for music in the pauses between sets).

CONS

- Having a live band is more traditional than hiring a DJ.
- Live music can create a fun, memorable atmosphere.
- Live musicians can really pump up the audience and get everyone dancing.

CREATING THE MOOD

There are many options to create ambience at your ceremony and reception. Choose from the following ideas to create memorable melodies.

Single instruments sound fantastic for a ceremony and can provide background music at a reception. The flute, harp, guitar, piano, and violin are good examples of instruments that are intimately connected with the romantic feeling of a wedding. One way to find a good instrumentalist is through a local high school or college. Also, if you are planning to book a band for the reception, consider asking a single member, such as the guitarist, to arrive a few hours before the others and play at your ceremony. Another cost-cutting option is to hire an instrumentalist for the ceremony and assemble your own playlist for the reception. A single instrumentalist will charge from $100 and up.

Booking a band can be easy if you already know somebody—or time-consuming if you don't. First, decide what type of band you want to hire, whether rock and roll, jazz, swing, or whatever you prefer. Then get referrals from friends, ask your reception location coordinator, or visit wedding shows and local nightclubs.

If you definitely want live music, and you are committed to staying on your budget, here are a few suggestions to help you search out and find musicians you like with a price tag of a few hundred dollars rather than a few thousand:

- Look for a band whose members already have day jobs. There are wonderful musicians who play together on weekends only and don't have the overhead a professional band would have.
- Consider hiring a high school–aged band. Eleanor and Jerry (profiled on pages 282–86) searched local jazz clubs and hired younger musicians with talent way beyond their years. The $200 they paid them to play was more than the musicians had ever received before, but way less than it would have cost to hire a professional band—or a DJ for that matter.

TIP

If you hear a tune on the radio that you would like to add to your wedding playlist, use an iPhone app such as Spotify or Shazam to capture the name of the song or artist.

- For a warm touch at your ceremony and reception, consider having child virtuosos perform. One New York couple, whose six-year-old daughter (from a previous marriage) was an adept violin player, arranged for her whole violin class to perform during their ceremony. There was not a dry eye in the place! A middle-school band would also be adorable. They may not play perfectly; however, the price (free?) and how cute they are will more than make up for any missed notes.

MUSIC SUGGESTIONS

A blend of traditional and nontraditional songs will appeal to guests who range in age and backgrounds. There are many sites that can help you sample music for free and create a custom playlist complete with the recorded music ready for an MP3. You pay per song. For starters try logging onto Weddingmusic.com, iTunes, Weddingmusiccentral.com, Topweddingsites. com, Myweddingmusic.com, Classicsonline.com, Soundextremeweddings. com, or Weddingmusicproject.com, among many choices. See pages 58–59 for a more complete listing of websites that feature wedding tunes.

The following list of recommended songs and instrumental pieces is not meant to be all-encompassing. New music is recorded all the time, and an entire book this size could be filled with available options. The songs below are wedding favorites that I have read or heard about time and again. Some are from the classical repertoire, while others are from rock, alternative, country, and other genres.

Consider your favorite artists, from the Rolling Stones to Adele or Josh Groban. Think about Broadway show tunes, for example, "Sunrise Sunset" from *Fiddler on the Roof,* or soundtracks from beloved movies, such as *Sleepless in Seattle.* In the words of Frank Sinatra, "Do It Your Way."

FOR THE CEREMONY

TRADITIONAL

"Amazing Grace"

"Ave Maria"

"Bridal Chorus" (a.k.a. "Here Comes the Bride"), Wagner

Canon in D Minor, Pachelbel

The Four Seasons, Vivaldi

"Ode to Joy," Beethoven

"Pomp and Circumstance," Elgar

"Wedding March (from *A Midsummer Night's Dream*)," Mendelssohn

NONTRADITIONAL

"A Thousand Years," Christina Perri

"Come Away with Me," Norah Jones

"Evergreen," Barbra Streisand

"Falling," Alicia Keys

"Falling in Love at a Coffee Shop," Landon Pigg

"First Time Ever I Saw Your Face," Roberta Flack

"Home," Phillip Phillips

"How Long Will I Love You," Ellie Goulding

"I Do," Colbie Caillat

"I'm Yours," Jason Mraz

"It's You," Terrell Carter

"No Ordinary Love," Sade

"Somewhere Over the Rainbow / What a Wonderful World," Israel Kamakawiwo'ole

"The Prayer," Celine Dion and Josh Groban

"The Way You Look Tonight," Frank Sinatra or Michael Bublé

"Truly, Madly, Deeply," Savage Garden

"Unconditionally," Katy Perry

"Waiting on a Woman," Brad Paisley

"When Love Finds You," Vince Gill

ROMANTIC TUNES FOR PRE-CEREMONY, THE COCKTAIL HOUR, DINNER, THE FIRST DANCE(S), AND SLOW DANCING

"A Kiss to Build a Dream On," Louie Armstrong

"A Whole New World" (theme from *Aladdin*), Peabo Bryson and Regina Belle

"All My Life," K-C and JoJo

"All of Me," John Legend

"All This Time," OneRepublic

"All You Need Is Love," The Beatles

"At Last," Beyoncé

"At Last," Etta James

"Because You Loved Me," Celine Dion

"Best Day of My Life," American Authors

"Better Together," Jack Johnson

"Bless the Broken Road," Rascal Flatts

"Breathe," Faith Hill

"Come to Me," Goo Goo Dolls

"Crazy Love," Van Morrison

"Everlong," Foo Fighters (violin version)

"Every Breath You Take," The Police

"Fade into You," Mazzy Star

"Feel So Close," Calvin Harris

"Fields of Gold," Sting

"Friday I'm in Love," The Cure

"Have I Told You Lately," Rod Stewart

"Ho Hey," The Lumineers

"How Sweet It Is," James Taylor

"I Cross My Heart," George Strand

"I Finally Found Someone," Barbra Streisand and Bryan Adams

"I Hope You Dance," Lee Ann Womack

"I Think I Want to Marry You," Bruno Mars

"I Wanna Grow Old with You," Adam Sandler

"In My Life," The Beatles

"In Your Eyes," Peter Gabriel

"Into the Mystic," Van Morrison

"Is This Love," Bob Marley

"Just a Kiss," Lady Antebellum

"Just the Way You Are," Billy Joel

"Kiss Me," Ed Sheeran

"Love Me Tender," Elvis Presley

"Love Song," Adele

"Love Story," Taylor Swift

"Make You Feel My Love," Adele or Bob Dylan

"Mama's Song," Carrie Underwood

"Maybe I'm Amazed," Paul McCartney

"Me & You," Kenny Chesney

"No Ordinary Love," Sade

"One," U2

"Overjoyed," Matchbox Twenty

"Rolling in the Deep," Adele

"Sea of Love," Del Shannon

"She's Always a Woman to Me," Billy Joel

"Stand By Me," Ben E. King

"Sway," Michael Bublé

"Thank You," Led Zeppelin

"The Way You Love Me," Faith Hill

"Then," Brad Paisley

"This Will Be Our Year," The Zombies

"Time in a Bottle," Jim Croce

"True Love," Pink

"Un Amor," Gipsy Kings

"Unchained Melody," Righteous Brothers

"We Found Love," Rihanna and Calvin Harris

"We've Only Just Begun," the Carpenters

"What a Wonderful World," Louis Armstrong

"Whenever I See Your Smiling Face," James Taylor

"Wind Beneath My Wings," Bette Midler

"With or Without You," U2

"Wonderful Tonight," Eric Clapton

"Yeah," Usher

"You & Me," Dave Matthews

"You Are So Beautiful," Joe Cocker

"You Are the Best Thing," Ray Lamontagne

"You Give Good Love," Whitney Houston

"You're My Best Friend," Queen

"You've Got a Way," Shania Twain

"Your Song," Elton John

DANCE MUSIC

"Ain't Too Proud to Beg," The Temptations

"Blurred Lines," Robin Thicke

"Brick House," Commodores

"Celebration," Kool and the Gang

"Cha Cha Slide," DJ Casper

"Crazy Little Thing Called Love," Queen

"Don't Stop Believing," Journey

"Feel So Close," Calvin Harris

"Gangnam Style," Psy

"Glad You Came," The Wanted

"Good Feeling," Flo Rida

"Happy," Pharrell Williams

"Holy Grail," Justin Timberlake and Jay Z

"I Gotta Feeling," Black Eyed Peas

"Jump Around," House of Pain

"Kiss," Prince

"Let's Go," Ne-Yo

"Love Shack," B52s

"Marry Me," Train

"Mirrors," Justin Timberlake

"Moves Like Jagger," Christina Aguilera and Maroon Five

"O.M.G.," Usher

"Push It," Salt-N-Pepa

"Raise Your Glass," Pink

"Respect," Aretha Franklin

"Save the Last Dance for Me," Ben E. King

"Sexy and I Know It," LMFAO

"Shout," Isley Brothers

"Shout," Lloyd Williams

"The Chicken Dance"

"The Wobble," Vic

"Titanium," David Guetta featuring Sia

"Treasure," Bruno Mars

"Twist and Shout," The Beatles

"We Are Young," fun. featuring Janelle Monae

"What Makes You Beautiful," One Direction

"Y.M.C.A.," Village People

FUN SONGS FOR THE GARTER TOSS

"Another One Bites the Dust," Queen

"Bad to the Bone," George Thorogood

"Foxy Lady," Jimi Hendrix

"Hot in Herre," Nelly

"I'm Too Sexy," Right Said Fred

"Legs," ZZ Top

"Super Freak," Rick James

FINDING A GREAT DJ

Word of mouth referrals are your best bet for finding a good DJ, especially from recent newlyweds or wedding vendors with whom you are already working, such as your caterer or your reception location coordinator. Also, you can search for local DJs on the web, perhaps using a ratings site like Yelp.com or Angie's List. Bridal shows, local bridal magazines, and wedding shows also publicize wedding DJs. The ideal DJ should be personable and have a great music library, own his or her own equipment, and have wedding experience—with a feel for pacing and for knowing when it's time for the first dance, when to throw in a slow dance, and so on.

Before finalizing the DJ's contract, be sure to meet with the DJ in person, attending a live gig, if possible. Go over the DJ's playlist and be sure it includes plenty of music that is your style, as well as any specific favorites that you require. Let the DJ know what, if any, music you absolutely *don't* want played. For example, if you hate disco and don't want to hear "Y.M.C.A.," be sure to spell this out upfront. It is important that you find a DJ with whom you feel comfortable and whom you believe will be responsive to your needs and tastes. Don't forget to check several references! The cost of a DJ ranges from $400 to $750 and up.

DJ AND BAND CONTRACTS

Once you have decided on a DJ or band, be sure to get a written contract. The following points should be included in the contract:

- Exact cost for their services
- Date and time of the wedding reception (ceremony, too, if anyone is performing then)
- The starting time when the DJ or band will begin to play, and the time they will end
- Exactly when they will be performing music during the event—during the cocktail hour, after dinner only, and so on
- How many breaks they will take, the length of the breaks, and if (and what type of) recorded music will be played during the breaks
- The names of band members or the DJ who will be present and acceptable backups in case of an emergency
- What they will wear to perform (tuxedos, white dress shirts with black pants, and so on) as well as what you *don't* want them to wear (e.g., T-shirts and gym shoes)
- What type of sound system and equipment they will bring
- What you are responsible for providing (e.g., chairs, electricity, meals)
- Any overtime or incidental charges that you may be responsible for
- Cancellation and refund policies

DO-IT-YOURSELF, NO-COST, OR LOW-COST WEDDING MUSIC

When we got married, music wasn't high enough on our priority list to warrant any real expense. Neither my husband nor I are musically oriented, so I asked a couple of friends for their help creating the playlist and making sure all ran smoothly at the ceremony and reception. These suggestions can help you out:

- If you are planning to go this route, find out if you will have access to an on-site stereo system. If not, arrange to bring your own or borrow one.
- Be sure to ask someone to be in charge of cueing the music on location (you will be far too busy to deal with this on your wedding day).
- Consider buying a wedding mix that will provide continuous play without your spending time recording or assembling a playlist.
- Look in your local public library (my library has a great selection), check out a CD store, or visit online music stores to find out what is out there that suits you.
- Make separate playlists for the cocktail hour, dinner hour, and dancing portions of the reception.
- Make sure the tempo of the music escalates with each new stage, and throw in a couple of slow dances, too.
- Blend your favorite artists together with favorites from other generations to ensure that everyone will get up and dance.
- Make note of what specific music you want for each stage of the dinner and dance, including the song you want to dance to for your first dance as husband and wife, and the songs for the dances with the bride and her dad and for the groom and his mom. The garter toss, bouquet throw, cake cutting, and the bride and groom's departure all may call for separate musical choices.

MUSIC, FOOD, AND FUN

Eleanor and Jerry's Wedding on August 5
100 guests in Allentown, Pennsylvania

PRIORITIES

1. Good food
2. Good music
3. Not too expensive yet stylish
4. To save the bulk of their available funds for their honeymoon
5. To have their friends and family present

Eleanor, twenty-eight, and Jerry, twenty-seven, were college sweethearts who originally met when they were both writing for the school paper. They had been living together for eight years when Jerry proposed on Christmas morning in front of his entire family. Jerry gave Eleanor a dozen long-stemmed red roses and got down on one knee. He then pointed out to Eleanor that one of the roses wasn't a rose at all; it was a jewelry box in the shape of a rose, and it contained a diamond engagement ring.

A few months later, when Eleanor and Jerry started looking at locations to tie the knot, they naturally went back to the college campus where they first met. But after hearing the high cost for using the wedding chapel, they decided to take a different approach. They wound up hosting both a 3:00 p.m. wedding ceremony and the reception that followed at their local Masonic temple.

LOCATION

Jerry described the room where they married as "a ritual room, where they confer honors in the temple. It was majestic and plush in appearance, with coats of armor, flags, an organ, and cultural symbols that made the wedding feel steeped in history. The room had a center floor area that was surrounded by seats in a circle; the chairs were upholstered with crushed red velvet and matched the deep red color of the carpet. It was kind of like standing in the middle of a very plush basketball court, encircled by all of your friends."

The reception was held in the temple lobby on the first and second floors. The walls, floors, and staircase were white and black marble; the lobby doors were held open to a view of the park across the street.

BUDGET

Wedding, reception site	$ 125
Dress, alterations, veil, and shoes	$ 500
Groom's clothing	$ 125
Food, catering, cake, rentals, beverages	$ 1,750
Photography	$ 0
Music	$ 125
Flowers	$ 125
Decorations	$ 65
Invitations	$ 65
License, minister	$ 65
Total	$2,945

DETAILS

Eleanor and Jerry's wedding was designed to be "a celebration of our relationship, our announcement to the world that our relationship means a lot to us." A friend of Eleanor's family, who is also a missionary, performed the nondenominational ceremony. There were traditional elements intertwined with poetry, philosophy, and self-written vows. Jerry explained, "We were concerned that in our souls and hearts we felt bonded to each other and committed. We know that difficult times would come. We were vowing to stay together regardless of the obstacles that came up." (See pages 307–08 for excerpts from their ceremony.)

APPAREL

Eleanor wore a white dupioni silk gown with a full skirt, a sweetheart neckline, and pearl-lined braiding that was sewn on the bodice in the shape of daisies. The dress was purchased locally in Allentown, Pennsylvania. Eleanor had made her own veil, but on the wedding day she forgot it at home, and there wasn't enough time for her to send someone to retrieve it. Fortunately, Eleanor was able to pull together a new veil on the spot! She took some of the tulle she had for room decorations and stole flowers from various arrangements in the room. She pinned the flowers into her hair, forming a simple headband, and attached the shoulder-length tulle.

Eleanor's maid of honor and two attendants wore full-length deep purple sheath gowns ($98 each). The dresses had a layer of sheer material on the top and a silk slip underneath. Jerry, his best man, and his ushers all wore traditional black tuxedos with vests.

MUSIC

During the ceremony, their caterer played the organ, accompanied by one of Jerry's friends on the acoustic guitar and another friend playing violin. "Rigaudon," by André Campra, was the processional, and Beethoven's "Joyful, Joyful, We Adore Thee" was the recessional. For a mid-ceremony hymn, everyone joined in to sing "Amazing Grace."

Jerry hired a high school–aged jazz band to perform at the reception. He had heard them play several times at a local coffeehouse and knew that they were good. "I was really nervous at first about relying on them. But they did a great job, and people danced. Everyone loved having live music."

Jerry, who is a writer in his day job and a musician on the side, is a member of an eight-piece jazz band. All of his fellow band members attended his wedding, and they all brought their instruments with them: drums, sax, guitar, and bass (there was a piano in the lobby already). In between sets from the hired band, Jerry's band either all jammed together or individuals performed instrumental solos. The music was a mixture of "jazz, rock and roll, John Coltrane, and Steely Dan–like rhythms."

FLOWERS AND DECORATIONS

The morning of the wedding, Eleanor and Jerry held a rehearsal on location. Afterward, they decorated the temple and arranged the flowers with the help of the wedding party. Then they sat down to a potluck luncheon before the guests arrived.

For her wedding bouquet, Eleanor carried a bunch of creamy pink roses with gladiolus mixed in. Her attendants carried similar flowers in smaller arrangements. Boutonnieres and corsages were also made with the rose-gladiolus combination.

For the ceremony and reception arrangements, they filled deep ceramic pots with gladiolus and a mixture of organic flowers and vegetables grown in Eleanor's mother's garden. The roses were purchased through a wholesale market. "The potted flowers sat on top of white columns and were so high, they stood twice as tall as us," remembered Eleanor. For added room decoration, they draped satin, tulle, ribbons, and flowers around banisters and down the staircase. They also put up a large bulletin board with a series of pictures of the bride and groom from babyhood through their engagement.

PHOTOS

Eleanor and Jerry chose not to hire a professional photographer. Instead, they asked a few friends who are avid amateurs to come early and take still pictures. Following the ceremony, the wedding party and immediate family went to the park across the street to take a few portraits. However, most of the pictures in their wedding album are candids that were taken by their photo-bug friends and a variety of guests.

FOOD AND BEVERAGE

Eleanor and Jerry are both vegetarians, and so their catered menu reflected a variety of meatless choices. At a finger-food station, for instance, there were miniature quiches, stuffed mushroom caps, rolled grape leaves, and cheese tortellinis. There was also a bread station where hollowed-out loaves of bread were stuffed with either peanut sauce or pesto and surrounded by sliced breads and vegetables for dipping. A fruit, cheese, and cracker station rounded out this light repast of hors d'oeuvres.

Their cake was a vanilla raspberry torte with raspberry Chambord filling, buttercream frosting, and a garnish of white chocolate curls and fresh raspberries. The caterer built a fountain out of lowball glasses and a rented base. The fountain had a flowing stream of whiskey sour mix. There was also a self-serve bar that included apple cider, ginger ale, colas, diet drinks, sangria, chardonnay, cabernet, Pete's Wicked Ale, Foster's, and black and tans.

Chapter Thirteen

WORDS OF WISDOM

o———————o

My most brilliant achievement . . . was to persuade my wife to marry me.
WINSTON CHURCHILL

U p until now, you and your intended have made many decisions affecting the overall feel of your wedding—the location, the theme, the wedding attire, what caterer to use. This chapter, filled with wisdom from past brides, grooms, and ministers, will help you tighten your focus and concentrate on the commitment that you are making to spend your life together.

First, it's time to finalize the guest list and decide just how many folks are going to be invited to attend your exchange of vows. Next, go over wedding invitation wording and announcements. Then, move on to the wedding ceremony, vows, and toasts. By the end of this chapter, you will have lots of ideas to help you design your own guest list, wedding invitations, and ceremony.

THE GUEST LIST

Many couples want to share their wedding day with close friends, family, and relatives, and so, while writing the guest list, they take stock of who those people are. By now, you have read several times in this book that the number-one way to save money on your wedding is to keep your guest list to a minimum. But saving money is not the only reason to trim your guest list. Many of the couples interviewed for this book kept the numbers down in order to keep a sense of intimacy while deepening their commitment. Over and over I heard newlyweds explain that on their wedding they wanted to spend quality time with each other and with the folks who meant the most to them. In many cases this included children from previous marriages. Many couples who were marrying for the second time spoke frankly about wanting to simplify their wedding this time around and celebrate the beginning of their new lives together as a couple and as a family.

Reverend Roger Coleman of Clergy Services Inc., in Kansas City, Missouri, specializes in small family weddings. Reverend Coleman realizes that contemporary couples face a real challenge when trying to keep the focus off of the externals and on the family, friends, and relationship. He suggests not "having more guests than you can spend one minute of time with. If you invite three hundred guests, spending one minute with each would take over five hours."

However, many couples feel obligated to invite business associates, distant relatives, and friends of their parents. Ways of avoiding this include eloping, inviting only the immediate family, inviting guests to a reception celebration but keeping the exchange of vows private, or giving in and inviting the masses and attempting to spend quality time with everyone. If you decide to limit your guest list, let others know what your plans are: to marry with yourselves only, with just immediate family present, or with just a few witnesses. Hopefully, they will understand the hard choices that you made and respect you for them.

Many couples, ourselves included, start out with a large list and decide to trim it down only after the expensive quotes from caterers and locations begin to come in. Our original guest list was 150, but by the time the invites actually went out, there were 80 on our guest list. We sent out an additional 25 announcements following the wedding.

KIDS OR NO KIDS:
DO WE REALLY NEED TO INVITE THEM?

When speaking with betrothed couples on how to prune the guest list, the question of whether or not to include kids often comes up. Here are pros and cons I've heard from brides and grooms who were trying to decide:

PROS

- We love kids and, of course, want to include everyone in our celebration. It's fun to see how they have grown and to get them out on the dance floor.
- We're afraid we will be offending people if we do not include everyone we know.
- Our friends and family have kids of all ages. We really want the adults to come, and if we don't include kids, several people will bow out.
- Guests who are coming from afar and have kids may not want to leave them in their home state. We do not want them to boycott the wedding for lack of a weekend sitter. If they do bring the kids, they've spent a fair amount to get everyone here, so we feel including them is the least we should do.
- We have kids from a previous marriage and/or a niece and nephew who will be the flower girl and ring bearer in the ceremony. It seems rude to let them attend but not let others bring their children.

CONS

- We need to trim the guest list to be within budget. Cutting kids out is an easy way to do so.

- Our event is formal and will end well past midnight. As such, we do not feel including kids is appropriate.
- It's too much work to keep kids under control. They would need a separate menu, toys, games, and maybe a sitter or two.
- We are not very tolerant of children and do not plan to have any ourselves. Why should we invite kids to our day?

Whatever you decide—yea or nay—on including the kids is completely your right. Just realize that you may lose some guests if kids are not included. It is not ideal etiquette to state anything directly on the invitation, for instance, saying "kids not invited." However, that does not mean it's never done. The traditional method of not including them is simply not to add their names on the invite, nor refer to John Doe and "family"; instead address the envelope to John and Mary Doe. Another option that I've seen on the invitation, directly below the ceremony information, is the specification "Adult Reception to Follow." Bear in mind there are people who will bring the kids anyway, unless you hold firm.

If children are included, you may want to have a kids' room or separate table; you will also need kid-friendly food choices, plus games and entertainment for them. Hiring a sitter or sitters may benefit all involved. Employing this strategy can keep the kids occupied and out of trouble, at the same time giving parents a break to enjoy the festivities.

INVITATIONS

Your wedding invitations should reflect all of the decisions you have made about the style of your wedding thus far. Whether traditional, informal, e-vites, or eclectic, there are many options to choose from.

Traditional formal invitations are engraved or embossed on white or ivory paper, which is usually a costly venture. Thermography (chemically raised lettering) can save some dollars, as can standard printing. Here are several more money-saving suggestions:

- Shop at a wholesale or discount stationery store.
- Utilize an office supply store for your invitations.
- Look on the Internet and in bridal magazines for budget-savvy stationery and printing.
- Have the invitations laser-printed instead of embossed or traditionally printed.
- Use a stock paper, parchment paper, or a preprinted paper instead of a custom design.
- Hire an art student to design and make your invitations.
- Have a friend or family member do the calligraphy for you.
- Make them yourself (see below).

Do-It-Yourself Invitations

In this day and age of computers, it is getting easier and easier to make your own invitations. We designed and printed our invitations, announcements, and reception cards on high-quality stock that was purchased from a stationery store. We spent $100 total, including postage, less than half of what the same store would have charged to do the printing. They turned out so well that when I told my mom and a few close friends that we did it ourselves, they didn't believe me at first.

Here are more ways to save money while making your own invitations:

- Handwrite or print your wording on a laser printer and then copy the original onto high-quality paper at a copy shop or print them yourself.
- Buy a computer invitation kit or CD-ROM. This includes software and card-stock stationery similar to the quality available through mail-order outlets.
- Use a print shop–style software program and your own paper to design a style that works for you.
- Shop office supply, paper or stationery, or online stores to

choose a paper style that you like: invitation stock, parchment, recycled, scented, or Japanese-style paper. Select envelopes and enclosure cards to match.

- Address the letters by hand yourself, writing with a gold, silver-toned, or calligraphy ink pen. Use gold- or silver-toned address labels for return addresses on the envelopes.

- Buy an embosser and emboss the invitations and/or envelopes yourself.

- Decorate with lace, stickers, rubber stamps, dried flowers, ribbons, twine, sponge painting, or original artwork, such as a miniature watercolor print. Enclose dried rose petals or heart-shaped glitter inside your invitations for an added creative touch.

- Scan baby photos or an engagement photo of you and your fiancé and design an invitation using them.

- It's much less expensive and eco-friendly to send e-vites. Some e-vites are even free! It's up to you if using this non-traditional method meets the formality of your event. If you do go this route, realize that you may have a few people who still are not computer savvy. You will need to send them something or call to invite them.

- You may want to send a save-the-date card electronically, then send paper invites. You could also follow up with an e-vite reminder a few weeks after sending invitations in the mail. For more on e-vites, including some vendor recommendations, see page 52.

OTHER COST CONSIDERATIONS

- Use plain instead of lined envelopes, or line envelopes yourself by attaching a glossy paper inside a plain envelope with rubber cement.

- Keep in mind that oversized invitations cost more, not only for the paper, but also for the postage.

- Order ten to fifteen extra invitations in case you make mistakes or need to add to your guest list. Remember that not everyone needs his or her own invitation. Couples or families residing at the same address can get one invitation, as can single friends who are bringing a date ("John Hass and Guest").

- Double-check the wording on your invitations before approving the draft or printing them yourself. Mistakes are costly to correct.

A MEMORABLE INVITE WITH HEARTFELT BLESSINGS

A Dallas bride whose wedding theme was based on her feng shui expertise designed a unique and meaningful invitation. Written on handmade paper, the invitation included wedding particulars on one side and Chinese blessing paper tied onto the other side by a sheer satin ribbon. Instructions were included to tear off the blessing paper, write down a blessing for their marriage, and insert it in a small envelope (provided). At the church, everyone put their blessings into the collection plate during their wedding Mass.

One month after the wedding, the couple pulled out the blessings and read them to each other in remembrance of their wonderful friends and the love they share.

INVITATION WORDING

Invitations are usually mailed four to six weeks before the wedding, but they are ordered up to four months ahead of time. If you expect guests from abroad or are getting married over a holiday weekend, send out invitations and/or a save-the-date postcard six to eight weeks ahead of time to alert everyone to block off their calendar. We sent out a newsletter a few months in advance, which included maps to the ceremony location, local hotel phone numbers (with advice to make early reservations), and other tourist information for anyone planning an extended vacation. Nowadays, you can send e-vites online, then follow with a formal invitation.

This information usually is included on the invitation:

- Day, date, and time (depending on the formality, these may be spelled out)
- Host of the event
- The bride and groom's names
- Where the reception will be (sometimes a separate card)

Mr. and Mrs. Daniel Brown

request the honor of your presence

at the marriage of their daughter

Margaret Ann

to

Mr. Jeremy John Smith

Saturday, the eighth of July

Two Thousand and Fifteen

at one o'clock ["in the afternoon" is optional]

Holy Name Church

314 Randolf Road

Deerfield, Illinois

When deciding the invitation wording, consider the style of your wedding. If it is traditional, pick up an etiquette book to be sure you understand customary protocol. Usually, whoever is paying for the bulk of the wedding has their name appear first on the invitation, followed by their child's name.

If you host your own wedding, no parents' names appear on the invitation.

We invite you to join us in a celebration of love

on the two year anniversary of the day we met

On this very special day

we will deepen our commitment

by sharing the vows of marriage

Carly McGuire

and

Geoff Kalinsky

Tuesday, the fourth of July

Two thousand and fourteen

at two o'clock p.m.

The Heidi House

65 Horseshoe Hill Road

Carmel, California

Reception to follow

Announcements are optional and can be sent to acquaintances and relatives who were not invited because of distance or inability to attend. Have a friend send out your pre-addressed announcements the day after your wedding. Ours looked like this:

Carly McGuire

and

Geoff Kalinsky

are happy to announce

we deepened our commitment

through the exchange of

Marriage vows

on Tuesday, the fourth of July

Two thousand and fourteen

Carmel, California

INVITATION AND ANNOUNCEMENT DETAILS

- If the groom's parents are hosting, change the format so the groom is announced first.
- If the host or hostess is unmarried, use the single full name.
- If the invitation is informal, you can delete the *Mr.* or *Mrs.*
- If either the bride or groom has been married previously and has children, wording can include their names as the hosts: for instance, "Kimmy Brown and Adam Smith invite you to the marriage of their parents . . ."
- If the reception being hosted does not include a traditional full meal, it is a good idea to subtly point that information out on the invitation or reception card. For example, "Light refreshments will be served following the ceremony" or "Cake and champagne will be served following the exchange of vows" or "Join us for a dessert buffet immediately following."
- If the wedding took place earlier and the invitation is for the reception only, invite the guests in this fashion:

Laura and Don Jacobs

request the honor of your presence

at their wedding reception

(date)

(time)

(place)

An alternative to the above formal style would read "Laura and Don Jacobs invite you to a reception in honor of their recent wedding."

Other stationery items can be purchased or made and may be included when sending the invitation:

- **Reception cards** are optional because the location information is often listed at the bottom of the invitation. When separate cards are included, it is probably because the reception is being held at a different locale. The following is a traditional reception card:

  Reception

  immediately following the ceremony

  Old White Country Club

  1225 Central Avenue

  Highland Park

- **Response cards** are standard and should be sent with a self-addressed-and-stamped return envelope. For informal weddings, you can avoid the expense of a response card by listing a phone number at the bottom of the invitation and requesting an RSVP.

The following is a traditional response card:

Please respond on or before

the second of July

M_____

will __ attend

- **Thank-you notes** to be used following the reception can also be made or purchased in the same fashion. Often they match the wedding invitation stationery.
- **Wedding programs** are yet another option. They help everyone follow the ceremony, and they also make great keepsakes. A wedding program usually lists all participants, includes the sequence of events, the words to any readings, the song titles, and may even include lyrics so guests can sing along. If you decide to have a program made, or to make one yourself, ask a friend or attendant to pass them out as your guests arrive for the ceremony.

WEDDING CEREMONIES

Planning the ceremony itself is a series of deeply personal decisions. If you choose to get married in a church or synagogue, use a minister in an outdoor setting, tie the knot at city hall, or marry in a wedding chapel, the ceremony is often preset, although you can often customize it. Ask the officiant in advance for a copy of the ceremony and ask him or her to point out the areas that you can personalize. If you are marrying with the help of a judge, a nontraditional minister, or a justice of the peace, you may be able to design every aspect of the ceremony yourselves. Talk to your officiant and decide what is appropriate.

TIP

A recent wedding I attended sent out a save-the-date magnet. In addition to listing the name of the couple getting married and the upcoming date, it featured a picture of the couple holding hands and prominently showing off the gorgeous engagement ring. It was a very cute and unique idea.

Most ceremonies these days include a processional, a welcoming of guests, several readings by family members or close friends, an exchange of vows, and a pronouncement of marriage followed by a kiss and the recessional. Other options are, of course, music, a blessing of the parents, the offering of the daughter by the father (sometimes the mother, a sibling, or a child may have this honor instead), a moment of meditation, a homily, communion, the lighting of a unity candle, the breaking of a glass at the end of the ceremony, and some type of symbolic gesture toward children from previous marriages, such as the offering of a Family Medallion (see pages 304 and 306).

The ceremonies, vows, and readings included in the following pages are for the most part nontraditional. They are intended to be a starting point for brides and grooms who are planning to write their own vows or design their own ceremony. While in the planning phase, be sure to ask the person who will officiate to join in the discussions and fine-tuning of the details. Mix and match readings, add a meditation if you want, include prayers and psalms, or avoid them altogether. Search online for a wide variety of articles, websites, ceremonies, and readings. Keep in mind that the ceremony should reflect who you are as individuals and as a couple, and with thought, research, and soul-searching, hopefully you will find wording and a ceremony that suits your needs.

CHOOSING AN OFFICIANT

Whether civil or religious, the officiant who you choose will play a major role in your wedding ceremony. It is important that you are comfortable with the direction that the officiant will take and that he or she understands what your priorities are regarding the ceremony.

Ask the following questions when interviewing potential candidates:

- Are they available for your wedding date?
- Can you personalize the ceremony?
- Are there any restrictions, rules, or regulations that you need to follow?
- What kind of counseling, if any, is required?
- What is the minister's fee for conducting the ceremony?
- Ask to see a copy of the ceremony that is commonly used so you can get a feel for the style.

If you are marrying in your church or synagogue, your officiant is usually supplied; hopefully, you already have a relationship with him or her. If not, it's a good idea (and required in most cases) to set up at least one counseling session with that officiant prior to the ceremony. If you are marrying at a wedding chapel, out of town, or at city hall, the officiant will usually be supplied and often is someone you have never met before. Gather as much information about the ceremony as possible, starting with the above questions.

The real challenge comes when you have to find someone whom you don't already know to share this special day with you as a minister or justice of the peace. In the best-case scenario, you either meet someone at another wedding or find a family friend to officiate. Other ways of tracking down the ideal officiant include asking for referrals at city hall, word of mouth, the phone book, a wedding planner, or the ceremony or reception site.

If you know someone who you think would be perfect but is not a registered minister, check with your local city hall. In some states, anyone can officiate by paying a small fee and being sworn in as a justice of the peace for a day. Another option is to have the person you choose apply for a minister license. The Universal Life Church, in Modesto, California, grants these licenses by online application and usually can process the request in as little as a day or two. Log onto ulchq.org/ordination or call (209) 527-8116 for further details.

LGBT WEDDING CONSIDERATIONS

In general, same-sex unions are nearly identical to traditional heterosexual unions involving a man and wife, although there are some minor differences:

- LGBT weddings are not allowable in all congregations or denominations. Check with your church and minister to see if you can marry where you attend.
- Decide how to dress for your nuptials: will either or both of you wear tuxedos, suits, wedding dresses, veils?
- Decide flowers: do you prefer boutonnieres, bouquets, or no flowers?
- Determine if someone will give one or both of you away during the ceremony.
- Will you have a best man, maid of honor, wedding party, and attendants?
- What readings and music appeal to you?
- How would you like to be referred to, for example, as bride and bride, bride and groom, groom and groom, or spouse and spouse?

Gay Wedding Planning Tips

- **Pick an LGBT-friendly location.** The last thing you want on your special day is discrimination! The same goes for the staff and management of the event. Make sure to stipulate that everyone involved must be gay-friendly! No exceptions.
- **Understand the legalities.** If it's legal in your home state, getting married there could be easier than having a wedding abroad.
- **Peruse websites for LGBT wedding-planning resources and vendors:** for instance, Gayweddings .com, Equallywed.com, soyourenGAYged.com, and Weddingwire.com.

The following is a collection of custom wedding ceremonies and vows designed to inspire you.

Merrilyn and David's Ceremony

This wedding celebration, a second marriage for both, was adapted from Reverend Coleman's booklet *Our Wedding Celebration*. David's child, A.J., who served as the best man, was given a Family Medallion as part of the ceremony. Family Medallions, rings or necklaces, and additional family ceremony literature are available from Clergy Services Inc. (For more information, log onto Familymedallion.com or call 800-237-1922. See pages 325–330 for more on Merrilyn and David's ceremony and reception.)

WELCOME

JUSTICE OF THE PEACE: *Throughout history, men and women have sought to recognize the great moments in their lives. On these occasions, they call first upon family and friends to share in their joy and happiness. Therefore, in the beauty of this setting, David and Merrilyn invite you to help celebrate their love and their marriage.*

[For the first reading, Pat, Merrilyn's college roommate, shared an excerpt from the book *It Was on Fire When I Lay Down on It*, by Robert Fulghum. For the text of this reading, see pages 321–22.]

VOWS

J.O.P.: *Are you, David, ready to enter this marriage and to be to Merrilyn loving, faithful, and supportive through all your days together?*

DAVID: *I am.*

J.O.P.: *Are you, Merrilyn, ready to enter this marriage and to be to David loving, faithful, and supportive through all your days together?*

Merrilyn: *I am.*

J.O.P.: *By these answers, your love for one another is affirmed. Please join hands and repeat after me.*

David: *Merrilyn, I take you as my wife, to care for you and trust you, to respect you and to laugh with you, to forgive you and be forgiven by you. I will be your best friend and partner in life. I will love you in good times and in difficult times, when we are together and when we are apart. I promise to be faithful always, today and for all our years together.*

[Merrilyn repeats the same, substituting the word *husband* for *wife*.]

AFFIRMATION BY GUESTS

J.O.P.: *And will you, their family and friends, give David and Merrilyn your blessing, and pledge to them your continued love and support? If so, please say, "We will."*

RINGS

J.O.P.: *The circle has long been a symbol for marriage. These circles are made of precious metal just like the precious nature of your relationship. Being unbroken circles, each represents unending love. As often as you look upon these rings, be reminded of this moment and the love you have promised.*

David, will you place this ring on Merrilyn's finger and repeat after me?

With this ring, I pledge to you my faithful love.

[Merrilyn then places the ring and repeats the same.]

PRAYER

[Al, Merrilyn's older brother, reads a Native American prayer.]

Now you will feel no rain, for each of you will be shelter to the other.

Now you will feel no cold, for each of you will be warmth to the other.

Now there is no loneliness, for each of you will be companion to the other.

Now you are two bodies, but there is only one life before you.

May you live in love and joy together, now and always.

FAMILY MEDALLION

J.O.P.: *Often marriage is viewed as the union of two individuals. In reality, however, marriage is much broader and more encompassing. As we give thanks for the love which brings David and Merrilyn together, we must also recognize the merging of families taking place and the additional love and responsibility family and friends bring to this relationship.*

As part of this newly created family, we acknowledge A.J. and the significant role he plays in the relationship celebrated today. David and Merrilyn will present A.J. with a Family Medallion, created as a symbol for family unity and in recognition of the hope and joy made possible through this marriage.

DAVID: *A.J., this medallion represents your importance in our lives and our continued love and support for you. Whenever you look at it, know you are loved.*

SECOND READING

[Nancy, a friend, reads an excerpt from *The Prophet* by Kahlil Gibran.]

Our children are gifts entrusted to us, not as objects to be controlled, but as human beings, each unique in their own personality, each separate in their own identity. You may give them your love but not your thoughts, for they have their own thoughts. You may house their bodies but not their souls, for they dwell in the house of tomorrow, which you cannot visit, not even in your dreams. You may strive to be like them, but seek not to make them like you. For life goes not backward nor tarries with yesterday. You are the bows from which your children as living arrows are sent forth.

[Following a blessing, the Justice of the Peace presents the newly formed family.]

J.O.P.: *It is my pleasure to present to you David and Merrilyn in their new relationship as husband and wife and their son, A.J.*

Eleanor and Jerry's Vows

Eleanor and Jerry's wedding (pages 282–86) was a mixture of traditional and nontraditional elements. The following text, adapted from *Letters to a Young Poet*, by the poet Rainer Maria Rilke, was read as their first reading:

It is good to love because love is difficult. For one human being to love another human being, that is perhaps the most difficult task that has been entrusted to us, the ultimate task, the final test and proof, the work for which all other work is merely preparation. That is why young people, who are beginners at everything, are not yet capable of love; it is something they must learn. With their whole being, with all of their forces, gathered around their solitary, anxious, upward beating heart—they must learn to love. . . .

Loving does not at first mean merging, surrendering, and uniting with another person. It is an inducement for the individual to ripen . . . to become world in himself for the sake of the other person: it is a great, demanding claim on him, something that chooses him and calls him to vast distances. . . . The claims that a difficult work of love makes upon our development are greater than life, and we, as beginners, are not equal to them. But if we nevertheless endure and take this love upon us as burden and apprenticeship instead of losing ourselves in the whole easy and frivolous game behind which people have hidden from the most solemn solemnity of their being—then a small advance and a lightning will perhaps be perceptible to those who come long after us.

[Following the first reading was a passage from Scriptures (Luke 7:36–50), followed by a homily. Then these pastoral questions were asked of Eleanor and Jerry.]

PASTOR: *Jerry, will you have this woman to be your wife, and will you pledge to be patient and kind to her and not to envy her and never to be boastful, conceited, nor rude; not to be selfish or quick to take offense with her, not to keep a score of her wrongs; and not to gloat over her sins; but to delight in all that is truthful between the two of you? And do you pledge to face all things together?*

JERRY: *I will.*

PASTOR: *Eleanor, will you have this man to be your husband, and will you pledge to be patient and kind to him and not to envy him and never to be boastful, conceited, nor rude; not to be selfish or quick to take offense with him, not to keep a score of his wrongs; and not to gloat over his sins; but to delight in all that is truthful between the two of you? And do you pledge to face all things together?*

ELEANOR: *I will.*

[Eleanor and Jerry wrote the following vows themselves. According to Jerry, in order to write the vows, "We wrote, revised, and rewrote what we wanted to say. Basically we wanted to unpack the phrase 'I love you.'"]

JERRY: *Eleanor, I take you to be my wife, to love and to honor and to respect for as long as you shall live. I promise to share with you and grow with you through your joys and your sorrows, your failures and your accomplishments. I shall try to be sensitive to your needs and to give you love and support as well as freedom as you strive to develop your full potential. I promise to try to always remember that you are God's gift to me. As a remembrance of these vows and as a symbol of my ever-growing love, I give you this ring.*

[Eleanor then recited her vows exchanging the word *husband* for *wife*.]

Antonia and Donn's Vows

The following self-written vows are from Antonia and Donn's wedding (pages 142–46).

To you, Donn/Antonia,

I vow to honor you with my complete trust, respect, laughter, and love;

I pledge to you compassion, in good times and in bad;

I vow to give you the freedom to pursue your adventure and to discover and follow your own bliss;

And I vow I will always cherish you, nurture our relationship, learn and create with you, and never stop giving thanks that we found each other.

Antonia also wrote a poem for Donn that she recited to all present.

Donn,

I hold your soul to mine

with cords of love stronger than silken spiderwebs

and mightier than the invisible ties that keep the moon and stars together.

I love you completely, unconditionally.

It is as if you have always been with me.

Now our union is as real as your ever-loving spirit.

Jana and Jeff's Vows

The following couple from Los Angeles, California, wrote these wedding vows to acknowledge thay they are going to grow and change, and do whatever it takes to keep their love fresh.

JEFF: *I promise to grow old along with you . . .*
To be willing to face change
As we both change,
In order to keep our relationship
Alive and exciting.

JANA: *I promise to keep myself open to you . . .*
To let you see through
The window of my personal world
Into my innermost fears and feelings,
Secrets and dreams.

JEFF: *I promise to share with you . . .*
My time, my close attention,
And to bring joy and strength
And imagination to our relationship.

JANA: *I promise to love you*
In good times and bad,
With all I have to give,
And all I have inside . . .
In the only way I know how . . .
Completely and forever.

[Read together by Jana and Jeff]

> *I now accept your love for me*
> *Without fear of tomorrow*
> *Knowing that tomorrow*
> *I will love you more than I do today.*

A Unity Candle Blessing

Many couples these days are including the lighting of a unity candle in their ceremonies. They each take a slender taper and light a large candle, their union symbolized in the two flames joining into one. This ancient Irish blessing is adapted by Reverend Roger Coleman, of Clergy Services Inc. from his booklet *The Blessing of Light*, a resource for incorporating the unity candle into your ceremony.

May the blessing of light be with you always,

Light without and light within.

And may the sun shine upon you and warm your heart,

Until it glows like a great fire.

So that others may feel the warmth of your love for one another.

The Prayer of Saint Francis of Assisi

This adaptation of the Prayer of Saint Francis of Assisi was read at my wedding and many others that I have attended over the years.

Lord, make me an instrument of thy peace:

Where there is hatred, let me sow love;

Where there is injury, pardon;

Where there is anger, forgiveness;

Where there is doubt, faith;

Where there is despair, hope;

Where there is darkness, light;

O Divine Master, grant that I may not so much seek

To be consoled, as to console;

To be understood, as to understand;

To be loved, as to love;

For it is in giving that we receive,

It is in pardoning that we are pardoned,

And it is in sharing our love with another,

That our hearts are filled with joy.

A Modern Adaptation of I Corinthians 13:4–13

A few couples that I interviewed included a modern or traditional version of this classic Bible passage in their ceremony.

Love is patient, Love is kind.

Love is never jealous or envious, never boastful, nor selfish or rude.

Love does not demand its own way.

It does not hold grudges and will hardly even notice when others do wrong.

It always protects, always trusts, always hopes, always perseveres.

There is nothing that love cannot face.

There is no limit to its faith, its hope, and its endurance.

Love never fails.

When I was a child, I talked like a child, I reasoned like a child.

When I became a man I put childish things behind me.

My knowledge is now partial, then I shall know fully, even as I am fully known.

There are three things that last forever: faith, hope, and love; but the greatest of these is love.

The following are selections of romantic readings and poems that are considerations for non-traditional ceremony readings. Refer to your ceremony site coordinator to see if there are any restrictions. For instance, many churches will stipulate exactly what Bible passage can be used as readings and which Bible interpretation is allowable. Poetry is often not allowed in religious ceremonies.

On Marriage
by Kahlil Gibran

You were born together, and together you shall be forevermore.
You shall be together when the white wings of death scatter your days.
Ay, you shall be together even in the silent memory of God.
But let there be spaces in your togetherness,
And let the winds of the heavens dance between you.

Love one another, but make not a bond of love:
Let it rather be a moving sea between the shores of your souls.
Fill each other's cup but drink not from one cup.
Give one another of your bread but eat not from the same loaf.
Sing and dance together and be joyous, but let each one of you be alone,
Even as the strings of a lute are alone though they quiver with the same
    music.

Give your hearts, but not into each other's keeping.
For only the hand of Life can contain your hearts.
And stand together yet not too near together:
For the pillars of the temple stand apart,
And the oak tree and the cypress grow not in each other's shadow.

An Irish Wedding Blessing

May love and laughter light your days,
And warm your hearts and home.
May good and faithful friends be yours,
Wherever you may roam.
May peace and plenty bless your world
With joy that long endures.
May all life's passing seasons
Bring the best to you and yours!
May the road rise to meet you.
May the wind always be at your back.
May the sun shine warm upon your face.
The rains fall soft upon the fields.
May the light of friendship guide your paths together.
May the laughter of children grace the halls of your home.
May the joy of living for one another
Trip a smile from your lips,
A twinkle from your eye.
And when eternity beckons,
At the end of a life heaped with love,
May the good Lord embrace you
With the arms that have nurtured you
The whole length of your joy-filled days.
May the gracious God hold you both in the palm of His hands.
And, today, may the spirit of love find a dwelling place in your hearts.
    Amen.

I Want Both of Us
by Hafiz

I want both of us
To start talking about this great love

As if you, I, and the Sun were all married
And living in a tiny room,

Helping each other to cook,
Do the wash,
Weave and sew,
Care for our beautiful
Animals.

We all leave each morning
To labor on the earth's field.
No one does not lift a great pack.

I want both of us to start singing like two
Travelling minstrels
About this extraordinary existence
We share,

As if
You, I, and God were all married

And living in
A tiny
Room.

In One Another's Souls
by Rumi

The moment I heard my first love story I began seeking you,
not realizing the search was useless.
Lovers don't meet somewhere along the way.
They're in one another's souls from the beginning.

From *Jane Eyre*
by Charlotte Brontë

"I have for the first time found what I can truly love—I have found you. You are my sympathy—my better self—my good angel; I am bound to you with a strong attachment. I think you good, gifted, lovely: a fervent, a solemn passion is conceived in my heart; it leans to you, draws you to my center and spring of life, wraps my existence about you—and, kindling in pure, powerful flame, fuses you and me in one."

The Key to Love

by Anonymous, 1st-century China

The key to love is understanding . . .
The ability to comprehend not only the spoken word,
but those unspoken gestures,
the little things that say so much by themselves.

The key to love is forgiveness . . .
To accept each other's faults and pardon mistakes,
without forgetting, but with remembering
what you learn from them.

The key to love is sharing . . .
Facing your good fortunes as well as the bad, together;
both conquering problems, forever searching for ways
to intensify your happiness.

The key to love is giving . . .
without thought of return,
but with the hope of just a simple smile,
and by giving in but never giving up.

The key to love is respect . . .
realizing that you are two separate people, with different ideas;
that you don't belong to each other,
that you belong with each other, and share a mutual bond.

The key to love is inside us all . . .
It takes time and patience to unlock all the ingredients
that will take you to its threshold;
it is the continual learning process that demands a lot of work . . .
but the rewards are more than worth the effort . . .
and that is the key to love.

One with Each Other
by George Eliot

What greater thing is there for two human souls, than to feel they are
joined for life—to strengthen each other in all labour,
to rest on each other in all sorrow,
to minister to each other in all pain,
to be one with each other in silent unspeakable memories.

The Bargain
by Sir Philip Sidney

My true love hath my heart, and I have his,
By just exchange one for another given:
I hold his dear, and mine he cannot miss,
There never was a better bargain driven:
My true love hath my heart, and I have his.

His heart in me keeps him and me in one,
My heart in him his thoughts and senses guides:
He loves my heart, for once it was his own,
I cherish his because in me it bides:
My true love hath my heart, and I have his.

On Second Marriages

This beautiful passage regarding second marriages was excerpted from Robert Fulghum's inspirational book *It Was on Fire When I Lay Down on It*. It was read during Merrilyn and David's wedding (see pages 304–306).

Weddings are usually thought of as fairy-tale times when Real Life is momentarily suspended. "And they lived happily ever after" seems possible, if only for a day. When my children were small and their daddy tried to end bedtime stories with the happy ending, one of them would always ask, "And THEN what happened?" How could I tell them that Cinderella discovered she was married to a guy with a foot fetish and that . . . the princess might have turned into a prince, but still had the personality of a frog and ate flies for breakfast instead of cereal? What I know about real life suggests those are not unreasonable answers to the and-then-what-happened question.

I tell couples, in mock seriousness, that the warranty on the wedding license is only good for twenty-four hours. The odds on a marriage lasting are 50-50 now, which means that a minister is often asked to perform a wedding wherein one or both parties have been previously married. They did not live happily ever after the first time around. But they know something now—about themselves, about real life, and about marriage. And their weddings reflect their wisdom.

For one thing, they know, as I know, that the real wedding and the real vows don't happen on the day of the formal social occasion.

There comes a time usually some days after the proposal and acceptance, after the announcement and setting of the date and all the rest, when there is a conversation between two people in love, when they are in earnest about what they've agreed to do. The conversation happens over several days—even weeks. Partly in a car driving some-where, partly at a kitchen table after supper, partly on the living-room floor, or maybe on the way home after a movie. It's a conversation about promises, homes, family, children, possessions, jobs, dreams, rights, concessions, money, personal space, and all the problems that might arise from all those things. And what is promised at that time, in a disorganized, higgledy-piggledy way, is the making of a covenant. A covenant—an invisible bond of commitment. Just two people work-ing out what they want, what they believe, what they hope for each other. With their eyes, they ask each other if they really mean it, and they do. Then they seal it with a whole lot more kissing and hugging than you'll see in public. And that's it. The wedding is done. All that's left to do is the public celebration, however they choose to do it.

I know this sounds like heresy—that the Church Fathers might not agree. But if you are married, you know it's true. That's why I always tell couples to pay more attention to what's going on in that talking time before the Big Day. They wouldn't want to miss their own wedding.

When couples come to me for a second marriage, they have al-ways spent most of their time and energy on that talking time and are a lot less concerned about the Big Day than they were the first time. They know that companionship in the kitchen around suppertime is vastly more important than the color of the bridesmaids' dresses. They know that good company and friendship count for more than good looks. And they know that marrying a frog is fine if you re-ally like the frog a whole lot and don't expect princely transforma-tions. . . . It's not as romantic the second time, but it's not without love. The love tends to be richer, deeper, wiser this time.

MORE VOWS AND READINGS

There are so many wonderful readings and other resources to consult to find fabulous vows, prayers, and ceremonies. If you're religious, talk to your minister or look in the Bible or your book of worship for appropriate readings. If you prefer poetry or alternative spirituality, the following books, pamphlets, and authors are worth some research:

- *Into the Garden: A Wedding Anthology, Poetry and Prose on Love and Marriage*, edited by Robert Hass and Stephen Mitchell, HarperPerennial, 1994.
- *Illuminata: Thoughts, Prayers, Rites of Passage*, Marianne Williamson, Random House, 1994.
- *Our Wedding Celebration, The Blessing of Light, and Celebrating the New Family (Resources for Including Your Children in the Wedding)* are booklets written by Reverend Roger Coleman, Clergy Services, Inc. (Call 816-753-3886 for further information.)
- The works of classic and contemporary authors, including Elizabeth Barrett Browning, James Joyce, William Shakespeare, George Eliot, Rumi, Kahlil Gibran, and Rainer Maria Rilke.
- Another alternative is to recite the lyrics to your favorite songs in place of a reading, for example, "I Hope You Dance" by Lee Ann Womack, Jim Croce's "Time in a Bottle," or Bruce Springsteen's "If I Should Fall Behind."
- Also consider whimsical text from a favorite book, such as *Oh the Places You'll Go* by Dr. Seuss or *The Giving Tree* by Shel Silverstein. A favorite poem could also be meaningful, for instance, "The Invitation" by Oriah Mountain Dreamer, or the essay, "Everything I Needed to Know I Learned in Kindergarten" by Robert Fulghum.

A WORD ON TOASTS

The best man usually offers the first toast, either during dinner, if champagne is flowing abundantly, or, if only one champagne toast is scheduled, right after the ceremony when the champagne is poured and served. Let him know ahead of time exactly where and when to begin the toasting. It can either be done standing (at a cocktail hour or reception) or seated (where the toaster stands up in their place and speaks so all can hear). A microphone is sometimes used.

The maid of honor usually follows with the next toast, and then it is open season for any members of both families. The toasts consist of funny stories on growing up or friendship in general and offers of welcome into their new extended families. The toasts work best if they are funny, sincere, move at a good pace, tell interesting (but not too intimate) stories of how the couple first met, and end with a sentimental twist. After each toastmaster speaks, everyone raises his and her glass to the newlyweds.

When the toasts are winding down (or the champagne is running low), you may want to extend a few toasts yourself: a thank-you to both sets of parents, to everyone who helped you with your special day, to family and friends for showing up, and to your new spouse for being as wonderful as I am sure he or she is.

With your upcoming nuptials in mind, I raise my glass and extend this Irish toast to you:

May you be poor in misfortune
Rich in blessings
Slow to make enemies
Quick to make friends
But rich or poor or slow
May you know nothing but happiness
From this day forward.

A GARDEN CELEBRATION

Merrilyn, David, and A.J.'s Wedding on May 19
61 guests in Hatfield, Massachusetts

PRIORITIES

1. Including David's son, A.J., in the ceremony
2. Keeping the wedding small and manageable
3. A casual outdoor garden setting
4. Tasteful
5. Not too much hoopla

Merrilyn, forty-four, was attending a working dinner at the Ritz-Carlton with several coworkers and their husbands, when her then-boyfriend, David, forty-three, ordered up a real surprise. When dessert came and the silver dome covering her plate was lifted, the words *Say Yes?* were written in chocolate ganache encircled with raspberries and a diamond ring.

After accepting David's proposal, they decided to get married on the five-year anniversary of their first date. Both had been married before, and they agreed that David's son, A.J., ten, should be the best man and master of honor. They did some research into ways to include him in their ceremony, and they came across a special ceremony and a Family Medallion from Clergy Services that they subsequently gave A.J. to include him in the bonding of their new family.

LOCATION

Merrilyn and David married in Hatfield, Massachusetts, in the backyard of Merrilyn's good friend and boss, Lisa. When they accepted Lisa's gracious invitation to hold the wedding at her house, they sent her two hundred yellow tulip bulbs as a perennial gift of thanks.

In order for Merrilyn, David, and A.J. to make a stylish entrance and exit, Lisa also lent them her red-and-white 1955 Ford Crown Victoria.

BUDGET

Wedding, reception site	$ 0
Dress, alterations, veil, and shoes	$ 290
Groom's and son's tuxedos	$ 50
Food, catering, and cake	$ 1,330
Food costs for what they provided on their own	$ 70
Beverages	$ 400
Rentals (tent, chairs, linen, china, and silverware)	$ 1,200
Photography	$ 400
Music	$ 45
Flowers	$ 200
Tulips for Lisa's house	$ 110
Invitations	$ 100
Minister	$ 0
License	$ 60
Family Medallion and ceremony booklet	$ 83
Total	$ 4,338

DETAILS

They held their ceremony at 2:00 p.m., on the steps leading to the garden. The tulips were in full bloom as were all of the flowers along the garden path. The justice of the peace stood on the first step leading to the garden, the two readers took their turns on the second step, and David and Merrilyn stood on the third, with A.J. beside them.

"Our ceremony contained elements of spirituality, but nothing religious in the conventional sense," Merrilyn explained. "I remember at one point thinking to myself 'This is perfect . . . exactly what I envisioned.'" (See pages 304–306 for the ceremony and pages 321–22 for an additional reading.)

APPAREL

Merrilyn wore her mother's 1945 wedding dress. It was a tea-length, satin dress with a V-neck, slightly off the shoulders, and tiny buttons running down the back of the dress. Merrilyn hired a seamstress to replace the lace, which was deteriorating, with pieces of satin from the original train.

As a wedding gift, Merrilyn's long-standing hairdresser styled her hair the morning of the big event.

David had previously worked as a model for a local tuxedo company, and he bartered more modeling in exchange for the floral garden-printed tuxedo that he wore. A.J. wore a Tasmanian devil vest and tie with his tuxedo.

Merrilyn and David had told all of their guests with children to bring a change of clothes for the kids to romp in. Merrilyn recalls that her seven-year-old nephew kept asking, "Now is it time to change?"

MUSIC

A good friend of Merrilyn and David's was put in charge of the music. He had an oldies collection, as well as jazz and some popular CDs. For the ceremony processional and recessional, they played "Going to the Chapel" by Yellowman. Other musical highlights included Rod Stewart's "Forever Young" and Merrilyn and David's song, "I've Had the Time of My Life," from the movie *Dirty Dancing*.

As a thank you for help with the music, Merrilyn and David gave their friend a $40 gift certificate to a music store.

FLOWERS AND DECORATIONS

Merrilyn held a simple spring bouquet interspersed with periwinkle-shaded flowers and tied with a matching satin ribbon. Merrilyn's mother and all of the young girls at the wedding were given corsages that matched the bridal bouquet. David and his father both wore matching boutonnieres.

The reception took place on the side lawn under a canopy tent (which also served as a backup in case of rain). Periwinkle tablecloths adorned the banquet rounds, and pastel floral napkins decorated each place setting. Wide periwinkle ribbons were wrapped around the handles of the small wicker basket centerpieces that sat on each table. The buffet table was covered with rose-colored tablecloths, and large wicker baskets held the food. Vintage photos of Merrilyn's mother wearing the original wedding dress were added decoration.

A friend of Merrilyn's is a purchasing agent for a local college, and she had to purchase flowers for a graduation that was the night before Merrilyn and David's wedding. She ordered the flowers in complementary colors, and after they were used at the graduation, she brought them over to decorate the tent (they returned them to the college the next day).

PHOTOS

The photography was done professionally but in a very informal fashion, with only a few posed portraits. They had a few family shots, a couple of specific groupings, but mostly candids. They used the husband of a longtime friend, and he gave them "a real great price." They then received a completed album as a wedding present.

Another photo-bug friend chronicled the on-site setup and everyone getting ready for the wedding. David's sister videotaped the ceremony and some of the reception, including footage of David, Merrilyn, and A.J. dancing. She then asked a few key people to give the happy couple words of advice on camera.

FOOD AND BEVERAGE

The following menu was a combination of foods provided by a professional catering company and foods prepared by Merrilyn with the help of a few friends.

MENU

Crudités of Vegetables

Fresh Fruit

Cheese Platters

Roasted Red Pepper Dip with Pita Chips

Spinach and Cheese Crostini

Assorted Dips and Crackers

Salsa and Chips

Cold Beer Shrimp

Hoisin Beef and Scallion Rolls

Grilled Pizzas

Miniature Orange Muffins with Smoked Turkey

Hot Dogs (for the kids)

Chocolates and Nuts

Chocolate Brownies

Carrot Cake with Cream Cheese Frosting

The cake was a three-tiered round creation that the caterer made from Marcel Desaulniers's book *Desserts to Die For*. The caterer served the wine, beer, champagne, sparkling cider, sodas, juice, and coffee that Merrilyn and David had purchased themselves. According to Merrilyn, "When it comes to the food, if there are things you can do on your own, it will really help to keep the costs down."

Chapter Fourteen

TAKE THE MONEY AND RUN

○————————○

When you sit down to plan your wedding, do you feel so much pressure from all sides that it makes you want to scream? If the answer is yes, you may wish to consider eloping or having a faraway wedding. There still are a lot of decisions to make with either of these choices: Where will you tie the knot? When will the wedding take place? And, why didn't you think of this sooner? This chapter will help you handle the details of an elopement or faraway wedding, avoid hurt feelings, and address after-the-fact receptions.

Even if running away from it all doesn't make sense to you, you'll still want to run away for your honeymoon, so tune in to the cost-cutting honeymoon tips on pages 339–40 for some nontraditional solutions.

ELOPING

There are definite pros and cons to eloping.

Pros

- You can get married whenever you want, on the spur-of-the moment or after careful planning.
- You will probably save a bundle of money.
- You won't be limited to a location convenient to your families.

- You won't be ruled by the expectations of your families.
- You can avoid on-site family conflicts.
- You can choose to have a progressive-style reception after the fact and celebrate with individual family members on your own terms.
- Eloping may eliminate a lot of pressure and stress.
- The focus will be on the joy and love you share, not family politics.

Cons

- Your family and friends may be angry or hurt by your decisions.
- You will miss having the people you love as witnesses when you exchange your vows.
- If you have the fairy-tale fantasy, the wedding on the run might not do it for you.
- You may feel a sense of remorse: "What if I had done it this way instead?"
- Your families may not get a chance to meet your spouse until much later.
- Your families may not get a chance to bond (for better or for worse).

THE DECISION TO ELOPE

Eloping and choosing to marry far away are both very personal decisions that have to be decided by the couple themselves. In writing this book and speaking to newlyweds, I've heard so many reasons why couples chose to elope, with or without their families present. I also heard several couples who didn't elope say if they had to do it all over again, they would choose to elope. Here are a couple of the stories that were shared with me.

- One thirtysomething couple was offered $40,000 by the bride's father, with the option to either throw a lavish wedding or elope and use the money as a down payment on a house. (It didn't take a rocket scientist to make that decision.) They notified their families of their elopement plans and wed in an intimate family-only ceremony held in a downtown San Francisco hotel penthouse. A few months later, I helped them cater their own dessert reception and housewarming party (see their menu on page 185).

- I was out to dinner one night in Oakland with a lively group, including some East Coast visitors and one of the visitor's local stepchildren. The stepson, twenty-seven, and his charming fiancée, twenty-four, began describing the building pressure they felt surrounding their upcoming nuptials. They said there were too many parties being planned on *both* coasts, and too many family members trying to outdo each other. Someone at the table jokingly suggested eloping (I swear it, wasn't me), and we got into a conversation about some of the benefits. Later that night, their stepmom got a call in her hotel room from the couple who had eloped to Lake Tahoe! In the ensuing weeks, after the major players involved had calmed down a bit (and stopped blaming the stepmom), parties were still held on both coasts, but instead of pressure, the newlyweds were filled with joy.

- An Illinois couple (in their mid-twenties) who share a keen sense of humor recently flew to Las Vegas for the weekend, rented a Cadillac, and tied the knot at an Elvis-themed drive-through wedding chapel. "We had joked about it ahead of time, but we really had a blast with the whole experience."

- A couple from Santa Cruz, California, married on the island of Kauai with ten guests present. "We wanted to have a very private, very upscale wedding. Inviting just our closest friends and family members meant that we could do just that." They had saved up airline miles and were able to get their flights for free. For the ceremony, they hired a wedding planning service, Island Weddings, who took care of everything: finding the perfect beach location, providing beautifully written vows, flowers, photography, and even a rain backup. (For more information on Island Weddings, call 808-828-1548.) The couple spent their first three days at the Princeville Hotel, where they also hosted their post-ceremony reception. The reception was held in a private dining room, which opened out onto a balcony with an incredible ocean view. A Hawaiian buffet was set up for the group, and a wedding cake was served following the feast. After their wedding weekend, they stayed another five days in Kauai at a north shore condominium. The cost of their wedding and honeymoon was $4,650.

- A couple of Irish Americans opted to elope to the Emerald Isle with both sets of parents in tow. They made arrangements and traded miles for plane tickets four months in advance so the international paperwork would be completed by the wedding date. Distant relatives they never met previously helped plan their Catholic wedding, including a cousin who was a priest. The small old-fashioned church was the perfect setting, complete with centuries-old stained glass and cathedral ceilings.

ELOPEMENT TIPS TO TEMPER HURT FEELINGS

The following tips are meant to help you smooth things over with friends and family who may be disappointed they will not get to witness your nuptials:

1. First, announce your plans as soon as possible to give people time to adjust before you elope or before you marry in a private ceremony.
2. Then, tell your family and friends how much you love them and how much you love your new spouse, and that you hope in time

they will come to understand and accept that you have formed a
new bond and are starting a new life. Remind them that you could
use all of their help and support.

3. Understand that your own feelings may get hurt by family members
   or friends who feel rejected. Healing takes time, and it would be
   wise to focus on the joy, hope, and love involved with your wedding
   instead of focusing on the negative. There will always be people you
   will not be able to please. Remember that it's important to please
   yourselves first and foremost!

CHOOSING A LOCATION

If you have decided to elope or marry out of the public eye, you might just go
downtown to your city hall to tie the knot quietly, and then hide out in a local
hotel for a day or two. Or maybe you know of the perfect wedding chapel in
the country only a few hours, or a few states, away. A phone call or two and
boom, it's a done deal.

Here are a few location suggestions to ponder:

BIG CITY. If you live in a small town, it might be exciting to run away and
wed in New York, Chicago, or San Francisco.

SMALL TOWN. If you live in a big city, it may suit you to escape to a small
town in Vermont, the Smoky Mountains, or the Catskills. Look for a wedding chapel or justice of the peace to make it all official.

EAST COAST/WEST COAST. Is marrying barefoot on the beach your
fantasy? There are fabulous views on either coast or over the Mexican border.

MOUNTAINS. Tie the knot on a Colorado skiing trip or while crossing the
Great Divide during a summer getaway.

WEDDING CHAPEL. You can find them all over the country, but look for
them particularly in tourist spots. Search the Internet for specific locales.

CASINO. Las Vegas has weddings down to an art, performing an average
of 8,400 weddings a month. Most of the big casinos have their own wedding chapels and bridal consultants. Some casinos specialize in a particular
theme, such as Excaliber Hotel's Canterbury Wedding Chapel, which can

provide medieval wedding costumes from $250 to $750. Other casino towns to consider include Reno, Nevada, and Atlantic City, New Jersey.

RESORT. If you are set on a faraway wedding, consider going to an all-inclusive (one set price includes all meals and activities) resort that will build your wedding into your vacation package. Sandals and Beaches both have packages at a variety of Caribbean locations. Consider using airline mileage to get a free flight. If you are already planning to visit a Disney resort for a family getaway, you may be able to add on a small wedding. It's definitely worth researching.

OTHER SUGGESTIONS include any tourist attraction, such as a national park or a ghost town, a cruise ship, an international vacation (do your research before you go), or a trip to Universal Studios or other theme parks (see sidebar opposite). Be sure to call the location you are considering and ask if they have specific wedding packages, and if so, what are the costs involved. Book as soon as possible to hold your date.

It would also be a good idea to review chapter 5, bearing in mind your priority to *get out of town*.

EVER THINK OF GETTING HITCHED AT AN AMUSEMENT PARK?

Silver Dollar City, in Branson, Missouri, is a circa 1880s family-friendly theme park in the Ozark Mountains; open mid-March until late December.

A rustic historic log cabin built in 1847 sits prominently inside the gates of the park. Known as the Wilderness Church, it holds Christian church services on Sundays and charming—yet surprisingly affordable—weddings any day of the week.

The quiet simplicity and picturesque setting provides the ideal backdrop for your once-in-a-lifetime moment. Packages start at only $400 for an elopement with the couple only and go up to a few thousand for a full meal with fifty-five guests. You can reach the wedding coordinator at 800-876-8962.

All packages include private use of the Wilderness Church, ordained minister, professional musician, wedding coordinator services, filing of the marriage license (you must provide the license), photo CD containing twenty professional photos (with copyright release), the use of a bridal bouquet and groom's boutonniere during ceremony, and a 6-inch heart-shaped wedding cake boxed for transport. Premium packages also include a horse-drawn carriage ride to the church, VIP parking, and park passes for the bride and groom to Silver Dollar City.

HONEYMOON IN PARADISE

A few couples mentioned that they were curtailing wedding expenses to save up for an exotic honeymoon. By researching thoroughly prior to traveling, you can find bargain fares to almost any locale. The following is the 2014 list of the top ten honeymoon destinations in the world according to Honeymoon.com:

1. Bora Bora or Tahiti (both in French Polynesia)
2. The Maldives
3. The Seychelles
4. Maui, Hawaii
5. Mauritius
6. Bali, Indonesia
7. Fiji Islands (also in French Polynesia)
8. The Cook Islands
9. Cancun, Mexico
10. The Bahamas, Caribbean Sea

PLANNING A WEDDING AWAY FROM HOME

When you have narrowed down your search to the city or country in which you want to marry, you'll need to pin down a ceremony location and begin to do the footwork to find out local marriage license requirements. In the United States, some states still require blood testing, while internationally you may need to submit documents months prior to the wedding announcing your intentions. Other requirements may be notarized or original birth certificates (and, in some cases, translated), divorce decrees, or a doctor's certificate. Find out what you need as far in advance as possible.

Determine what city or country you are leaning toward and do as much research as possible to find hotels, wedding sites, and/or a wedding coordinator. Let your fingers do the walking and utilize the phone book, do an Internet search of the area, call the local tourism bureau, and look in your library for guide books of the area, checking for their recommendations. If you already have a hotel picked out, call and ask their concierge for suggestions and help pulling it all together.

For the most part, this book was written for couples who want to be their own wedding coordinator. But if you are marrying outside of the area in which you live, you will probably need some help. If you're going back to your hometown to get married, perhaps your mother, siblings, or a childhood friend can do some legwork for you. But if you are marrying out of state or out of the country, you may wish to hire an on-site wedding coordinator or use an all-inclusive service that will take care of everything for you.

If you're using professional people to coordinate the wedding (and possibly all of your travel accommodations), be sure they send you in writing (1) the contract, (2) their suggested ceremony, (3) any brochures they have, (4) a list of references you can call, and (5) the requirements for legal marriages in their area. Check to be sure that your date is available; find out if a deposit is required, and if so, how much; what type of payment plans they offer; what the cancellation policy is; and if wedding/travel insurance is available for an additional fee. Pay for all of your travel arrangements by credit card, if possible (which makes it easier to get a refund, if needed). Ask your coordinator(s) to update you in writing of any changes.

If time and money allow, it would be smart to visit your location and meet with everyone who will be involved in your wedding. Obviously, if you decide to wed in Jamaica, for example, that's probably not going to be possible; in that case, be sure you feel at ease with whomever you hire to put together the wedding. Talk on the phone with the officiant who will perform the ceremony and ask your on-site coordinator as many questions as you need to feel comfortable.

OFF-SEASON SPECIALS

A couple from Indiana married at Sandals Jamaica for under $5,000! Their off-season package included airfare from Chicago, a six-night stay, all meals, and the wedding.

How did they do it? Lots of research. They found an amazing deal that was an online-only special. Plus, staying for six nights earned them a free basic wedding.

A NONTRADITIONAL HONEYMOON

Here are some cost-cutting ideas for a nontraditional honeymoon:

- Spend a few days locally or within a few hours' drive of your wedding. Then save up your money after the wedding and go on a blow-out belated honeymoon six months later or on your first anniversary. After our wedding, we drove up the California coast and rented a house with a Jacuzzi for a few days. Six months later, we spent a week in Cozumel for our fantasy honeymoon.

- Rent (or borrow from family or friends) a romantic getaway cabin or house. You could also look into house swapping if you want your dollars to go extremely far. But near or far, find somewhere you can decompress in privacy!

- Register for a honeymoon with one of the honeymoon registries popping up these days. This option is for the bride and groom who already have everything they need. After registering with a honeymoon specialist or travel agency, they send out postcards announcing the information. Miss Manners would definitely not approve, but if you don't need another toaster, check Honeyfund.com for more information.

- Consider camping together if you are avid outdoor enthusiasts. One couple I interviewed registered for backpacking gear and cut the costs of their ten-day honeymoon by backpacking half of the time and staying in decent hotels the other half. Another option is to rent a camper and tour a specific region or see some of America's greatest natural wonders, for example, Yosemite or the Grand Canyon.

- To have a fabulous honeymoon while staying within your budget, do your research. Call in advance or search the Internet to check availability and look for great bargains. Ask travel agents and hotels if there are specials or packaged plans available (e.g., free airfare) or trade in frequent-flier miles. Consider B and Bs for affordability (note that not all B and Bs fall into this category) and do as much research as possible when finding and booking your destination.

Additional honeymoon registry and Internet travel information is on page 61.

SURPRISE: MARRY ME FRIDAY?!

Stacey and Trent's Elopement on September 19
4 guests in Clearwater, Florida

PRIORITIES

1. Intimate, just us
2. Simple and easy
3. Memorable
4. A surprise for Stacey
5. Barefoot on the beach

Stacey, thirty-seven, and Trent, thirty-nine, met in Cincinnati, Ohio, on Match.com. Stacey said she knew on their second date that he was "the one." After a year of dating, Trent and Stacey discussed getting married on several occasions. "We knew we wanted to spend our lives together. I wasn't sure when we'd make it official," Stacey shared. Trent chimed in, "We both had been married before. In my case I had a huge formal wedding. No need to do that again—or to have a long engagement. This was it for both of us."

LOCATION

A few weeks before they were set to visit his parents near Tampa, Florida, Trent had started researching options online. He made a reservation through the company Affordable Beach Weddings (affordablebeachweddingsflorida .com). He also ordered a black diamond engagement and wedding band set for Stacey with a matching band for him. He kept it all a secret from Stacey, but his parents knew what he was up to.

BUDGET

Wedding, reception site	$	425
Dress, alterations, veil, and shoes	$	0
Groom's clothing	$	0
Food, liquor	$	0
Photography	$	0 (included in the package)
Makeup, hair	$	0
Flowers	$	0
Decorations	$	0
License, minister	$	50
Total	$	475

DETAILS

On a Tuesday night as Stacey returned home from work, Trent proposed. The following Thursday morning they got on their prearranged vacation flight to Tampa airport. Since their flight was delayed, after landing they had to hurry to get their marriage license secured before the government offices shut down for the day.

Friday morning, Trent, Stacey, his parents, the officiant, and the photographer met on the beach in Clearwater at 10:00 a.m. It was a slightly overcast day with a touch of mist, not too hot and not too cold. You could see the ocean for miles. It looked like it might rain, but, luckily, it held off while the couple exchanged vows. People wandering by stopped, gathered around, and watched as the couple tied the knot with the stunning natural ocean setting as the backdrop.

"Our wedding was so easy. It went quickly. It was what God wanted," said Stacey. As part of the ceremony, they poured white and blue sand into a keepsake heart-shaped vase, symbolizing combining their two families into one. They both have children—five in all—from other relationships. They wanted this moment in time to be just the two of them, with his parents as the witnesses. They called their kids afterward to let them share in the joy.

APPAREL

Both Trent and Stacey wore clothes they had purchased for their vacation. Stacey had bought a mauve spaghetti-strapped cotton dress for only $50 at an Ohio boutique. It was calf length with tulle below the waist. She said it was perfect for the occasion, and it is multipurpose so she will get lots more use out of it. Likewise, the $9 white cotton button-down shirt Trent bought was going to get lots of wear beyond its first appearance at his wedding.

PHOTOS

"The photography lasted longer than the ceremony," shared Trent. "In total about an hour. The photographer took over 250 photos. Our package included a CD with 30 photos of our choice. We can purchase more if we want."

OFFICIANT SERVICES

"The package also included the officiant, the legal filing of the marriage license, use of a silk flower arrangement, a keepsake copy of the wedding vows, a keepsake copy of the marriage certificate, a decorated table, and the perfect spot on the beach," according to Trent.

Trent and Stacey's wedding was everything they had imagined: elegant, affordable, and easy, a wonderful surprise elopement and a cherished way to start their new lives together.

Chapter Fifteen

AND THEY LIVED
HAPPILY EVER AFTER . . .

○———————○

Grow old along with me! The best is yet to be,
The last of life, for which the first was made.
ROBERT BROWNING

As your wedding date approaches and you check off the items on your list one by one, it may seem some days that the whole event is taking on a life of its own. Don't let it! So much comes up in the course of the planning: what his folks want, what her folks want, what the couple wants. This final chapter includes tips for bringing it all together: how to make your wedding uniquely your own, avoiding family conflict, some final details to take care of, de-stressing strategies, and a final to-do and financial checklist.

Throughout the book, I have given you advice about setting priorities and selecting what suits you (vows, dress, food, wedding site) to create a wedding ceremony and reception that reflect who you are. Creating such a loving salute to you both at times takes courage. Some people may prefer that you use the cookie-cutter approach to planning your wedding. Others may not understand interfaith marriages in which both parties want to respect and include some reference to their beliefs. Your families may not appreciate where or when you have decided to hold your wedding or some other aspect of the choices you have made. There are so many areas where your loved ones can support or deny you that an engaged couple can feel very vulnerable.

Robert Fulghum, the writer and philosopher quoted earlier in the book (pages 321–22), refers to family baggage and politics as "land mines." It is important to avoid the land mines that can be set off so easily around a wedding. You may choose to ask specific family members to refrain from their conflicts with each other or their judgments of you during your wedding period—a peace treaty of sorts. There are complete books written on dealing with such issues as planning a wedding with divorced parents, the forming of stepfamilies, and interfaith or interracial marriages. It's beyond the scope of this book to delve further into these issues, but I do want to suggest the following de-stressing strategies:

- Remember why you are getting married.
- Reaffirm your love for each other with a kiss and a warm hug every day.
- Take care of yourselves, eat right, sleep well, work out, and meditate, if you so choose.
- Pamper yourself, get a massage, massage each other, spend time with friends.
- Celebrate life and relationships.
- Breathe deeply.
- Always keep in mind that this wedding is about love, community, hope, and joy!

FINAL DETAILS

TRANSPORTATION. Arrange transportation to and from your ceremony and wedding site. This could be driving yourselves, hiring a limousine (call around for the best deal), borrowing a classic car, or having family members drive you. Also, remember to give all out-of-towners directions/maps to your locale.

REHEARSAL DINNER PARTY. You'll want to decide in advance whether or not to host a rehearsal dinner party. If you have many guests coming from out of town, it would be gracious to have some sort of informal gathering on the eve of your wedding. If you are extremely budget-conscious, as we were, consider a simple meal in your home, or the home of a friend or family member. We hosted ours in the community room of our apartment complex. It was a great way to introduce family members and begin the bonding before the big day.

SPECIAL WELCOME ITEMS FOR OUT-OF-TOWN GUESTS. Items could include: a card or note welcoming them, maps of the area, a flyer with details about the weather, the area, where to sightsee, plus an overview of the weekend's festivities.

GIFT BASKET. It could include a six pack of bottled sparkling or still water, assorted chips and snacks, sunscreen, and lip balm.

TOTE READY FOR KIDS. It might feature an Uno pizza-delivery coupon card, puzzles, a pack of cards, MadLibs, fruit snacks, a microwave popcorn pack, and an in-room movie voucher.

GIFT REGISTRY. Traditional couples register at department stores for china, silverware, and furniture. But there are lots of other options. Perhaps you already have everything you need, or maybe your wedding was on a tight budget and you feel you shouldn't be asking for such luxurious gifts. There are many more practical and perfectly acceptable places to register these days, including Home Depot, Sears, JCPenney, or Target. See chapter 4 for Internet resources.

GIFTS FOR THE WEDDING PARTY AND PARENTS. It is common for couples to give gifts to their wedding party and parents as a remembrance of the occasion, and a thank-you for their participation. In keeping with the budget theme, the only real rule of thumb is to buy or purchase the gift from your heart. Think about the people you are giving the gift to, and buy or make something they'll treasure. One bride who was having a tea searched flea markets and garage sales for a teacup for each bridesmaid that reflected her personality. She then filled them with a satchel of tea and a note of thanks. Keep in mind that you don't have to spend a lot to show your appreciation.

GUEST COUNTS. Depending on your contracts, you may need to give your caterer a final guest count one week before your wedding by collecting RSVPs and tallying the numbers. You may need to call and check up on a few people if you haven't received their answer. It is a good idea to keep a running tally from the time the invitations go out. Check off by each name if they are or aren't attending, and how many will be coming. If you are planning to do a formal seating chart, this information will be invaluable when you sit down to decide who should sit with whom, and whom you should definitely keep at opposite ends of the room.

THANK-YOU NOTES. If you are already keeping a tally of invitations sent out and RSVPs returned, it would be smart to add a few extra columns to your list so you can check off if you receive a gift from each person, what the gift was, and a column to check when you send a thank-you note. Promptly send the note, and refer to the gift that was sent in the note. Usually the notes are handwritten and signed by either the bride or groom.

CONFIRM WITH ALL OF YOUR VENDORS. A week or two before the big day, phone and confirm the date, time, and place with each of your vendors (minister, photographer, florist, etc.). Also, tell them who is going to be your on-site coordinator (maid of honor, best man, mother of the bride), let them know if they can get final payment from the coordinator, or turn to them with any problems that come up.

PACK A WEDDING EMERGENCY KIT. Bring it with you on the big day. I recommend filling a gym bag or tote with items you hopefully will not need but that could save the day if they are on hand. My list of essentials includes masking and cellophane tape, straight and safety pins, needle and thread in basic colors, sunscreen, lip balm, bandages, backup contacts and saline eye solution (if applicable), eye drops, hand lotion, razor, scissors, medicines (including prescriptions, aspirin and/or acetaminophen, allergy medicine, Benadryl, antacid), sanitary napkins or tampons, two extra pairs of panty hose, hair supplies (brush, comb, volume spray, blow dryer, curling iron or straightener, hair spray, bobby pins), makeup for touch-ups, toothbrush and toothpaste, mouthwash, clear nail polish, nail file, earring backs, and tweezers; flip-flops or ballet flats for dancing are useful, too. It's also a good idea to keep extra copies of the wedding schedule on hand.

WRITE OUT A TIMETABLE FOR THE WEDDING AND RECEPTION. Be sure that you have thought out how you would ideally like the timetable to flow. Give this information to your coordinator/helper and be sure all vendors understand this as well (e.g., caterer, photographer, DJ).

OUR TIMELINE
FOR A 2:00 P.M. WEDDING

11:00	Bridal party met onsite to get ready.
1:00	Bridal party has portraits taken.
2:00	Guests are ushered around the gazebo leaving an aisle for the bride.
2:15	Ceremony begins with the walk down the garden path.
2:30	Ceremony concludes; the groups moves to the patio for sparkling cider toasts.
2:45	Picnic baskets and lawn cloths are handed out for appetizers. Photography continues.
3:00	Guests are invited to start through the buffet line.
3:30 or 3:45	Dancing begins with Gary and Kathleen's first dance; the bridal party dances.
4:30	The cake is cut.
5:00	Bouquet and garter are tossed.
5:30 or 6:00	The reception ends.

COORDINATE WITH YOUR ON-SITE WEDDING HELPER(S). Be sure you know ahead of time who will help with the ceremony: who is in charge of the music or pointing out who is who to the relatives, and who will take care of the many post-ceremony details (send out announcements, tape envelopes to presents, and get the presents back to your house)? Also, know who will be returning all rentals, tuxedos, equipment.

DOUBLE-CHECK THE WEATHER BEFORE LEAVING FOR THE WEDDING. Either tune in to your local weather channel or read the newspaper. Take it from me—it's best to be prepared for everything: sunscreen, umbrellas, a shawl. I spent the morning of my wedding calling friends to see if anyone had a white shawl because I thought it would be foggy and cold (as it was the day before, during our rehearsal). On our wedding day, the fog lifted a half hour prior to the ceremony. The sun was so bright, and I was completely unprepared for it (no sunscreen) that I got second-degree burns all over my exposed shoulders and neck!

TO TIP OR NOT TO TIP. Before doling out extra dollars to the on-site staff, check contracts to be sure you haven't already included a tip. Most caterers, for example, include a gratuity in their price quotes or final contracts.

SO LONG, FAREWELL. Based on your personal preferences or the restrictions at your reception site, you may choose, or decide to forgo, the showering of rice, bubbles, or confetti prior to leaving on your honeymoon. Assign a helper to pass out whatever you decide will be used to bid you adieu. You may want to reserve a hotel or honeymoon suite at a location close to your reception and travel the following day if you are going on a honeymoon.

Lastly, a friendly reminder for you and your spouse-to-be. Please do not to lose sight of what the day is truly about. Don't sweat the small stuff. Instead, focus on starting your marriage out on a sure footing. Enjoy the day, the guests, and each other as you celebrate becoming a married couple.

FINAL CHECKLIST

Confirmed	Deposits Paid	Amount Due	Final Cost	
Invitations, thank-you notes	_____	_____	_____	_____
Wedding site	_____	_____	_____	_____
Reception site	_____	_____	_____	_____
Dress	_____	_____	_____	_____
Alterations	_____	_____	_____	_____
Veil	_____	_____	_____	_____
Shoes	_____	_____	_____	_____
Groom's attire	_____	_____	_____	_____
Attendants' and Kids' attire	_____	_____	_____	_____
Caterer, food	_____	_____	_____	_____
Beverages	_____	_____	_____	_____
Cake	_____	_____	_____	_____
Rentals	_____	_____	_____	_____
Flowers, decorations	_____	_____	_____	_____
Photography	_____	_____	_____	_____
Videography	_____	_____	_____	_____
Band, DJ, or tapes	_____	_____	_____	_____
Officiant	_____	_____	_____	_____
License	_____	_____	_____	_____
Other _____	_____	_____	_____	_____
_____	_____	_____	_____	_____
_____	_____	_____	_____	_____
Total	_____	_____	_____	_____

ADDITIONAL COSTS

Confirmed	Deposits Paid	Amount Due	Final Cost	
Engagement and wedding rings	_____	_____	_____	_____
Wedding night lodging	_____	_____	_____	_____
Honeymoon plans	_____	_____	_____	_____
Rehearsal dinner	_____	_____	_____	_____
Other _____	_____	_____	_____	_____
_____	_____	_____	_____	_____
_____	_____	_____	_____	_____
_____	_____	_____	_____	_____
_____	_____	_____	_____	_____

MORE TO DO (CHECK OFF AS COMPLETED)

_____ Ceremony planned

_____ Vows written

_____ Music playlist

_____ Gifts for attendants

_____ Gifts for parents

_____ Marriage license

_____ _____

_____ _____

_____ _____

_____ _____

_____ _____

_____ _____

_____ _____

_____ _____

CHEERS TO
BRIDES AND GROOMS

○———————————○

feel so blessed to have interviewed dozens of couples about their incredible, unique, and memorable wedding experiences. Only afterward did I feel that I understood *why* these wonderful weddings transcended their price tags. These weddings were indeed priceless, because by asking for and receiving help from friends, and simplifying their wedding expectations, the community of loved ones around each couple grew stronger. The creativity of designing a ceremony and personalized reception helped each couple better understand and share their priorities and who they are. And instead of stress, support for each other deepened their bond.

In each interview, newlyweds shared with me their own wedding and courtship stories. These interviews were so intimate, they left me in awe. Some people I spoke with I knew beforehand, and now I have a better understanding of them. Others were complete strangers who filled me in on every detail, from how they met to their special day. I am so grateful for the inspirational and romantic stories shared with me, and I am thankful to have the opportunity to pass along these innovative ideas. As one bride remarked to me, "If I could do it all over again, and spend ten times the amount, I wouldn't change a thing!"

My wish is that your marriage be as priceless as your wedding. May the hope, love, and joy you share continue to grow and flourish, and remain with you always.

Congratulations and best wishes,
Kathleen Kennedy

ACKNOWLEDGMENTS

I am grateful for the most amazing gifts that resulted from our priceless wedding, my kids, Nick and Michaela Kovalsky. They have brought joy, gratitude, change, growth, and a myriad of other treasures into my heart and life. PRICELESS! I'm also thankful for their understanding and support as I revisited every aspect of this book.

This book would never been written without the support and encouragement of my wise and talented agent, Liv Blumer, and her husband, Bill Blumer, who seamlessly handles details behind the scenes.

I am so appreciative of my Potter Style senior editor, Aliza Fogelson. How fortuitous that she became engaged and wed during the revision and editing process. Her finesse, ideas, questions, suggestions, and eagle eye not only shepherded the update, she also brought the viewpoint of a soon-to-be bride to the table. This second round of *Priceless Weddings* is all the better for it!

I confess to being nervous when a new editor was assigned in the eleventh hour. Happily, from the very first phone call, I knew Amanda Englander was going to be a wonderful partner. Her enthusiasm, professionalism, and sense of urgency made clear I was in very capable hands. I am eternally grateful for her help and support!

Kudos to the design team who designed a great book the first time around, and to Claire Vaccaro for making it even more relevant and compelling to the eye for this edition. Wow, y'all are so talented. I am also thankful to the Potter team, including Debbie Glasserman, Joyce Wong, Kathy Brock, Ana Leal, Kevin Garcia, Doris Cooper, Aaron Wehner, Marysarah Quinn, Stephanie Huntwork, Lauren Velasquez, Danielle Daitch, and Kate Tyler.

My appreciation goes to the Three Rivers Press team and Pam Krauss, who brought my original vision to life when they initially acquired and edited this book. Dan Rosenberg helped me organize my thoughts for both the update proposal and the revision. I am in debt to him beyond what money can buy. Likewise, Carolyn Hart Bryant, held my hand—and taught me restraint of pen—or the first edition.

Writing and rewriting a book takes a village. I've been beyond lucky for the incredible support system I've amassed, including: Pat and Katie Kennedy, who have gone above and beyond to help me and the kids. Not sure what I did to get such a great brother and sister-in-law, but I praise God every day for them being in my life. The same holds true for Aileen and Dan Miller, Peggy Hayden, Alicia and Nick Soto, Maya Blum, and all of my wonderful friends, relatives, mentors, and the many people I've met, worked beside, and have been in awe of throughout my career. Only wishing Tom Fitzpatrick and Ora Kennedy were here to witness this rebirth. Glad to know they are guiding me from above.

Friends, creatives, and experts that I owe a nod of thanks to include: Ann Eicher, Craig Cuzmanko, Angela Muchmore, Sandy and Bre Griffith, Jim Hermann, Tina Harlan, Peter Reinhardt, Gina Deleone, Tim Kennedy, Kelli McKinney, David Slaughter, Judy Kennedy, students at the Culinary California Academy, Cheryl Forberg, Antonia Allegra, Laura Krohn, Jana Joy, Julie & Kristin Fitzpatrick, Tara Coughlin, Gary Kovalsky, Ann and Larry Walker, Tess Young, Kim V, and everyone who helped plan and execute my priceless wedding. That day still reigns as the best wedding I ever attended. I'm hoping all who use this book feel the same exact way about their own nuptials and wedding celebration.

Above all, my gratitude goes out to the brides, grooms, families, friends, and wedding professionals whom I interviewed for this book or who are reading it. May you all live happily ever after.

INDEX

invitations, 8, 290–301
  e-vites, 52, 292
  Internet resources, 51–52
  keeping track of RSVPs, 348
  money-saving tips, 290–93
  post-wedding announcements, 9,
    295
  response cards, 299
  save-the-date mailings, 294, 300
  when to send, 293–94
  wording on, 149, 290, 293–98
Island Weddings, 334

Las Vegas weddings, 76–77, 334, 335–36
LGBT weddings, 86–89, 302–3
licenses, 8, 338
loans, 35
locations, 8, 69–113, 120. *See also* out-of-
    town weddings; themes; wedding
    profiles
  A–Z ideas for, 72–74
  beverages and, 163
  elopements and out-of-town
    weddings, 78, 124, 331–36, 338–43
  equipment rentals and, 80, 82, 147, 151
  finalizing the contract, 85–86
  flowers and, 131–32
  food and, 80, 82, 83, 84, 147, 150,
    151–52, 158, 178
  honeymoons, 337–38, 339–40
  investigating venues, 78–84
  LGBT considerations, 303
  money-saving strategies, 40, 74–76
  music and, 82, 270, 271–72
  outdoor weddings, 72, 73, 74, 84
  questionnaire, 70–71
  Silver Dollar City theme park, 337
  unique locations, 77–78, 80–81
  wedding chapels, 76–77, 335
luncheon menus, 240

main dishes
  recipes, 198, 214–22
  store-bought suggestions, 221
makeup, 108–9

manicures, 109
marriage licenses, 8, 338
marriage mission statements, 22–23
McGlone, Julie, 261–62
menus. *See also* caterers
  changes to, 167
  dessert menus, 166–67, 184–85
  DIY menu ideas and planning,
    178–81, 199, 237–43
  working with a caterer, 154, 155,
    159–60
minister licenses, 302
mission statements, 22–23
mothers. *See* parents
Muchmore, Angela, 273
music, 8, 267–82. *See also* themes;
    wedding profiles
  for the ceremony, 268, 270, 271,
    272–73, 275, 277
  DIY music, 267, 276, 281–82
  DJ and band contracts, 280–81
  DJs, 268, 274, 279–80
  evaluating priorities, 269–70
  Internet resources for, 47, 58–59,
    276, 279
  live music, 268, 270–73, 274,
    275–76
  locations and, 82, 270, 271–72
  for the reception, 268–69, 273,
    277–79
  specific suggestions, 272, 277–79
  unique processionals, 269

nails, 109

officiants, choosing and booking, 8,
    301–2
online tools. *See* Internet inspiration
    and resources
outdoor weddings. *See also* wedding
    profiles
  location ideas and concerns, 72, 73,
    74, 84
  themes for, 121, 122–23, 124, 125–26
out-of-town guests, 8, 47, 61, 347